CW00395008

MOTORCYCLE TALES

FROM EUROPE

James Rendall

CONTENTS:

Introduction

I would like to speculate that you, dear reader, are in possession of this book as a gift because some well-meaning friend or relative has seen the cool picture on the cover, the word 'motorcycle' and thought of you, 'cos you have a bike? And that's great, and you should thank them (and so should I). If, on the other hand, you are the kind of free thinking, devil may care individual that purchased it yourself on a whim then more power to your exhaust pipe sir (or, indeed, madam).

May I just answer a couple of questions you may have before we move on. The more observant among you will have noticed the sub-title claiming 'six riders' but the cover features a mere five. This is because I couldn't find a decent photo with us all on (sorry Kev). Next, my name is James Rendall (note the spelling) but I am not related to Ruth Rendell, a proper author, so this book is not a thriller or a psychological murder mystery, sorry. Also, I was born in Grimsby and still reside locally but, unfortunately, I have never met Guy Martin (local Hero) although I work just up the road from him.

So that's the negatives dealt with let's look at what this book is all about and why I have decided to 'have a go' at writing and then publishing it. For a start, should someone who can't spell, has a CSE grade 2 in English and, worst of all, an insubordinate attitude to the correct grammatical use of the apostrophe seriously consider writing a book? Probably not, but let's do it anyway.

You may well enquire as to the purpose of the contents within? Well, on researching the possibilities of self-publishing a certain phrase kept cropping up, 'Vanity Publishing'. This I took to mean I wanted to see my name on the cover of a book. I can-not deny there is an element of truth in that but what I would really hope to achieve is for you to primarily enjoy reading but ultimately perhaps encourage you to 'have a go at Europe' if you haven't already done so.

I have been riding motorbikes since sometime in the early 1980s. I stopped regular riding when I could afford a car but returned to it later on in life. I didn't sell my 1977 Kawasaki KH400 but it languished in the back of the garage for years. Rather foolishly I got back into bikes by purchasing a Fireblade, a great bike but worlds apart from the KH400! I went to local bike nights, did track days, came close to effecting the premature demise of my wife and I then took IAM and RoSPA training. I ventured further afield to the Cat n Fiddle run, North Yorkshire and the Lakes but eventually ran out of ideas and realised I was going to the same local places and using the bike less and less.

I needed some fresh ideas and that's when I jumped at the opportunity to join a couple of guys I knew on a weekend trip into Europe. We loved it and have continued a regular pilgrimage to our near neighbours ever since. The trips have increased in duration from three days to eleven or twelve as we have tried to visit different places each year and the group has varied in size from six to three. You don't need to be Charley Boorman, Ewan McGregor or Nick Sanders. You don't have to sacrifice loved ones or gainful employment for years and you don't even need a 'proper' bike to enjoy riding in foreign parts, as I hope to demonstrate.

For some reason on these trips I decided to make a few notes of where we had been, what we had seen and what we did as I went along. This spiralled into an essay that I produced at the end of each year which I hoped would be vaguely humorous. "You should write a book" they said (well one person said that, possibly).

You will note that I have included mileage and durations at the start of each day. These are lifted straight from my plans but should only be used as a very rough guide (means we got lost a bit sometimes). Also, I don't intend lecturing about 'correct' clothing or luggage or whatever but I would suggest a degree of planning before setting off and recommend restricting the majority of riding days to a maximum of 200miles. Inform your insurance company, obtain travel insurance and consider break-down insurance. Finally, and despite rumors to the contrary, not everyone speaks English (although many do), talking louder won't help so maybe a brush up on a please and thank you in foreign tongues might help.

Oh, one more thing. There are no pictures in the book but should you wish to view a selection of the many we took I have made a twelve minute picture show and stuck it on YouTube. My friend Steve Blythin kindly allowed me to use a selection of his music to accompany the show making it a muti-media experience. If you wish to view it get your popcorn ready, go to YouTube and search for the books' title "**Motorcycle Tales from Europe**". It's the modern way. That's the introduction waffle over with, thank you for reading it let's get started.

Chapter 1.

Something For The Weekend? (3 Days).

Some friends of mine, people I had worked with in the past, invited me to join them on a weekend taster trip to France. When I began talking to two others about this the group swelled to six. The idea was to travel to France during the Friday, spend Saturday exploring our chosen region and then to return home on the Sunday. I had never toured much beyond Peterborough before but I fancied giving it a go.

Booking the ferry using P & O proved interesting as we managed to get three different prices for the same voyage on the same ship using a Motorcycle News reference number. Prices from various sources varied considerably but using a MCN code we managed to obtain a reasonable figure for the return crossing including bikes. I had no luggage but the consensus was that the Oxford Humpback magnetic tank-bag would suffice to which I added a cheap tail bag and copious bungees. I had a two piece leather suit but thought it prudent to purchase a two piece waterproof over suit, just in case. The French hotel we were to use was sourced, as so many things can be, using the Interweb with virtually no hassle and we were good to go.

So who are these people and what do they ride? Introductions are in order I feel. Let's start by saying we were all born in the late fifties and early sixties to give you some indication of an age group. Firstly there's 'The Boss'. I have named him thus as he rides a Harley Davidson something or other and has the most European travel experience. Festa, named for a liberal attitude to food sell-by dates and one dodgy looking photograph which made him look like the uncle in the Adams Family. Festa also has the oldest bike of the group a ZX6R Ninja. Kryten, I have named after the character in Red Dwarf due to a badly fitting helmet that leaves amusing marks on a hairless head. Kryten shares my addiction to bike changes but has a CBR600F for this trip. Desperate Dan, well this name chose it's-self, due to Dan's' notorious always hungry for 'something savoury' appetite. Dan's' choice of steed is a BMW 1100RS. Chippy was my least original choice of name given his trade as a joiner but he, like me, rides a Fireblade. The groups' motorcycling experience and abilities vary widely but when we met up for our only group ride to a local bike night we all seemed to hit it off instantly ('Kindred Spirits' as Henry Cole would no doubt say).

Friday – Home to Dover (240miles 4hrs 30mins) – Calais to CharlieVille (210miles 3hrs 15mins)

The day in June dawned dull and damp. We all met up at a pre-arranged point (outside Morrisons) and set off at 5:30am into the drizzle. The pace was a little too polite at first so I decided to take the lead on roads that we were all familiar with. Not long after the weather began to improve and we made excellent progress down the A1 to join the M11 and the M25. Sports 600s have a tank range of about 130 miles, which meant a couple of welcome stops on the way down to Dover.

I am 6'2" and riding my Fireblade I had begun to cease up a bit by the time of the first stop. Now I can hear all you BMW and Pan riders chuckling away in your Belstafs but at the time I still wasn't old enough for a "sensible" touring bike with an armchair for a seat, heated grips and a CD player! This was my first attempt at touring with the Blade; it's a truly versatile machine but requires a few compromises.

At the Dartford Crossing I was overtaken by Chippy the other Blade rider keen to lead us over the bridge. Unfortunately his enthusiasm led to us over taking the lines of patiently queuing cars and ending in the only empty, unmanned, booth. A rather cross looking lady let us all through, cheers luv, bikes are free and a bit of a nuisance I gather. Dover seemed to be reached in next to no time, in fact we were about an hour early so we caught the earlier ferry, no-one seemed to mind. Passport checking was interesting; I was waved through after being checked still wearing my crash helmet and sunglasses (things may have changed a bit since then)!

We all stood back and watched our bikes being lashed down by the burley sailors; a strop is hooked to a mounting point in the floor, chucked over your seat and ratcheted tight on the other side. I was told you should not attempt this yourself, as should your machine fall over you will not be insured. We waved bye-bye to blighty and its' white cliffs while the rain clouds gathered ominously overhead.

Just over an hour later we slipped into Calais and were soon offloaded and on our way. No clamber for leadership now! Lots of anxious glances towards the slightly more experienced and calm Boss Hogg, the Harley rider. Boss was up for the challenge and led us straight to our next petrol stop. It's noticeably cheaper in Euros and no more difficult than at home to fill up "Numéro deux, s'il vous plait" (number two please) and a quick "Merci" being all that is required. Failing that you can revert to the true Brit version and hold up the requisite amount of fingers. With tanks replete we decided to take advantage of our slightly earlier arrival in France and stay off the fast toll roads opting to view the various towns at a more leisurely pace.

Our revised route took us West along the familiar sounding A16 before joining the E402 towards Montreuil. At Montreuil we headed east along the N39 towards Arras. Shamefully, I am not fully aware of the battles fought in the area but we were all struck by the amount of British, Canadian and Australian cemeteries that we passed on the route. Such open and beautiful countryside had clearly been witness to some of the worst horrors man can inflict on his fellows.

In contrast to we began to witness the better side of human nature. Almost every fellow biker acknowledged us with a friendly wave or gesture. Not just the often begrudging nod of the head seen in Britain, but full waves, thumbs up or amusing leg shaking. It seems a left leg out means Hi if you are passing in the opposite direction, or I have seen you in my mirrors please pass me. This is acknowledged by a thank you with the right leg extended.

With some very pleasant miles under our belts it was time for a coffee break. We pulled into a likely place and ventured inside. It seemed to us that each time the door was opened a Cockerel struck up. The locals made nothing of this and I was pushed to the front to order the drinks, my wife is a French teacher so that made me the "expert". Unfortunately I am not a student of French but the drinks duly arrived, err, without milk. (Le café avec le lait).After some time we became more accustomed to our café environment and began to notice that the Cockerel sound was getting louder and more frequent.

We realised that one bloke was fastening talons to live birds ready for a fight. Not something we are used to in England and time to leave the café we felt.

In the far busier town of Arras we struggled to keep our six riders together as we encountered traffic lights, junctions and roundabouts. At one junction cars honked us while we waited as we had missed the filter light. Some got through but the last two of us got caught by the red light. We sat there watching the traffic mayhem unfold in front of us, knowing where we wanted to go but having no idea as to how to get there. The green light jolted us into action, but just as we were about to move the cavalry arrived in the form of two Gendarmes on mopeds going in our direction. We tucked in close behind the mopeds and dived through the melee without incident.

After the confusion of Arras we emerged back to the beautiful French countryside and the not so crowded roads enjoying once again the shaking legs of our fellow bikers. We passed through Cambrai to join the N43 to our destination, a pair of merged towns either side of the river Muse called Chareleville Mezieries, in the Ardennes region near the Belgian border. It seemed that each village we passed through had just had a shower as the roads were just drying out. We never caught the rain up but enjoyed the steady progress through the broken sunshine. We stopped for a breather in one village as a marching band came past. We waved at the young musicians as they proudly followed their flags and they enthusiastically waved back giggling and laughing, a nice bit of Entente Cordiale n'es pas?

Once we'd worked our way into CharlieVille (as it became known to us) we arrived at a traffic light controlled T-junction. With the lights at red we gathered tightly together trying to decide whether to go left or right, no one knew. As the lights turned green, and with confusion still reigning, Festa, the last rider in the group shouted something and pointed to the right.

We were outside the hotel! To the confusion of the local traffic we all turned into the small covered passageway that led to the hotels' garage. Relived laughter replaced the sound of our bikes as we each turned off our engines, we'd made it. We checked into the hotel where pigeon French met pigeon English and breakfast was organised (probably). I had practiced some of the phases my wife taught me but I was lost when asked any questions. Our hosts seemed genuinely pleased to see us and I would love to have been able to share a more in depth conversation. The petite lady showed us to our adequate rooms and we were fascinated by her attire as we thought she looked ready to hit the town. The most striking item was her excessively long white pointy shoes which echoed as she walked over the bare floorboards.

A quick check to make sure we all had twin beds, not the much feared doubles; dump the tank-bags and a quick shower. My room-mate, Kryten, came out of the shower and thanked me for letting him have the double bed, I replied "You're not getting it to yourself", his face was a picture! We hurriedly dressed and then it was out into the warm evening to find the restaurant recommended by the charming lady at the hotel. We weren't sure of the directions so we ended up in an English themed pub watching the European Football Championships in French on the big screen, drinking German larger and eating Pizza, how cosmopolitan!

Saturday - Charleville-Mézières to Bouillon, Belgium (80miles 3 hrs).

A peep through the curtains at the morning revealed that sort of mist that promises a nice warm day to come. After breakfast there was an air of excited anticipation as we dashed to don the uniform of the touring motorcyclist. The garage erupted to the sound of six bikes bursting into life and the sight of six pathetic childish grins crossing ageing faces as cold engines began to warm.

We filed slowly down the passageway and onto the road out of town. Unleaded petrol, sans plomb, was taken at a small village on the edge of town. The owner seemed pleased of the custom and then ran out to take a photograph of the Harley at his pump (there's no accounting for taste!).

Someone had been told that a town called Bouillon, just across the border into Belgium was nice so that's where we were heading. Certain members had even created extra luggage capacity in the hope of tracing cheap cigarettes so the mention of Belgium had greatly appealed to the great white fag hunters.

Now it may seem odd at this point but no-one really knew where we were going. I had been told that the original three had mapped the area, they hadn't really. The only map we had been one cobbled together using a web-site and a large amount of sellotape, it seemed to suffice. The roads to and around Bouillon are breathtakingly beautiful. The route we chose included the Rue de Lingue following the lazy meanderings of the river Semois and its' valley. Accents and descents through tree lined curves and small picturesque villages flowed effortlessly, a great time to be riding a bike. Everywhere seemed lush, green and refreshing. We made numerous crossings of the slow flowing river over bridges built as much to be aesthetically pleasing as any practical value it seemed.

On arrival Bouillon did not disappoint. It is guarded by a castle high on a hill above the village and entered through a short tunnel beneath the ramparts. Once again the wide river Semois joins us and we park our bikes along-side it. With the engines quickly turned off peace returns briefly. More bikes stream through and this seems like a place lots of people come to from France, Belgium and Germany. It does not have all the usual tourist tat, just nice coffee and cake shops, which we made full use of (no fag shops though). I bought a local paper for my wife to read when I got home. I could have gladly watched the world go by drinking coffee and eating cake sat looking up at the castle perched above us in the sunshine all afternoon. This was made more enjoyable by reports from home that it had been raining virtually non-stop since our departure, shame that.

Back in the saddle again and back into more fantastic country. We stopped to admire a superb view at a dusty roadside pull in. Below us was a huge loop in the river and a village set around a hill in the centre. A couple of dozen other bikers joined us before speeding away urgently up the hill and into the trees. Off again and this time the road straightened out, as if, like me, it needed a stretch. A Buzzard flew overhead and while it captured our attention Kryten claimed to have seen two wild boars in the field close to the road. These are the sort of roads that you ride with your visor up taking pleasure from simply breathing deeply and smiling.

The villages seemed to get prettier and town clocks chimed dainty tunes to mark the passage of an exhilarating day. So caught up in all of this were we all that when anyone bothered to check the time it was about 8:00pm and we had no real idea of how far away the hotel was.

It was with a hint of sadness that we headed back to the hotel, it had been a wonderful days' riding. On the way back the fag hunters stopped in desperate search of their quarry. The rest of us promptly got lost in CharlieVille (or went to see the rest of the town, depending on which version you choose to believe). Strange how none of this stuff matters when you're not at home.

Quick shower and a change of clothes and then we were back out to find somewhere 'less English' for a meal. In a large square we found several menus to peruse. Suddenly we were confronted by a young girl dressed in an odd smock with a pillow stuffed up it, awful lipstick and wearing comedy bottle bottom glasses and a daft wig. She offered us a tray full of seashells. Looking around I saw several accomplices laughing, one with a video camera. Boss Hogg asked, "Do you want some of these yo-yos? (Our name for the Euro). This seemed to please the crowd and after depositing untold riches into her tray we received two shells in return. I have since asked my wife if this is some little known French custom but she and I remain clueless.

No sooner had we got rid of the mad mademoiselle than we were approached by another man smiling and saying "Otel le Pelican" (a bit like Rene from 'ello 'ello). Now we were staying at the Hotel le Pelican but how did he know this? Had word got round this French town that six clueless British misfits were on the loose? Monsieur 'Otel Le Pelican pointed to his restaurant and sitting in the window was the long suffering Madam from our 'Otel reception. We waved and smiled but figured that she had probably had enough of us lot and wouldn't want us cluttering up her Saturday night off.

It was getting late so we found a reasonable looking place and went in to sit down. Oh this was true French all right, not a word of English spoken or written and six hungry bikers to be fed. After a short bemused silence during which furrowed brows stared at the menu it was unanimously decided that this was the wine list! All eyes fixed on the language expert, err that'll be me then. After some elementary French the menus arrived. We're none the wiser and it probably showed. Boss announced that his wife had thoughtfully packed him a phrase book, err but it was at the hotel.

Suddenly a cheery French accent appears over the back of the seats, "'Aving une problem avec zer menu?" he asks smiling. "Do you speak English?" we excitedly enquire and he is inundated with requests for translations. We return to our ponderings when Monsieur Smiley receives his meal. "Hey English look at me" he taunts smiling once again over the back of the seat. He waves his hand over his veal and pommes frites so that we can smell how good it is "Good yes?" he says. "We'll have six of them luv" we shout "and six beers!" Spurred on by this cultural exchange of language Festa decided to thank the waitress for his food using a bit of the native lingo "Gracias" he said confidently. She probably thought you are Spanish we assured him!

Maybe it was because we were six bikers, or maybe it is a quiet town but there was absolutely no hint of trouble or loutish behaviour anywhere that night. Families were out, even late at night, and that led to a really friendly atmosphere. The French seemed genuinely pleased to see us and I am led to the conclusion that this we hate the French and the French hate us is complete Sun reader / white van nonsense.

Back to the hotel and final preparations are made for the journey home in the morning and I watch Krytens' attention to detail with some amusement.

Sunday – CharlieVille to Calais (210 miles 3hrs 15mins) then home (240miles 4 hrs 30mins).

Breakfast over and the final bill settling commences. Pigeon languages suffice and we bid a fond farewell to our delightful hosts. In the garage an elderly Belgian gentleman is press ganged into taking a group photograph. At first he is nervous, who can blame him, but after much pointing and arm gesturing our Belgian Lord Litchfield performs the deed and even waits around to see use leave, despite his wife's' keenness to seek sanctuary in the car.

Our route back is to be the quickest we can find, N43 up to Cambrai and then join the fast French Auto route A26 to Calais. As we progressed on the minor roads a minor issue began to develop. I had slightly overdone the intake of tea and orange juice at breakfast and now it was time to find somewhere to offload. I was at the back and kept thinking there's a place to stop but by then it had passed by. Ever onwards we rode through countryside now devoid of shrubbery until my minor issue had developed into a major space hopper sized issue just as we entered a busy town. When we stopped on a roundabout my eyes crossed and the word FULL became clearly visible across the lens. She's gonna blow! Then I spied the neatly tended shrubbery in the centre of the roundabout and knew I had found the place. I kicked the side stand down, abandoned my bike on the roundabout and, after an excruciatingly long time faffing with the zips on my leathers while performing the dance of the incontinent, finally released the pressure. Oh what joy, oh what bliss, oh s**t I hadn't noticed the overlooking office block or its' amused occupants. Why does peeing outdoors take so long anyway?

Petrol is a bit of an issue in France on a Sunday we discover. Small garages are closed and larger 24hr ones are card operated, only not by any cards we took. Luckily we finally found a garage that took cash in Hirson and were soon back onto the A26. The A26 is a toll road and it cost about a fiver to get to Calais. This is a fabulous experience for someone from England. I think the speed limit is 80mph, although the French go faster, but there is hardly any traffic and the surface is mostly smooth, it's great. You collect a ticket at the start and pay at the tollbooth at the end of your journey, easy, quick, clean and efficient, doesn't sound much like home does it?

In Calais we have one desperate detour for the fag hunters. Oh dear, it seems French law prohibits the sale of tobacco on a Sunday after midday. Whiskey is ok though and Boss fills his saddlebags. We pass strict French passport control by answering the test question correctly, "What nationality are you?" I answer "British" Festa answers "Yes" we are all waved through with no further ceremony. The ferry is much busier on the way back and the rain clouds come out into the channel to greet our return. As the white cliffs fill the portholes we don our waterproof everything.

Back on English soil we weave our way out of the terminal and up the hill past the multilingual "Drive on the left" signs. The rain starts and I wish I could just be home. The rain gets heavier and heavier as we get closer to London, this is unpleasant stuff. I start to see the signs for Dartford Tunnel through my rain spattered visor but it doesn't seem to be getting any closer. Despite the rain the general pace of the mass of vehicles hardly slows until tailbacks of queuing cars forces it to. Motorcycles seem to be coming from all directions and filtering between the frustrated rows of motorists.

The rain gets heavier and the filtering gets more frantic, where are all these bikes coming from? Turns out we were caught up in a mass exodus from the Brands Hatch round of the British Superbike competition, I am only used to riding down the local duel carriageway! At the Dartford Tunnel three lanes of cars are swelled to seven by filtering bikes. The tollbooths release one car and four bikes each time the barrier is raised. The tunnel echoes to the roar of bikes and cars and I can't wait to get away from London. Others in our party seem to have relished the filtering and are grinning from ear to ear when we finally stop for fuel somewhere north of the capital. We are all soaked but the rain seems to be easing off.

The final push sees sunshine and showers; we even notice some farmer has his field sprinkler system running. As we approach home it is beginning to get dark. We all park up for a last chat and goodbye. It has been a great trip, 1100 miles, in great company, a real education. We have shared some good times, had some good laughs and we've only been away for the weekend.

Chapter 2.

Vosges - French Mountain High (3 Days).

In the dull, dark and cold of winter I am in the process of organizing the next trip to visit the neighbours. This years' folly will be to the Vosges Mountains close to the German and Swiss borders. For this trip we wanted to head further south and managed to add an extra night. Over the preceding months we had poured over maps of the roads at our chosen destination like schoolboys with a copy of Playboy. To negate the long dull ride down to Dover we decided to try the overnight ferry from Hull to Rotterdam's' Europort thus arriving in Europe bright eyed and bushy tailed ready for the journey. We reasoned that we had travelled around 450miles in one day on our previous trip and set that as a guide distance.

Thursday - Home to Hull (40miles 1 hour).

We all meet up again at Morrisons but this time it is for the brief ride to Barton Upon Humber for a penny pinching portion of fish 'n' chips (rather than pay for a P&O feast). After washing it all down with some fizzy pop we make our way over the magnificent Humber Bridge to the North Sea Ferry terminal in Hull. Through passport control we ride upwards to gain access to the ships vehicle deck. After being directed to an isle for bikes in the center the first surprise was that we had to strap the bikes down ourselves, last year at Dover this was done for us. This led us to a dilemma, how tight should the straps be and what if the crossing is a rough one? We glanced round and nervously observed the more experienced travelers making light of the job.

As the Pride of Hull ship slipped out of its' dock on time at 9pm we sorted ourselves out in the slightly claustrophobic cabins, one 2 berth and one 4 berth. The 2 two berth is a tight squeeze with bike luggage, leathers and helmets to stow but the four berth is almost impossible and tests just how strong friendships are. After some good humored jostling we headed into the public area and settled into the Irish Bar to watch the P&O Players show. Hummm, it started with "Reach for the Stars" and never really recovered. Time for bed.

Friday – Europort to The Vosges (400miles 6hrs 30mins).

After a good nights' sleep on what must have been a friendly North Sea I am awoken by the urgent tones of my alarm clock and I feel a little disorientated. There are no windows in the cabin and therefore no way of knowing what time it is. Out on deck I spy something beginning with W, yep, Windmills, so this must be Holland. Fill up with a bacon and egg breakfast before we're unleashed onto continental roads like winners of a supermarket trolley dash. Rotterdam to our destination in the Vosges Mountains of the Alsace was a full days hard riding so we needed to make swift progress.

Everything started well and we made good time to our first petrol stop. After this the weather began to play a rather dismal hand. Rain started to fall and made boring motorway riding even harder work. This seemed to be less of a worry for The Boss; mounted comfortably on his Harley and protected from the worst of the elements by a huge screen he even rested his feet on the protruding chrome leg guards. I did my best to lie as low as possible across the tank-bag peering out through the Blades' tiny screen Thinking about it we must have been a curious sight as a group. Sports bike riders in a racing tuck trailing behind a casual dude on a Harley.

We came up to a standing queue of traffic at one point and began filtering. We filtered and filtered for mile after mile through completely stationary traffic. The further we went the more the people were out of their cars. There were numerous impromptu roadside picnics with tables and chairs set out, some had to be moved to let us through. When we reached the front of the queue we saw nothing holding up the traffic but Lorries whose drivers were wandering about with seemingly not a care in the world, the French certainly do know how to protest. We were all thankful to have been on two wheels at this point.

Later on, possibly in Luxembourg, we stopped for petrol again and were most confused by the procedure. No you don't fill first and then pay but rather pay first then fill. So work out how many liters we each require and go in to pay? Nope, you have then to work out how many Euros worth of petrol you require and pay accordingly, must make perfect sense to someone, but not us!

As the day wore on our enthusiasm wore thin. It rained heavily again and our only rest bite came at the anonymous filling stations. Concentration became more taxing and it was while looking for somewhere to fill up we had one of our scariest moments. The Boss in front took a turn off the motorway to look for fuel and while most of us managed to follow, Chippy missed the turn and locked up his wheels going sideways several times before stopping well past the exit. Some confusion followed and we temporarily lost contact. A little further on we stopped again and, using mobile phones, the stray was returned to the fold.

As we eventually neared our destination fatigue led us to miss our road and we travelled about 40 miles in the wrong direction, not too bad after 400 miles though. After consulting the map a route was selected and this turned out to be a fabulous choice. We were now off the motorways and fast A roads and into more rural areas. The roads got hillier and twistier and our spirits began to rise once again. We eventually arrived dripping wet at our hotel in the Col du Bussang about 10 hours after setting off from Rotterdam.

The hotel was fantastic. The web-site said it's 95% bikers and it certainly looked like this was the case. The owner, Mark, came out to greet us and admire the Harley; he has one himself he tells us. Inside the first thing that strikes you is the varied biking memorabilia, particularly the half size Harley model made out of cane. We are to be three to a room and although they are sparsely equipped everything required is there and clean.

Showered, refreshed and changed we all meet in the dining room come bar come lounge. Our host offers the first round of beers on the house and although there is no choice, an excellent meal arrives soon after. The room has an exceptionally pleasant and welcoming atmosphere. We are seated around a large wooden table and feel warm and relaxed after the long day. The Boss asks if we should order wine to go with the meal and several bottles are duly consumed.

Our host flits effortlessly between his guests and we are struck by how he can change languages with ease. Turns out Mark and his wife Ida are Dutch and able to speak English, German and French fluently.

Sleep comes swiftly following the consumption of wine and beer and I am only partially woken in the night by an odd sensation from my feet. I half open an eye to see Kryten tucking my feet back into bed while on his way to the loo! Well what are friends for?

Saturday – Touring day (80miles 3hrs).

We assemble for breakfast and the talk of snoring and flatulence is soon replaced by expectations of the coming days' ride. The rain clouds seem to be dispersing and it looks like we are in for a great day.

Our route takes us back the way we came over the Ballon d'Alsace. The D465 Rue du Ballon d'Alsac road is a biking gem, a mixture of predictable sweeping bends through forest and small villages. There is very little traffic and at times we catch the sound of the Boss scraping the footrests of the Harley on the tighter bends. After 20 miles or so of excellent riding we tumble into the town of Masevaux in the Haut-Rhin department and decide to take a break.

We park up in a square that could only be in France. There is a fountain in the middle; a huge wooden carved scene in one corner and a market seems to be going on just over the river bridge. The sun is shining and the day is warming pleasantly as we head off towards the market doing that slightly uncomfortable walk we all do in riding gear carrying helmets. The sound of an over revved trails bike spoils the atmosphere as a 'yoof' hurtles past. Moments later we see him clip the end of a railing and end up in an embarrassing heap on his arse right in front of concerned shoppers. He is soon remounted and off like a scolded cat, oh to be young.

The Boss buys cherries we all share and I head off to look for the toy I promised my young son. We rejoin for a coffee at a pavement café sitting in the sun people watching and listening to the chatter of French Saturday shoppers. Somehow this is so much more agreeable than the same situation in my local corporate fronted high-street.

After some instructions as to how to actually get out of the town from the nice lady at Maurer the Boucherie et Charcuterie we head off on the D466 towards the towns of Thann then Cernay and the start of the D430 Route des Cretes. This mountain road was created by the French military during World War One and follows line of a ridge to prevent the Germans from observing French troop movements.

We start to climb out of the busy town of Cernay and the roads and views get steadily more spectacular. No chance for great speeds but more of what motorcycling is all about for me. It's that feeling of control, balancing brake and throttle tucked in behind the screen of the bike while you sweep from bend to bend to hairpin and back under a canopy of lush green foliage through which sunlit shadows dance onto the road (quite poetic for CSE grade two English eh?). The air seems clearer and fresher here and we are heading towards the 1424m summit of the Grand Ballon, I just don't want this to end. It's good to be here in early summer as most of the route is closed in the winter by snow.

The higher we climb the more we notice an increasing number of motor-homes parked up lining the side of the road. Higher still and there is what seems to be graffiti in the road. It turns out that this is one of the climbs on the Tour de France due through the next day. As we round one bend near the top there is a small Mexican-Wave from some smiling motor-home dwellers accompanied by an encouraging "Allez, Allez, Allez!" as we sweep by, such a great atmosphere.

On top of the Grand Ballon the views are breathtaking and there is a small village of every conceivable type of motor-home. We stop outside La Vue Des Alps café and take time drinking it all in. On a balcony outside the café we sit eating cakes and drinking coffee with a beautiful French landscape stretched out towards the Swiss Alps on the hazy horizon. After a while and almost unspoken, we all start to move back towards the bikes and gear up with great anticipation of the next run.

Off we go along the ridge eventually breaking clear of motor-homes to give uninterrupted views from plateaus before descending through bend after bend in glorious verdant surroundings. Around one bend we can hardly believe our eyes. Bearing in mind we are a long way up a mountain there is a guy pedaling up on a penny-farthing! He has a support crew, it seems, but he is pedaling the thing up a mountain and even has the energy to smile and wave at us as we pass, amazing.

The Route des Cretes should take us through the towns of Le Markstien and Gerardmer and over the 1,139 m Col de la Schlucht but we are brought to an abrupt halt by barriers in Le Markstien. We ride past the barriers, the way one can on a bike and come to a stop behind a large crowd who are lining the street. Having parked the bikes we set out to find out what the hold-up is and soon discover the Tour de France is due through in about an hour. The sun is out, the sky is blue and this was too good an opportunity to miss.

As we watched an assortment of vehicles drove by throwing freebies into the crowd prompting a scrum. Dan managed to capture a ridiculous umbrella hat thrown into the throng and there's an amusing photo of him proudly sporting his prize with a disgruntled fella in the background who also wanted it. The atmosphere was like that at the Cleethorpes Carnival Parade, but at 30mph, err, and in the sunshine up a mountain, so not like Cleethorpes at all really? Anyway, as The Tour drew closer we could see the locals craning their necks to watch the live TV coverage through peoples' windows. Several helicopters replaced the Storks that were circling overhead and the noise from the crowd began to build to fever pitch.

The sound of whistles being blown to alert the crowd accompanied the increasing shouts of "Allez! Allez! Allez!" A wave of noise swept past just in front of the leading group of riders and there we were, in the front row, inches from Lance Armstrong and friends at full tilt, we could almost smell the drugs. Over in an instant but incredibly impressive and something you have to witness first hand to fully appreciate. The chasing pack blasted past not long after in a blur of colour and power. It was about three in the afternoon by now and these guys had been pedaling like that since about ten in the morning and still had a way to go, awesome.

We milled around with the crowd for a while before returning to our machines for the trip back to the hotel. Our preferred route was blocked due to The Tour, which meant a trip back via some less well cared for roads. Some "interesting" riding here as the roads were being used by everyone else who had been watching The Tour. It was quite busy but still steep and twisty but in places there were opportunities for some creative overtaking of sluggish motor-homes. At the hotel our crash helmets can hardly contain the grinning faces within, our enthusiastic chatter replacing the sound of the bike engines. Mark told us The Tour was due to pass right outside the next day so we needed to away fairly smartish in the morning or the road would be closed.

After a refreshing shower we met for dinner and continued to rattle on about the very varied day we had just enjoyed. As the evening progressed the wine seemed to flow as easily as the conversation with the friendly surroundings completing the scene. I don't think any of us wanted to go to bed and admit that it was all over.

Sunday - Col du Bussang to Europoort (400miles 6hrs 30mins).

The next morning we awoke to the promise of another warm and sunny day. Breakfast was a swift affair with all of us trying to eat enough to see us through an expected tough day ahead. Mark, our host, was busy setting up his barbeque ready for his anticipated hungry Tour de France punters as we loaded up the bikes but was cajoled into taking a rare group photograph, 'one for the album Gromit'. When the six engines burst into life, temporarily disturbing the peace, we all waved a reluctant goodbye as we filed past the barbeque and headed for home.

Before the red wine had taken command last night we had concocted a plan that basically involved retracing some our previous days route to Le Markstien before continuing north on new roads eventually joining the boring motorway further on. All started well and we were soon racing through the mountains once again in high spirits. It couldn't last! The Tour was in the region again and we ground to a halt unable to get round all the blocked villages and roads. The decision was reached to abandon the interesting roads for the motorway as we needed to be in Rotterdam in time for the ferry.

The familiar names of towns and cities passed by in a blur as we hurried ever north. After about an hour and a half we had covered around 100 miles and began to look for our next fuel stop. We were on a motorway so this shouldn't be an issue we thought. Wrong! As the miles ticked by there were no petrol stations to be had anywhere. When we did find one, it was credit card operated, unfortunately not with any card we possessed (I believe this situation has since been rectified and UK cards now work fine). Buzzards circled overhead and this was getting serious. Most of the bikes had around a 140 mile known tank range and we had covered 120 by this point. Further down the motorway we again turned off and this time sent Chippy and Dan in search of fuel but they returned empty handed. Nothing for it but to press on to the next biggest town, Aubange in Luxembourg, 20 Km away.

We seemed to be entering the European incarnation of Royston Vasey and things did not look good. The few confused locals we accosted were treated to desperate pointing to petrol tanks and responded by pointing vaguely further on. At a roundabout going nowhere and with no one around we stopped again. We were so close to running out that it was time to send out individual scouts. Then we heard the sound of a wasp in a bean tin. A bemused young moped rider was flagged down and received the internationally recognized petrol tank point. He smiled and most of the group followed him. Heaven only knows why, but two miles further on our young hero led us to a road with no less than six open petrol stations side by side, a veritable petroleum oasis. None of us ran out of petrol and all of us were amazed how far our bikes could go on vapour.

From this point on fuel was not a problem and we slogged our way ever northwards towards the ferry. It seemed endless, like a weekend spent priming your skirting board, as we churned out mile after mile on featureless motorway. At one petrol stop though we were reminded by the one wise man in our midst, Boss, "You can only go as fast as your Angel can fly" Profound dude.

At around 6pm we eventually arrived at Europort and crashed out into our claustrophobic cabins. Being clean once more after a shower raised some daunted spirits and we sat back to watch the P&O players. "Reach for the stars, Climb every mountain higher!" Oh no not again! We beat a hasty retreat to the sanctuary of the bar where we discovered the telly and live Moto GP from Laguna Seca, that'll do nicely then. A few pints later Nicky Hayden had won (great days those) and it was time for bed.

Monday – North Sea Ferry Terminal Hull to Home (40 miles 1 hour).

Up just after the bing-bong we skip breakfast and stand in silence up on deck watching the familiar landscape surrounding the Humber slip by before we docked in Hull. We resisted a strong urge to stay on the ship and made our way into the congestion that is Hulls' morning rush hour. After much filtering we popped like Champagne corks out of the traffic and crossed the bridge for home. After several near misses with some "me first" car drivers (welcome home) our last treat was to be breakfast at Morrisons supermarket.

So that was it for another year. I think we all felt that 400miles in a day is too far to be enjoyable but the roads around the Vosges Mountains were nothing short of spectacular. We have barely scratched the surface of this region and would love to return someday.

Chapter 3.

Black Forrest Get-out. (4Days).

Thursday - Home to Hull (40miles 1 hour).

Although we are good friends it is rare for us all to be together at the same time except for our continental trips. But as we gather outside Morrisons supermarket the group's rapport is instant. The Boss has decided not to join us this year as, unbelievably, his passion for motorcycling has been overwhelmed by his love of Golf, plus his wife says he can only do one or the other. GOLF (FFS!). The early evening June sunshine is warm and there is a high degree of excitement and expectation in the air. I have updated my Fireblade to a newer model this year and for a short while we cast a critical eye over each-others bike preparations. Tyre wear is discussed as Festa still has the same tyres as last year. My tyres, although legal now may not be so law abiding on our return. Just what is contained within the miscellaneous luggage so carefully attached to each bike is intriguing. Desperate Dan's' legendary small and expensive BMW tank bag is thought to have only the capacity to hold one can of baked beans. Speculation is rife as to each-others' minimalist approach to touring clothing and hygiene products.

Soon we are performing the dance of the touring motorcyclist. This involves standing on one leg while trying to slot the free limb over the seat in between the low rise tank bag and the jumble of bags and elastic that is amassed on the rear of the motorcycle. Festa, the most vertically challenged member of the group is performing a most gymnastic and entertaining display. When we eventually set off we fall naturally into formation behind Chippy the recently designated pathfinder and are soon eating our now traditional pre-sailing fish and chips on a bench outside a grocery store 30 miles away in Barton. The discussion now focuses on chain lubricant manufacturers' claims to "Low / No Fling" oils. The generally agreed conclusion being that these were somewhat exaggerated (or "bollox" as someone so neatly put it).

Greasy chip papers dispensed with we head off across the Humber Bridge to catch the evening ferry from Hull to Rotterdam.

This year's trip takes us south of Rotterdam to the promising looking Schwarzwald region of Germany (that's the Black Forrest to us guys). As a bonus the married members of the group have managed to blag another extra day away from their nearest n dearest. Having a mixture of shift and day workers in the group meant that the date kind of chose it's-self, but happened to neatly coincide with the World Cup finals. This became evident as we queued to get onto the fully booked up ferry behind the George Cross bedecked tatty camper van emblazoned with the legend "Max n Paddy's' European Tour". For some reason this vehicle drew the attention of the customs officers

Once aboard we were a little shocked to find that the method of securing our bikes provided by P&O this year was blue rope. Previously we have used webbing that could be tensioned using a ratchet system. We were told that the rope was as a result of some knob-heads inclination to cut the webbing rather than releasing the tensioning device, seriously guys! Having squeezed into the accommodation and slipped into something more comfortable we settle into what passes for "entertainment" on board. Namely Captain Charisma the bingo caller followed by a curious looking musical ensemble who proceeded to torture a selection of forgotten hits of yesteryear. Still the beer was ok as the Humber coastline slipped past to make way for the North Sea.

Friday – Europort to Wolfach (440miles 7 hrs)

We are woken at 06:00 by the ships "Bing Bong" announcement that breakfast is now available. Feels odd because we have a cabin with no windows and it's pitch black. As we stumble towards the smell of cooking the views from the windows reveal the windmills and promising sunshine of Holland.

Suited, booted and replete of a full English breakfast we sit in the fumes of the ships car deck eagerly awaiting our turn to exit into the continental sunlight beckoning us through the open door to the off ramp. The sunshine soon warms our leathers as we make our way through customs to the motorways beyond, with only a slight hiccup as our pathfinder back-tracks to find a lost glove.

From here I would like to report that the journey along the continental highways and byways was smooth and effortless, but that would gloss over the very long and arduous following hours. Trying to tuck in behind what little fairings our sports bikes offer while relentlessly churning out the miles has no pleasure for me, and I suspect, most of the others. As we join the German autobahns the pace is fast and furious. We are regularly pushing past the 90mph / 130 kph marks on our speedos in order to stay with the traffic. Festa does a sterling job at the rear soaking up the pressure of so many tailgaters; even so we still have to frequently move over to allow much faster traffic by. Couple this with some of the worst driving standards I have ever been unfortunate to witness and you see why the autobahns, for me, are a necessary evil.

To break up the monotony this year we had planned a brief stop at the Nurburgring, as we were passing so close by it would be rude not to. After trawling the internet during the planning stages we believed that "The Ring" would be open for us to have a go round. Since then we had just about talked each other into "Riding The Ring" (careful smutty minds) despite the warnings and horror stories that abound.

We followed the signs to Nurburgring and parked outside the grandstand. The noise of screaming bike engines from the track sounded serious and any bravado we may have had, began slowly evaporating. When we eventually found our way into the grandstand the guys on track were really giving it some and we got worried. They all seemed like proper racers and not the odds n sods we were expecting. Time was pressing; none of us fancied mixing it with these guys on track as they were definitely racers so we made a tactical withdrawal to a nearby café.

Note: To anyone wishing to follow our foolish example, on our return home we were informed that there are TWO Nurburgrings. One is a GP Circuit and one is the old 13mile long public road. You follow the signs for the Nurburgring from the autobahn but then look for signs to the Nordschleife apparently. Bugger. It may also be worthwhile pointing out that you want Nurburg not Nurnberg (the war crimes place). If you are contemplating "having a go" then http://www.nurburgring.org.uk/ is an excellent place to start gathering information, just remember to read all of it!

At the café our traditional British complete lack of language skills lead us to eating ice creams, good, and drinking fruit tea, not so good, but welcome at this point. After this stop we fumbled our way back to the autobahns to continue our South bound progress. At one garage we were given a small pack containing visor wipes, biker friendly or what! Me thinks these Europeans are a little ahead of us Brits in some areas. As luck would have it Germany were playing Argentina in the World Cup and the traffic started to thin out. Better still the match went into extra time! Bonus! By the time we reached our turn off at Offenburg (about 50miles south of Baden-Baden) they were into a penalty shootout.

As we made our way through the smaller towns to our destination it became apparent that the host nation had won. It seemed every person in every town had turned out to celebrate. People hung from buildings, out of cars and lined the streets cheering, hooting horns and waving the national flag. What a noise! What an atmosphere! What a time to stop and look at the map! With GB plates we were the subject of much banter, all of it very good natured I must add! Unforgettable and absolutely brilliant!

It was after 8:00pm, some twelve hours and over 500 miles of riding, when we turned into our destination town parking up near the tourist information board. Wolfach is about in the centre of the Schwarzwald and billed as a 'very pretty town of character'. This was not immediately evident from our lay-by view. We had stopped close to an industrial bit. Our fears however, were soon proved unfounded as we slowly made our way to the town centre and located our Hotel. Pretty as the numerous pictures we all took home with us. Traditional buildings lined a cobble stoned road with bars and café seating spilling out onto the pavements. Patrons sat under sun kissed umbrellas watching the world, and five sweaty English bikers, pass by.

In our hotel a wedding celebration was in full flow but, after a little confusion, we are shown to our rooms. At the first room, for two people, my fellow biking chums come out laughing. As my room-mate Kryten and I enter the room I understand why. There before us is a double bed! Our eyes quickly scan the room for an alternative but there isn't one.

Thankfully, on closer inspection there are at least two separate mattresses and two duvet covers...phew! Well it was ok for Morecombe and Wise. Turns out the other three guys have a double and a single. The loud snoring Chippy got the single.

We are told we can store our bikes in the hotels' garage which is round the back. Now it may have been the relief at the end of the journey but I found myself in the street sat on my bike in T shirt, boots and leather trousers. Two German chaps approached calling for me to do a burn-out. If I was capable of such antics I would have gladly obliged but I just shook my head and rode round to the garage. Kryten followed shortly afterwards dressed similarly and was approached by one particular local. It was Herr Plod who was not overly impressed by the lack of protective headgear. Turned out that the local nick is next door but one to our hotel. Humble pie and pushing the bike to the garage got him by with a finger wagging.

We unpacked, showered and quickly ordered a round or two of well-earned beer. We wanted them bigguns like the locals but one round got so lost in translation that the beer tasted of flowers... must be something to do with the sleeping arrangements? By now it was too late for a meal in most places and our own ever hungry Desperate Dan was looking a bit pale. As luck would have it we managed to find an Italian owned bar and ordered pizzas from an extremely likable waiter who spoke excellent English, result! Despite the absurdity of the bedrooms, sleep came very swiftly that night.

Saturday – Wolfach to Baden Baden and back (100miles 3 hrs)

I awake looking straight at Kryten, yikes! Get up swiftly and head on down to breakfast. The table is an absolute delight and the other guys are already tucking in to the range of breads, meat and cheese. Outside the world is already being warmed by bright sunshine and we anticipate a great days riding, err, but we need to be back early to get a good seat in front of the big screen in the bar across the road as England are playing Portugal tonight.

The roads immediately outside Wolfach do not disappoint. We head out through a valley, passing lovely villages with streams running beside the road. At one point Kryten's arm starts flailing towards a field on our left. A large brown bird is circling in the distance and Kryten is convinced this is an eagle.

We are on the B500 heading north towards the spar town of Baden Baden, England football teams' home for the duration of their stay in Germany. The road twists and turns its way over hills and valleys until it joins the Black Forest Ridgeway at just over 2000 ft. above sea level. The views are intoxicating and we can't help but make frequent stops to enjoy them. When we do stop we are often approached by native folk eager to talk bikes and to offer route or destination advice. All warn of over-zealous police on Sundays ready to ring many Euros into the cash registers at motorcyclists' expense, so, much like Blighty then. The biking community as a whole are a pretty friendly bunch but here in Germany we are probably experiencing this spirit at its best. Most passing bikers wave hands, arms or legs (unlike the begrudging nods of most British bikers) even the ones that ride like prats here!

Baden Baden town centre is approached through a long tunnel, an excellent place to drop down a couple of gears and listen to those ever so slightly illegal race cans in full voice (queue childish grin). The sun is very hot as we park up and walk into the PEDESTRIANISED area looking for a café. This is a very stylish town full of miscellaneous well healed Europeans. Will we catch a glimpse of any WAGs out spending in the many designer shops we wonder? I go off to buy the German merchandise I have promised my young son and struggle a bit. England stuff yes but German stuff is more difficult. I eventually return with a German football shirt and a flag. With temperatures over 30°c our sight-seeing is slow but enjoyable. There are fountains and running water, statues and grassed areas all clean and refreshingly graffiti and vandal free. Posh cars abound but no Posh and Becks.

Before long Kryten has itchy feet and it's time to make our way back to Wolfach for the big match. We choose the same B500 route back as it's so damn good. In a lay-by on top of a hill we stop and buy strawberries and honey. The strawberries are shared around and we gaze out towards the top of a ski run on the opposite side of the road. A passing hiker is cajoled into taking our photograph; it's the one on the front cover of this book.

Back in Wolfach we are soon showered, changed and out sitting in the chosen bar with large beers waiting for the match to start. Incidentally, I don't know if this is peculiar to this bar but the Germans seem to be hopeless at pouring a beer. They stand the glass under the tap causing a large foam head to form and then wait for ages to top it up. Anyway, not wishing to court too much controversy I choose to wear a Brazil shirt having been told that women like a Brazilian. (Someone later pointed out to me what this meant, I feel a bit foolish now!). Others in my group chose a much bolder display of national pride. There are not many here who share my companions' interest in the game and the locals seem to find our presence amusing. The bar owner's son seems a little tentative with his Portugal flag but is encouraged to watch the match with us. I say us but, not being a fan, I wander off to explore our host town. What a lovely place it is too. The buildings are mainly traditional, a river winds its way through and is crossed by several bridges. I find a pathway that leads up to a viewpoint and stand bathed in the warmth of the early evening sun surveying the town and the wonderful valley stretched out in front of me.

Upon my return I hear the sound of familiar exasperated English voices and peer through an open bar window to see four tortured faces glued to the TV screen. I re-join the group for the penalty shoot-out. One doesn't need to know much about football to be able to hear the words "England" and "Penalty" to know the result! What happened next, as we left the bar, was a little more confusing though. Portuguese flags began to appear and then the honking of car horns began to get louder. Why were the Germans celebrating England loosing with such enthusiasm? We made our way across the street to our jolly Italian friend to enquire. Turns out we were in a small town were around 500 of the population were of Portuguese descent due to some past factory or other.

A smiling young lady from another table makes her way over to practice her excellent English, commiserate with us and tell us that, as she was Portuguese, the best team won. We wanted to say bollox they did yer diving bunch of cheats, in that traditional sporting way of defeat, but thought a wry smile, a shrug of the shoulders and a bit of banter seemed more appropriate.

We ordered another very nice meal and then sat and watched France play Brazil. Yes that's right Brazil, and me trying to be all neutral in my Brazil shirt. Everyone in the bar wanted to see France win, me included for that matter. Surprisingly for a team I want to win France actually managed it. Everyone in the bar was cheering and then I heard "Hey, Brazil you lose again, ha ha ha" As I drifted off to sleep that night I found myself reflecting on the day, like a closing scene from "Open All Hours" Football, it's a funny old game really.

Sunday – Wolfach to Lake Titisee tour (140miles 4hrs).

The next day breakfast was taken with more warm sunshine outside and a gentle breeze wafting through the opened doorway of our hotel. The early risers and quicker eating members of the group went off to explore the view of the town I had so enthused about yesterday. Upon their return we were soon ready for another days riding, this time to the south around the amusingly named Lake Titisee (yes there is much Carry-on humour to be had in this land) and once again we would be using the B500.

The southern section of the B500 doesn't disappoint. As the road begins to snake its way towards Titisee we pull into a lay-by to replenish lost fluids in the increasingly warm morning sunshine. A farm house perches on a grassy hill while an old tractor is turning grass in the gently sloping valley that stretches out beneath us and the smell wafts up to greet us.

After our arrival in a busy Titisee we park alongside the numerous other bikes on the side of the road. We walk towards the lake down a pedestrianised street lined with what I shall term 'classy tat shops' and inviting cafes. The sound of a brass band ignites a wave of euphoria from Kryten and so we pitch up at the nearest café while he goes to investigate. From a friendly, but non-English speaking waitress, we tentatively place our orders.

I can't resist the lure of a "Schwarzwälder Kirschtorte" (Black Forrest Gateaux done properly!) and coffee. Desperate Dan is fancying 'something savoury' again. The brass band strikes up and we sit feasting on gateaux and the view of the picturesque lake that expands before us.

The town of Titisee is a health resort and Lake Titisees' claim to fame is that it is the largest and / or the highest natural lake in the Black Forest. The vista from our seats suggests it is far more than just a big lake. There are many families out enjoying the water bourn activities but beyond that lay the lush green of the rolling tree covered hills. The Black Forest gets its name from the dense cover of evergreens and from Titisee a 6 mile trail around the lake leads up beneath the canopy to the Hochfirst Mountain, so it said on the sign near the bikes. Not that we had time for any of that.

After a brief mooch around the various bikes parked alongside ours we ride along the B31 road through the Höllental Gorge (Hell's Valley Gorge) looking for a sinuous route up to the 1284m high Schauinsland Mountain. We turn off and the road soon starts to climb through woods which give way to open meadows. The grass in these meadows is largely being turned by hand and seemingly by every generation of the farmer's family and friends. It's hot work and I am pleased to be only a casual observer.

At the summit we rest our hard working bikes in the shade of some trees and begin to explore. I am struck by just how much effort has gone in to providing cycle tracks and walkways. During our tour of the region I had noticed cycle provision but up here demonstrated such commitment to it. I could easily imagine my family and I enjoying riding and walking the many pathways that radiate from here.

I have my photograph taken next to a sign saying "Bikers Paradise" overlooking a magnificent view. More glorious views are found when we stumble across the Schauinsland Cableway (Germany's longest two-way cable car system, apparently) bringing more people up from the Rhine valley town of Freiburg.

Back in the saddle again and it's all down-hill from here, and how! We had chosen a small but twisty looking route from the map and were now plummeting back down the mountain on a narrow winding road. We were not alone either. This being a Sunday there were many folks with similar ideas. The local biker population in particular seemed almost suicidal in their pursuit of "making good progress". Not sure if this was a bit of bravado on seeing the GB plates or if they really are that crazy. Granted excellent machine control but this seemed to be matched by an uncanny ability to see round blind corners. If they weren't bonkers enough the road race style cyclists hurtling downwards on thin tyres wearing nothing but Lycra and fly speckled grins are next level crazy.

This is a very long descent through more woodland and remote hamlets interspersed with the odd hotel or farm building. At one corner there is a hotel with people milling about. As I tip into the bend my rear wheel lets go, for one brief heart stopping moment, on some hot tar over banding. As my bike wriggles beneath me searching for grip I experience that 5p - 50p feeling as part of my anatomy attempts to keep me in the seat. Later I discover I am not the only one to "enjoy" this as Dan reports a similar experience and we wonder if the people milling around that bend come to witness just that.

At last we come to a halt in a small town called Todtnau where it appears to be carnival day. Due to the heat some of our party changes into an odd combination of shorts and biking boots locking sweaty leathers and helmets to their machines. Now, looking like extras from a Village People video, we move toward the centre of activities. Another brass band is playing in front of the church. The irresistible smell of cooking is everywhere and Desperate Dan is on the case. As the rest of us lap up ice cream Desperate D re-joins us with some savoury meat-fest thing in a box, his own version of Nirvana.

On a hill above the town wriggles what looks like a dry toboggan run accessed via a chair lift from just over the road. It's called the Hasenhorn Coaster and yes, the guys who run it will look after our gear, splendid fellows. Soon a small band of middle aged kids are sitting grinning and swinging our legs off the chairlift heading up the hillside.

After a surprisingly long ride to the top we stand looking back on the shrunken town and then at the fully armoured lads about to hurtle back down on mountain bikes, maybe next time. Soon we are each strapped onto our plastic sledge on rails awaiting our turns to be told "No use zee brakes" by the jovial man in charge before accelerating southwards at a fairly rapid rate. What a fantastic buzz chasing down a steep hill being thrown around the many twists turns and bumps of the course while seeing the town getting closer and closer and the bends getting tighter and tighter...yeee haaaa!!

We all want another go but time is against us as we have a meal booked at our hotel. We liked Todtnau, it's great to happen across something that much fun. Our route takes us back through Triberg a town with shops that proclaim '1000 clocks in stock' but more temptingly the highest waterfall in Germany, TRIBERGER WASSERFÄLLE with a descent of 163 m. Alas we must miss this as we are beaten by our own clocks. From Triberg the route has its moments but I think we are all ready for the promise of that shower and food.

It's amazing how good it feels to be in fresh clothes, showered, clean and sat outside with cool beer. The menu requires some interpretation, no English, but our waitress copes admirably. The resultant meals really complete what have been an extraordinarily pleasurable couple of days. When our host and chef joins us later for a chat we are positively gushing praise but just can't establish exactly what fish dish veggie Kryten has consumed. We make our beers last as long as possible as none of us wants to admit it's over and we must face the arduous return journey to the ferry.

Monday – Wolfach to Europort (420miles 7hrs 15mins)

Auf Wiedersehens are exchanged after an early breakfast and we are soon leaving Wolfach far behind as we try to swiftly put some miles in towards our Rotterdam by 7pm target. Away from the Black Forest minor roads we are once again blasting down the endless motorways with Herr BMW for close company.

Our plan is to break up the journey with a slight detour to Esch-sur-Sure, a highly recommended village in Luxembourg, a good half way back. We experience some confusion at a toll booth to a French PÉAGE, or was it a Belgian one, they all look the same. It would seem that for some you get a ticket and pay at the end and on some you pay at the start. Also, from our experience, the PÉAGE is a favourite place for lurking Gendarmes eager to swell their piggy banks with speeding fines.

Later we manage to get hopelessly lost in Luxembourg City centre and spend a very hot and frustrating hour or more trying to extricate ourselves. When we do find the way out and arrive in our recommended stop off it looks beautiful. It is set in a dramatic loop of the River Sauer but a quick glance at our watches confirms we have no time to enjoy it or the ruined castle perched above.

Food has to be a swift affair at a filling station on the motorway before continuing onwards. Chippy takes these opportunities to draw on a well-earned fag. Kryten's badly fitting helmet requires him to apply Sudocrem to an increasingly sore red patch at each petrol stop. Dan remarks that it looks like the same seagull is crapping on his head each time we stop. It is a rare moment of humour in the mundane madness of the motorway. At last we start to see the signs for 'Europoort' (but don't be fooled if you do this route as I am convinced the ring road leading there takes in half of Holland!) and make our ferry with about an hour to spare.

The crossing back is a much more subdued affair. The ferry seems almost empty and we are all tired and sad it's over for another year. Sadder still when Captain Charisma turns up doing the bingo to about half a dozen uninterested passengers! Even sadder than that when the musical entertainment strikes up. No-one wants to stay up late tonight.

Tuesday – North Sea Ferry Terminal Hull to Home (40 miles 1hr)

Following the Bing-Bong announcement that we are nearing Hull we get suited up ready to joust with the rush hour traffic. In the car deck I receive a text welcome home message from my young son and can't wait to get moving. My fellow travellers are all due back at work today and will ride straight there from the ferry, so I am the lucky one.

We weave our way in between the endless trail of stationary vehicles and head back over the bridge waving farewells on the motorway slip road. I make it back home just in time to be waiting for my son as he arrives at his school gates, perfect!

That was it for another year. Probably the best trip to date and a very tough one to follow. We are all still buzzing about it when the emailed photos start doing the rounds a few days later and the talk turns to plans for next year. Can't wait! Oh, and after a little research by my multi-lingual wife I am able to inform Kryten that the fish he ate was a member of the dolphin family....Oh my god he's eaten Flipper!

Chapter 4.

Good For Your Harz. (7 Days).

Thursday - Home to Hull (40miles 1 hour)

Anyone who knows me will tell you I don't do rain on a bike, it's no fun, it's cold and it's dangerous. But here I am sat outside Morrisons in the pouring rain and howling gale about to set off on our annual pilgrimage to the near continent. It's June and the forecast is not looking good for our destination either, bugger! I am not a happy bunny. I have seriously considered jumping ship from this tour. My companions, however, have few such concerns and my wife thinks I'm a wimp (she's right of course). I have to go; we have been planning this since we returned from last years' jaunt.

I think my mood is further exasperated as I have changed my bike since our last trip. I am now the proud owner of a new Aprilia RSV Factory (sex on 2 wheels) that until an hour ago was sat gleaming, warm and dry in my garage. For the record Kryten also has a new steed, a little yellow Suzuki SV650 of which he is equally proud and which was equally clean not long ago. Neither machine would be in any sensible persons' top ten best touring bikes but with a little compromise they will still do the job.

So, where are we off to this time? The town of Bad Grund in the Harz Mountains, part of the Saxony region of Germany. Yes, I know you've never heard of it, neither had we but it sounded good when I came across it by accident on the internet. Most of us thought it worth a go but Kryten did his best to sow the seeds of doubt. "I've looked it up and it's on the same latitude as Manchester so it will rain." This view was further enhanced by a Wikipedia entry that stated 'Because of the heavy rainfall in the region the rivers of the HARZ MOUNTAINS were dammed from an early date'. Oh dear. We spent last years' trip in the Black Forrest area and it was sunshine all the way so this trip had a lot to live up to...and it was already raining!

With all the stuff a bloke needs for a few days away tightly packed inside bin liners inside waterproof luggage covered with waterproof covers I creep my bike out from the limited shelter into the elements. My waterproof over-suit is zipped and Velcro'd up to my neck, I am wearing over boots (over my boots), thick waterproof gloves and a neck warmer. On the busy motorway there is spray from cars and my visor steams up (what fun!). Crossing the Humber Bridge we are bullied by a vicious cross wind which sees us displaying some rather impressive lean angles. Chippy, the lead rider, has all our toll money which saves the gloves off, fumble for change, gloves back on routine so enjoyed by following traffic.

It is a routine that cannot be avoided as we make our way through customs towards P&Os "Pride of Hull". Behind us are a couple on one of those Ewan McGregor BMW things. Through the rain we ask where they're heading. "Corfu" we are told and I thought they were joking. No joke, they were off for a three week European jolly through all-sorts of countries using around five different ferries on the way, crikey! I think they were hoping for better weather at some point though.

Inside the ships vehicle deck we begin to emerge from our wet clothing and start the task of removing the carefully fitted luggage from the bikes. Everything is soaking wet and a smell of exhaust fumes permeates the air. Next comes the tying down of the pride 'n' joy. I have an unlimited supply of rope and make full use of it; the bike looks like it's just read Fifty Shades of Grey. Now I have to transport all my gear to the cabin, up-stairs and through narrow corridors pushing past a melee of equally lost passengers.

Not everyone fanny's about like me of course, some of my friends are actually quite normal (with one notable exception). When I finally find the cabin Festa is just emerging, dry, changed and ready to make his way to the bar area for a shandy (or something). I am last to get sorted of course. It is a small cabin, there is much wet gear to attempt to dry and I feel the need to organise now rather than after the shandy takes effect later on. It never ceases to amaze me that even though I packed just a couple of short hours ago I can never find anything.

Eventually I extricate myself from the confines of the on-board accommodation ready to join the rest of the group. We all sit in the "entertainment" area listening to Captain Personality on the microphone laughing at his own inaudible jokes before being treated to the musical talent that is "Chicomania". Ok, so they're better than last years' offering, a bit.

Out of the windows and through the wind and rain the horizon can be seen gently rising and falling as Blighty slips silently past. The ships' Captain informs us we will enjoy what he terms a "moderate crossing" tonight. As alcohol begins to have effect and the sea gets all moderate, the journey back from the bar or toilet becomes more comical. Simply aiming at the table is no guarantee of arrival there-about. Oopps, I've just remembered my seasick pills! I have an interesting trip back to the cabin which is right at the pointy end of the ship, the bit that goes up 'n' down the most. I am not a good traveller. I get car sick and bus sick and am a white knuckle flyer, rubbish aren't I? I hope to goodness these little pills work their magic tonight!

Friday – Europort to Bad Grund (333miles 5hrs 45mins).

BING – BONG! "Guter Morgen die Herren und Damen" The ships tannoy has burst into life. It's six o'clock European time, so that's five o'clock in real time. I have slept on the top bunk in a room shared with Festa and Kryten. I have listened to the waves crashing against the ships' hull and a rattling picture all night, but I haven't been ill so the pills have worked. Festa was out like a light but Kryten had spent the night listening to that rattle. We make our way to the breakfast buffet bun fight and find that Chippy and Desperate Dan have been up ages. The weather around the windmills is foggy but it's not raining…yet. The consensus is that we will not wear the wet gear until we have to. Replete of full English, clad in moist leather and carrying all our possessions we join the race to the vehicle deck. Europe, shrouded in fog, beckons through the gaping hole of the ships door, but first there's the little matter of releasing bondage bike.

Free at last after passport control we immediately take a wrong turn and start heading back to the ship. This is soon put behind us as we begin to make good progress towards our destination some 333miles away down the Autobahns. I am conscious of the Aprilias' limited tank range and soon gesture to Chippy I need to fill up. When we stop I am met with puzzled looks. Turns out I have set my Speedo for kilometres which in turn had set my trip meter to kilometres (plonker!).

We had an on off relationship with our waterproofs throughout the journey which meant that my tank range did not impede progress any further. To be fair to the bike I think we have quite a well matched tank and bladder range, when the tank is empty the bladder is full! I can find little else to say about riding a motorcycle down a motorway. It's not what they are for; it's a means to an end, a necessary evil to be endured. The good part about bikes, of course, is their filtering abilities, something we made abundant use of through the myriad lorries we encountered (especially near junctions and roadworks). It was quite noticeable the difference between Dutch and German driving. The Autobahns are fast and furious places but they make for rapid progress.

The last sixty miles or so is taken off the autobahn to avoid travelling around Hanover. As it turns out this is a good move as road works around there are causing major hold ups. Navigation now is more difficult and progress seems much slower but we arrive in Bad Grund after a flawless display by Chippy who lead us the whole way. Ok, so now we've gone a bit wrong in our excitement at finding the town. We occupy a bus shelter and get the map and instructions out. We'd taken just one wrong turn which was soon sorted and from the bus shelter we went straight to the hotel.

The Hotel in Bad Grund is run by ex-pat couple who are both outside immediately to greet us with the warmest of welcomes. With introductions and handshakes competed we are ushered inside for most welcome beers. "Leave your gear on the bikes guys, no-one pinches stuff round here" we are assured. Beers are poured and conversation turns to the journey and bikes. Our host is excellent and very knowledgeable. Turns out he is an ex. sidecar and solos racer and an ex MCN journalist (nobody's perfect).

With that in mind and for the purpose of this tale I will name him Foggy, after the superbike champion and king of the jungle. "Do you guys fancy a three course meal?" he eventually asks. Daft question really, after a day on the Autobahns eating junk. We are shown to our very spacious rooms, one each this year, before we unload the bikes and dive into the showers, bliss!

Outside it is starting to rain once more as we assemble for the meal. Ok, so this isn't the greatest culinary experience in the world. Soup, followed by, err. two German sausages with two hash browns and some tinned veg. with a finale of, "ta da", two blobs of ice-cream. Not good, but worth it for the look on Desperate Dan's face as he poked the undercooked sausage things. It did get better away from the table as the night slipped by in a mixture of good humoured chat and more beer.

An IAM group turned up later in the evening and Foggy hurried to welcome them in the same manner he had for us. Seems one of their less popular members had got left behind during an arduous trip that had not been helped by a five hour delay on the ferry. Tempers were frayed but after a beer and some of Foggys' cheery patter things calmed down. "Do you fancy a three course meal guys?" he asked them. It was a good time for our lot to checkout our footwear and try not to laugh. When the "sausage surprise" began arriving we decided it was time for bed, big day tomorrow, a ride-out with Foggy.

Saturday – Ride-out heaven knows where (120miles? 5 hrs)

Wake up, after a night of heavy rain, to a cloudy but drying day. Downstairs the breakfast table displays what will become familiar fayre. Small glass of orange juice, one egg, two small bread buns, one pot of coffee, one small pot of jam, one small plate of butter and a plate containing one slice of cheese and one slice of ham each, one large plastic container with cornflakes and two small jugs of milk. Foggy greets us with a beaming smile and asks if anyone would like a pot of tea, we all do.

We tuck in and soon clear the table. Foggy flits back and forth as the IAM group begins to filter in. They will be joining us on the ride out today. Well some of them will be as the rift that opened up on the journey yesterday spills into today. The less popular member had not found the hotel until around two in the morning when the rain was at its heaviest so some would be having an "easy" day. We accept

Foggys' offer of more tea which duly arrives. A more apt description would have been "more water" since no further teabags were to be sacrificed this morning. Even the thorough pummelling each bag received barely managed to stain the liquid that crawled out of the pot. Time to get ready for the day while the IAM guys "get stuck in".

An air of excited anticipation drifts around outside as bikes of all shapes and sizes are lovingly prepared for the day. One bloke has an enormous Goldwing with what can only be described as a barbecue rack low down at the back. He proudly informs us he usually tows a trailer containing everything but the kitchen sink. I resist a strong urge to suggest he considers the purchase of a car for future trips. All but one carries a pillion. The one has sat-nav. and video camera mounts all over his bike and sports an "IAM INSTRUCTOR" yellow florescent bib, apparently he isn't married.

Foggy has the cool confident manner of being at one with familiar proceedings. Clad in a plain black two piece leather suit he is by far the most vertically challenged rider amongst us, even Festa is taller, but he commands respect. The old CBR 1000 he rides is no looker and shows all the signs of a machine that is the practical tool of his trade. Foggy does not burden his bike with all the nonsense we seem to need either and is soon ready for the off.

This is it, the beginning of what we have ridden all this way to do. Old bikes, big ugly bikes, flash sporty bikes and a little yellow SV650 all burst into life together filling the tiny street with exhaust gasses and noise. It really doesn't matter what your choice of machine is, riding in the company of others is a good craic. The sun is chasing away the remnants of last nights' rainfall as one by one we snick into first gear, release the grip of the brakes, ease out the clutch and file out and away from the hotel, sounds echoing around the little town.

Up to the top of the hill leaving Bad Grund below us we join a still slightly damp main road and the pace quickens. Foggy heads off into the first set of bends closely followed by most of the hi-viz team, us and then Quentin Tarantino on the camera bike. The road twists and turns, rises and falls through tightly packed forest with an occasional glimpse of a lake or a view. Not that there is much time to digest any of it, this kind of riding demands full concentration. The bends are many, fast and flowing, one leading naturally into another. You search for clues as to where the road will go next, check the rider in front for brake lights and strain to see as far into the bend as possible. Am I in the right position on the road? Have I selected the right gear? What's that idiot with the camera bike doing now?

We turn off and begin to climb out of the trees to the top of a hill. We haven't been going for more than about 40mins or so but it's a good time to stop and catch your breath. Torfhaus is little more than a car park with the usual café and gift shop. In the winter this is the start of a ski run or two, but in the summer it is a meeting point for bikes. The views of the surrounding country are nothing to write home about but there is plenty to tempt the eyes around the car park. The Kawasaki Club arrives with a goodly mixture of 70s and 80s machinery. Chippy, however, is none too impressed with Quentin Tarantino, it seems, as he has a tendency to fiddle with the equipment while riding which slows him down unexpectedly. If Chippy had his way the camera would be filming some most unusual scenes, probably of more interest to the renal unit of the medical profession than to the biking world though.

Time to go again and it is our turn to provide the entertainment as we leave the car park. A slightly odd, miss-matched, group of GB plated bikers winds its way back down the hillside. Foggy leads us round more and more curved tarmac now almost completely dried by the increasingly warm sunshine. We pass by open meadows and farm buildings, past a lake and through some very German looking villages. The architecture is clearly different to our own with greater use of wood from the surrounding forests and roofs designed for heavy falls of winter snow. Villages present brief moments to take in something other than riding. The slower pace allows one to focus on the intricate detail of a building, goods on offer on a market stall or on the expression of a face as we pass by (or just ogle a curvy Fräulein of course! Wunderbar!).

After a much longer ride we pull in to an unpromising looking car park with a café. It doesn't look like much but it has a really good atmosphere about it. "Tea mit Milch bitte, und ein Kuchen bitte"

"Dank" As Foggy is busy elsewhere one of the IAM pillions fulfils the vital role of translator. I attempt to copy her and am rewarded with a little international Banta, smiles, a cup of tea and a piece of cake. I couldn't understand a word of how much it was so I sneak a peek at the till. The lady try's to tell me in English and we meet somewhere in the middle, brilliant!

We all gather outside in the hot sunshine and chat about the ride. It's all good stuff. The tea is welcome and the cake is delicious (no idea what it is though). Foggy tells us that the disused building on the opposite side of the road is the old customs house where the East West border used to be. A high fence, guards with dogs and machine guns used to divide this area. When the Berlin Wall came down it took several days for the news to reach this part of the country. Once it had the guards just seemed to vanish overnight and the locals began to dismantle the barriers. We had been riding in and out of the old East and West all morning.

In the car park bikes of all shapes and sizes come and go. The odd flash git pulls a wheelie as they head out and the sound of "enthusiastic riding" can be heard resonating around the surrounding hillsides. It's time for us to join them once again. Our group files out tucking in behind Foggy for some more fun. The fun soon comes in bucket-fulls as we chase each other down through valleys and up over crests, passing farms and hamlets. The group gets stretched out through the bends and from my position as rear gunner I catch fleeting glimpses of the ribbon of bikes leaning one way then the other like a well-orchestrated set of tumbling dominoes.

Eventually Foggy leads us into the town of Stolberg, a World Heritage site. The half-timbered houses of this medieval town date from 15th to 18th century and it's lovely. Where the road narrows past a round clock tower we ride into a small square. The tarmac road has turned into cobblestones and we arrive near a restaurant. There are bikes everywhere and it's a struggle to find somewhere to park. Everyone is sat outside enjoying the warm early afternoon sunshine and watching the bikes go by. We settle on the table just outside and order some of Foggys' recommendations; well it was either that or play food roulette with the German menu.

The sound of chattering voices interspersed with laughter is interrupted only by the clatter of the local tourist horse and carriage, oh, and the sounds of bikes coming and going. It struck me that this is so much different than it would be at home. Bikes in this kind of environment would be tut-tutted at while young children would be shepherded into the protective arms of worried parents. Here everyone stops to watch the bikes and to listen to the various exhaust notes, a KTM with Akraprovic cans sounding particularly fruity as it made its way in to the square.

After lunch we have a quick shuftie around to stretch our legs. Foggy says he has never known it to rain while he has been coming here, just then it started to rain! Anxious faces scan the skys as we huddle under the restaurants awning. The square quickly clears as alfresco diners seek shelter inside. Thankfully it's just a shower and we are soon on our way again. Panic hits the front of the group almost immediately, Kryten is leading! Kryten only ever leads onto the ferry, he gets disorientated otherwise. I am in second place and refuse to take the lead as the sight is too funny to miss. We slow to such a pace it is difficult to keep moving. Eventually Foggy takes pity and comes back to the front to lead us to the petrol station.

Before long one of our IAM friends hurries to the front to halt the group as we have lost one of their number. We all pull to the side of the road when we hear a bit of a crunch going on at the back. The enormous BMW thing has toppled over sending its lady passenger tumbling into the street. With many hands making light work the huge beast is righted (and the bike is put back on its centre stand to…sorry, couldn't resist).

Once more with a full complement we head off to the garage. The touring bikes don't need to stop as often as the sporty ones, especially the Aprilia, so it's not long before we are all off to the next junction, a tricky left turn with traffic lights. The front one or two make the turn but one bike gets a headlight flash from an oncoming car and starts the turn. Foggy tells us later that flashed headlights mean "look out I am here" not "through you go mate" as at home. I have never seen such a big bike, with passenger, turn so tightly and remain upright. Left a large brown skid-mark in the road though.

Now we were in for a real treat, 6km of hairpin bends starting at Kelbra up and over Kyffhauser, a 470m high forested mountain ending back down in Bad Frankenhausen. There are, we are told, 35 bends up to the top, and a similar amount down the other side presumably. The roads have dried out nicely by the time we reach the first bend and begin the accent, and what an accent! The bends just keep coming. I didn't bother counting them as I was a little busy hauling the bike from side to side. I began to adopt a slightly odd looking racing crouch, trying to hang off the bike a little bit more. Not that I think my speeds demanded such antics, just because it feels so good and, in a curious kind of way, it seems to help me focus on the sheer enjoyment of it all. More bends and with little other traffic the bobbly bits on the edges of my tyres start to brush against this beautiful mountain tarmac. I'd like to make it clear that I don't claim any knee down action here, just getting the bike over further, turning more quickly and driving out more smoothly (I just hope there's no IAM boys video footage of this to burst my bubble).

When we eventually reach the crest I am ready for a break, my eyeballs are pushing against my visor and I don't think I've blinked for the last fifteen minutes! No stopping now though as Foggy legs it down the other side. Foggy had warned us to be a little more careful on the way down as some of the bends are less predictable. Wise words well heeded as I follow everyone downhill and brake lights come on from the, by now, slightly over confident group in front. I feel sure we all have a tale to tell of a slightly misjudged hairpin or two if we are totally honest. It seemed even further down than it did up and I am almost praying for it to end.

I am gripping with my knees to keep the weight off my aching wrists but it feels like I am performing a never ending handstand. Sounds like a complaint, but inside my helmet I am grinning from ear to ear as the ground begins to level out on the approach to Bad Frankenstien, fantastic stuff!

Out of town and the necessarily reduced mountain pace is soon picked up as we begin our return journey. Having over five years of them there hills 'n' valleys experience means Foggy knows all sorts of ways to keep up the enthusiasm and, enthusiastic riding is what we are about as we crack on along some flat swift smooth roads. The

IAM guys' bigger touring bikes were beginning to take their toll so I guess it was with some relief that we stopped back at the border café once more. Helmets were almost thrown off as we couldn't wait to share our experiences of the last couple of hours. I think Foggy got the message that we were all blown away by it all as the little guy in black was surrounded by cheesy grins. Tea and cake was taken outside and we chatted to the sound of gently pinging engines while calming down and adjusting to slower thought processes. I sat staring at my bike at one point; I almost felt I had let it down by not scraping the pegs, or scuffing that last bit of rubber from the very edge of those super sticky tyres. The Aprilia sat on the gravel of the car park nonchalantly pinging away and I swear I saw it shake its head.

Soon we are off again on the final push back to the hotel. The road seemed familiar and I begin to think we will soon be back. Foggy had other ideas and we take a left turn through more contorted forest roads. The group becomes more thinly spread out and we have more of our own judgements to make approaching bends. Just as we are getting into a groove the black clouds that have threatened us for the last mile or so start to release their contents. The rain starts to fall, slowly at first but all too soon there is a deluge and it becomes almost impossible to see. Even through the protection of leather I can feel the force of each drop as it pounds down. Foggy does not stop. I can feel bits of me shrinking as the cold water begins to percolate through, yuck! After about ten minutes of this, though it seemed like longer, we spied the familiar turn off to Bad Grund and our hotel. The shower had just about abated by the time the last engine was switched off.

Desperate Dan was not a happy chappie. The helmet had barely been torn from his head before he launched into an Anglo-Saxon worded protest about not stopping to don wet gear. Foggy calmly replied we would all have got even wetter had we stopped, which I think was probably true so we resolved to take the piss out of Dan instead. Kryten performing an excellent re-enactment of the helmet off dummy spitting incident got us all, Dan included, back laughing again. "That was some 'Spirited Riding' there Kryten" says Foggy (praise indeed). Kryten's ill-fitting helmet will never be the same again. "Fancy a beer guys?" asked Foggy. I think the word is used way too much these days but it seems totally appropriate for what we had just experienced, Awesome!

After an all too brief phone call home, a shower and a change of clothes we are heading out of the hotel and down the hill into the town for dinner. The rain has stopped and it is a warm and still evening with few people about. Foggy has booked us into the restaurant and we are lcd to a waiting table. There are some familiar faces here already. It's our IAM friends and they've started without us. Fortunately this gives us the opportunity to choose not only from the menu (written in English at Foggys' request apparently) but also from the food being enjoyed in front of us. After an amazing days scratching in the company of friends where the food is excellent, the beer cool and plentiful we top it all off with apple strudel, can life get better? We walk slowly back up the hill to the hotel passing struggling IAM folk. Foggy was going to bed but stays to share a last beer or two with us all. It is gone midnight when I finally turn out the light to let go of the day and drift quickly off into a deep and contented sleep.

Sunday – Harz Discovery Tour (165miles 6 hrs).

Fortunately I have remembered to pack my alarm clock as it is the only way I am to make it down to breakfast in time. My room is bedecked by motorcycle gear hurriedly hung from every available protrusion in an attempt to initiate some form of drying process. I am last down to breakfast and find everyone tucking into exactly the same fayre as yesterday, yum. Today we shall be off exploring on our own and the sun is already chasing away the clouds. Foggy has given us plenty of advice as to where to go and what else there is to see and we can't wait to get started.

It's a great atmosphere outside the hotel first thing in the morning. There is an air of expectancy, anticipation, camaraderie oh and fag smoke. Leathers are zipped up and buckles snapped into place. Ear plugs are poked into position before the crowning moment when the helmet is eased into place and firmly strapped on. These are scenes reminiscent of the 'A Team' before they go and sort out the bad guys. Those who complete the task first (usually Festa) sit coolly waiting aboard their machines. Those who have to faff about rechecking everything (that'll be Kryten and me then) are still pulling on a glove or hunting down a stray earplug. But suddenly we are all ready, keys are being turned, starter buttons prodded and dormant engines sparked willingly into life. A glance and a nod confirms we are all ready and Chippy leads us away from the hotel and up onto the main road.

With yesterdays' run fresh in our minds the pace is a more confident one than that of our previous trips. You have to come to this area to fully appreciate how superb it is for riding a motorcycle round and how it can re awaken a true passion for just riding for fun. We soon take the left turn recommended by Foggy and start heading into a steeply sided valley with a fast flowing stream for company. The air feels fresh and inviting after the rain as we twist and turn our way further onwards and eventually upwards. We are heading for the mediaeval town of Goslar, a world heritage site, as recommended by most guides for the area and Foggy. In the cold war, Goslar had been a major garrison town for the German army and later the Border Police but as we enter it there are no signs of this recent history. We park up in a large space reserved for motorcycles and begin to review the ride, more smiley faces.

Foggy has assured us that no-one pinches anything around here but we can't break the English fear and expend some effort securing things. Once done we head towards the pedestrian part of town with the squeak and creak that accompanies the motorcyclist on foot. We enter a large cobbled square surrounded by exquisite architecture and with a fountain bubbling away in the middle. There are tables outside cafes and we sit down in the shade cast by one of the large umbrellas. Tea is eventually coaxed out of our attractive, non-English speaking, Fräulein waitress, albeit of a fruity nature, and we sit soaking up the sun and surroundings

There are many tourists here, mainly German and Dutch but I detect the odd American accent disturbing the peace. The owner of a horse drawn carriage plies his trade along with the far less agreeable 'Tonka Train' thing that comes clanking into the square. A crowd is gathering and on the stroke of mid-day we find out why. A clock perched high above bursts into life chiming out a classical piece of music. Doors open at both sides and various scenes are played out by automatons as they wobble in and out of the building. This is a quite extraordinary display as it keeps on going for five or ten minutes enthralling the crowd gathered below.

It is rather warm as we leave the café to explore the town. I break away to find a suitable present for the expectant 6 year old back home while the rest of the group checks out a variety of sites the town has to offer. This area is famous for tales of witches and Walpurgis Night on April 30 is an old pagan festival when witches are believed to ride on broomsticks to places of pagan sacrifices in the Harz Mountains. So my choice of homecoming gift this year was a witch on a broomstick. What six year old boy wouldn't want one of those?

We meet back at the bikes and are just getting ready when the gallant team IAM turn the corner. After a brief chat we work our way back out of Goslar and onto more of those roads this time heading towards the 75 m high, 260 m long Oker Dam (German: Okertalsperre). When we stop to admire the dam some guy on a Suzuki Bandit comes screaming up the valley leant hard over dragging a knee around the bend in front of the café. Looked great but it so nearly ended in disaster as a family of cyclists were occupying part of the road and Bandit Berk had to alter his line mid corner.

Time to consult the 'Harz Motorrad-Karte'. Oh yes, this is another example of the Germans love of bikes. They actually produce a map of the area highlighting all the best biking routes and it's in a strong waterproof form, brilliant. Can you imagine us in the UK endorsing such a thing for say North Wales? I think not.

We plan our next route but to be honest there doesn't seem to be a bad one amongst them. Everywhere we go there seems to be another great set of bends or a view or both to discover. Proof, if it were needed, that God truly is a biker and this is where he takes Mother Nature for a pillion ride to blow away the cobwebs.

After some more excellent scratching around another corner a familiar café comes into view and we stop for a bite to eat, a drink and a grin. This time I will try the Currywurst and pommes frites so highly recommended by Uncle Fester (not usually a person whose eating habits I would normally follow, but this stuff looked tempting). 'Tis the food of the Gods and swilled down with a cup of tea sets me up for what remains of the afternoon.

We decide to go and 'do' the thirty five bends of the Kyffhauser again but navigation becomes an issue and we get a bit lost in a town called Nordhausen. This turns out to have the rather unexpected twist of us riding over cobbles and tram lines only to find a tram coming the other way straight at us. Chippy wisely pulls quickly into a side road. What the f…?

After seeing most that the town has to offer, i.e. not much, we eventually find a garage for petrol before escaping back into the sanctuary of the surrounding countryside. On a road out of town our group is passed on a series of bends by a local rider on a Yamaha R1. It is hard to describe just how fast this guy was travelling. He was scraping his knee fully cranked over with the rev counter buried somewhere near the red zone on the wrong side of the road in a fashion Mr. Rossi himself would have been satisfied with. I think we all watched and listened in amazement as he screamed away into the distance. Quite how anyone builds that sort of self-belief is beyond me but I have to admit to being secretly somewhat impressed.

After the struggle of Nordhausen and the ride to the base of Kyffhauser Chippy elects to have what becomes known as a 'Magnum Moment' and looks for an ice cream shop in Bad Frankenhausen. If he had planned it we could not have been more fortunate for we stopped next to surely the very best ice cream shop in the region. You know it's good when you have to wait in a queue of locals that stretches out the door. The ice cream is exceptionally delicious, reasonably priced and very welcome as we sit with the sun beating down in the small square. Time is getting on and those bends beckon us on.

The climb starts just outside the town and we are soon winding our way up and over the mountain. Somehow there seem to be more bends this time as we take more turns than a drunk on a unicycle. Most of the bends are smoothly predicable with the odd hairpin that tightens or keeps on turning just to keep you on your toes. In the lay-bys on each corner small groups of bikers gather to watch others make their way past. As we pass by a couple follow us down and are soon hot on our heels. I stick out a leg to encourage them to pass admiring the skills of those who 'know the road'. I am too embarrassed to try the racing tuck knee out stuff myself at such comparatively low speed but am buzzing none the less inside my helmet. There are very few cars on this section of road and those we see coming the other way seem to be very aware of the bikes. At the bottom of the hill the fast guys are just preparing to go back up for another go as we pass by and regroup in the town. We have all had such a blast coming down and, in hindsight, we should have gone back to sit in a lay-by ourselves.

We must now make our way back to the hotel but the fabulous roads just keep on coming. I don't claim to know the history of the place but I am guessing the Romans had no part in road building in this area. In fact if the roads in the Harz were public servants, they'd be politicians...there isn't a straight one here! Oh, tell a lie, there is one straightish bit right through the middle, top to bottom and it contains the only known speed camera in the area. You know where it is because it's near the only bridge on the road. We make full use of this road as we make swift progress back to the hotel. When I say straight though, it is more a series of connected curves, but that is straight for this area.

Back at the hotel we reflect on another superb day over a beer or two with Foggy. Yesterday was a long day so we had initially planned to take it easier today. Turns out we had actually covered even more miles on our own such was the fun we were having. When we mention we have ridden over Kyffhauser again Foggy tells us that there is an unofficial record up and down that particular section. It is held by a guy on a 125cc race bike with slick tyres. Also, despite most traffic choosing different routes, the road has been recently resurfaced. This is because the area attracts so many bikers. I ask if the locals get a bit pissed off with all the bikes? Foggy tells us that the Harz area suffers from high unemployment so bikers bring in much needed revenue. So much so that when the Mayor of Bad Grund tried to impose a ban on bikes he did not get re-elected!

There seems to be little time for relaxing in the shower before we are heading off to the restaurant in town. Our IAM friends are already there when we arrive and we swap tales enthusiastically over the fabulous meals. I am thoroughly caught up in it all. Normally I don't drink very much or eat red meat yet here I am on my third or fourth beer tucking into pork based Schnitzel and loving it. Kryten too is having a great time 'entertaining' the ladies of Team IAM with his muscular salt grinding prowess, what a tart!

We are the last out of the restaurant and slowly make our way back up towards the hotel. We are given a friendly wave by one of the waitresses as she parks her car at her house nearby, she could have given us a lift! Over one last beer Foggy tells us that when he first moved into the village he used to send customers to the restaurant but they couldn't understand where all the English people kept coming from. It was only when he got talking to the waitress neighbour down the road that all became clear and the menu translated into English. Anyway, it's past my bed time and I am knackered, another brilliant day drifts into a deep sleep.

Monday - Bad Grund to Colditz (150miles 2hrs 30mins).

When booking the hotel I had organised with Foggy to keep our rooms for a night while we rode off to visit a long held ambition of mine, Colditz Castle. Despite Foggy suggesting there wasn't much there we couldn't let the opportunity pass by without seeing for ourselves.

Keen to get going we were up for an early start quickly demolishing the breakfast offerings and securing overnight luggage onto the bikes. We headed out of Bad Grund to join the B243 which fed us onto the 38 and 14 Autobahns. Here we endured the usual jousting with German luxury vehicles for a couple of hours but at least the rain stayed away.

At last turning off the Autobahn we were soon able to enjoy the far more pleasing sight of the eight hundred year old town of Grimma. Despite its name Grimma likes to be known as the "Pearl of the Mulde River Valley" in the heart of Saxony, interesting just what advertising folk can dream up sometimes.

Exiting the Pearl of the Mulde River Valley it's not long before we spy the sign that announces we are entering the town of Colditz. For me having grown up watching the BBC TV series (Bernard Hepton as the Kommandant, David McCallum, Jack Hedley and Robert Wagner to name just some of the captives) and playing the 'Escape from Colditz' board game with my brother in the 1970s, actually arriving in Colditz was almost unbelievable.

Colditz Castle (Officially named OFLAG IVC - Officers Camp IV C), was hidden behind the "Iron Curtain" for over 50 years and yet now I was sitting on a motorcycle I had ridden here from England looking up at the huge walls. Truth was, ironically, we couldn't find the way in!

Once an entrance was located we crossed a cobbled courtyard to book ourselves in for the night. Oh yes! When I researched the visit I found part of the old guards quarters had been converted into a Youth Hostel. Better still we were told to leave our bikes inside and were given a set of keys to the gate in case we were out late (never an option in the board game as I recall).

We had arrived a little early but the guy on reception let us into our room to get changed as we had booked a guided tour starting at 2pm. Eager to get started we arrived at the small museum gift shop and found our guide waiting for us. She introduced herself as Steffi Schubert and spoke excellent English with a German accent. Steffi told us a large group had cancelled their visit so we would be her only guests for the tour which would last around two hours (we had chosen the Extended Tour which included most of the escape places - Pat Reid Cellar, French Tunnel, Glider Loft - Price: 18,00 € adults – cash only).

First we had a tour of the small museum were Steffi told us a brief history of the castle. In 1829 it became a mental hospital for the "incurably insane". In1864 a new hospital was built and it remained a mental institution until 1924. Between 1914 and 1918 the castle housed both psychiatric and tuberculosis patients, nearly 1000 of whom died of malnutrition. When the Nazis gained power during1933, they converted the castle into a political prison for communists, homosexuals, Jews and "undesirables" (probably motorcyclists).

From 1939 it was under the control of the Wehrmacht and used as a POW camp for Allied officers of high rank. It became a high security prison because some prisoners were known for their attempts to escape. They reckon there were more guards than prisoners. The Germans thought it escape-proof, the allied inmates proved them wrong. There were more than 300 escape attempts and over 30 successful ones.

Some of the more well-known prisoners here included, RAF flying ace Douglas Bader, Desmond Llewelyn (later known as Q in 17 James Bond films), Capt. Pat Reid, British escape officer at Colditz who later wrote of his experiences, Airey Neave who became a Conservative MP and Col David Stirling, founder of the Special Air Service.

Out of the museum we walked across the cobbles to trace the route taken by Pat Reid, Ronnie Littledale, Bill Stevens and Howard Wardle. Under cover of darkness they sawed through window bars in the prisoners' kitchens, climbed down onto the roof of the German kitchens and crept to the workshop door on the far side of the courtyard. They expected to find it unlocked but it wasn't so they moved round until they came to a cellar in the corner used for storing potatoes. The group spent several days hiding in the potato store before climbing out into the moat through a small air vent, Steffi showed us the vent and said she was perfectly happy for us to try it but we wisely declined. Seems the group stripped naked to wriggle out, facing backwards. Splitting into two pairs and disguised as Flemish workmen, all four made it to Switzerland.

Moving to an outside area called the Tiergarten where prisoners were taken for exercise Steffi told us that the French were the most prolific escapees and on April 11, 1941 French Lieutenant Alain Le Ray became the first. He hid in a terrace house in the park during a game of football and managed to reach neutral Switzerland. I later recounted this to some French friends we have (one of whom teaches German) and they had never heard of Colditz. I rectified this later that year by sending them the BBC box set for Christmas.

In the Tiergarten Steffi removed a lose cover from a drain and told us of escapes by Dutch prisoners. Lieutenants Hans Larive and Francis Steinmetz hid under the manhole cover emerging after dark to climb a wall before taking a train to Gottmadingen and reaching Switzerland three days later. This route wasn't discovered and so Dutch Major C. Giebel and Lieutenant O. L. Drijber used the same method for another successful escape.

Back inside Steffi allowed us to have our photographs taken standing on the theatre stage while she told us of the first British officer to escape. Lt Airey Neave and Dutch officer Tony Luteyn created a concealed hatchway underneath the stage and through the ceiling of a disused corridor. The disused corridor ran over the prisoners' courtyard gate to a building used as German officers' quarters. Dressed in fake German officers' uniforms, Neave and Luteyn descended the stairs and simply walked out of the castle for a successful "Home Run".

There were many more failures than successes which meant some time in "the cooler". We were shown the route of an elaborate tunnel built by nine French officers. It started at the top of the clock then descended 8m to a cellar through the space where the clock's weights and chains would have been. From this cellar they tunnelled under the floor of the chapel cutting a way through thick wooden beams before tunnelling down again breaking through into the Tiergarten. Unfortunately after all this effort Steffi showed us where the tunnel was discovered.

One of the more audacious plans was dreamt up by pilots Bill Goldfinch and Jack Best. With the help of numerous others they built a glider from bits of wood and nicked sleeping bags in an attic hidden behind a false wall. The plan was to break through the wall at the end of the attic and use counterweights to catapult it along a runway built on the ridge of the roof in front, which was hidden from the view of the Germans. The war ended before they could carry out the plan.

Steffi's in depth knowledge extended to many more stories, some quite humorous, but looking out over the Tiergarten she told us there was one confirmed fatality during the escape attempts. After receiving a 'Dear John' letter British Lieutenant Michael Sinclair attempted a repeat of the French vault over the wire escape. A security guard shouted a warning but Sinclair failed to stop and was fired on by other guards. A bullet hit Sinclair on the elbow and ricocheted through his heart.

I am sure that our tour lasted well over the two hours but all too soon we stood looking out over the town and the river from a vantage point while Steffi finally pointed out the flight path the glider would have made had it flown. Her final speech was interrupted by a man who she knew and embraced briefly before returning to us.

After Steffi had finished her talk she introduced us to the guy who turned out to be Tony Hoskins, owner of UK based glider maintenance / repair company. In 2012 his team was commissioned by Channel 4 Television to build a radio-controlled, full-sized replica glider in the Chapel attic. Once completed it was successfully flown from Colditz for a Channel 4 documentary and now forms part of a museum display in the Chapel Attic. It proved that the plan could have worked though as Steffi pointed out had the glider been launched today it would probably have landed on the Lidl supermarket.

We chatted with our fellow ex-pat for a while and he suggested we all go out for a meal that night as he was on a business trip and was tired of being on his own. This suited us fine as we had no clue about where to eat so we left him to catch up with Steffi and went back to our room in the guards' quarters.

Tony picked us all up and took us over the bridge and through some smaller roads to Gasthaus u. Pension Zur Kutscherstube (probably). He had spent several weeks in the town during the building process and was a mind of information. Certainly we would have never found the restaurant without him. We sat outside catching the remains of the suns' rays and seemed to be the only ones dining. The waiter / owner also greeted Tony as an old friend and spoke pretty good English.

Even with his grasp of the English language though our host still had trouble with Krytens' vegetarian requests but a solution was found, salad and chips, while the carnivores tucked into a superb local meaty feast. Numerous German beers were consumed as Tony continued to delight us with his knowledge of the town, the castle and his travels while we swapped stories of ours.

On the way back to the hostel in Tony stopped his car on a hill overlooking the castle which was lit up, its' white-washed walls resplendent against the darkening evening skies and a photo opportunity if ever there was one, shame I forgot to bring my camera then, bugger!

Tuesday - Colditz return to Bad Grund (165miles 4 hrs).

Awake to another sunny day in a prisoner of war castle. Breakfast is the usual hostel fayre of bread, jam and coffee but we are soon walking out of the front gate and crossing the bridge escaping the confines of the castle to have a quick look around the town. We find the sloping main square (Markt) with its cobbled surface surrounded by a collection of traditional looking older buildings. Unfortunately the square seems to double as a car park and aside from the town hall (Rathaus) at one end and a couple of restaurants there is little to hold our attention. When we return to the castle I have a quick look around the gift shop and find a Colditz Castle T shirt for my son but am disappointed they don't have my size in stock.

With a quick change of clothes out of 'civvies' and into biking gear we load up the bikes and pay the man. Sat astride my bike I take one last look around the imposing walls before turning the key and pressing go. The Aprilia bursts into life and is soon joined by the other four bikes our mixed exhaust notes reverberating around the courtyard. A brief glance over my shoulder and after nods all round we move out through the side entrance to leave the castle in peace once more, hardly Steve McQueen though.

Across the river we retrace our steps through 'Pearl of the Mulde River Valley' to the A38 Autobahn for another sparing session with the German motoring public. This time we turn off onto A71 briefly before an exit to the town of Artern and on towards Bad Frankenhausen.

In Bad Frankenhausen we miraculously locate the B85 and can once again indulge ourselves in the hairpin bend-fest up and over Kyffhauser towards Kelbra. With the odd car swiftly dispatched I gesture to the guys to come past me as I know they'll be eager to push the speed a little more than I am comfortable with.

So off we go again, the mountain to one side and Armco barriers to the other with the greenery of the surrounding forest blinkering the view ahead. On some bends I notice the Armco is painted red and white and set slightly back from the road as if to provide a small run-off area for the overenthusiastic, ran out of skill mid corner riders. This only goes to enhance the illusion of this being a race track rather than a public highway. Dotted along the side are occasional warning signs depicting leaning motorcyclists as well there might be judging by some of those hurtling down towards us.

We do not have the place to ourselves as is confirmed by a quick flash of approaching headlights in my mirrors. Several experienced German plated bikes blast past leant hard over and pick off the plucky Brits in rapid succession before their engine notes drift away into the distance.

I don't care, I have decided to do my own thing at the back and have assumed my version of a racing crouch once again shuffling from side to side and poking a tentative knee out towards the apex in the hope that it might make contact with the ground at least once. It doesn't! I am concentrating hard trying to look further ahead, brake, turn, and accelerate up from second to third gear brushing the double white lines in the centre of the road before braking, dropping down a gear with a blip of the throttle and turning in again. It's an all-consuming ride but if my confidence begins to grow beyond my skill level it is abruptly brought back down by a bend tighter than anticipated and a close up view of unforgiving Armco.

Once over the crest I notice I am beginning to lose touch with the group on the decent. I think the extra momentum that riding downhill gives just knocks back my confidence a little further and I find myself lapsing into overly cautious mode. I gather my thoughts and manage to get a more even rhythm going as I chase the group from bend to bend each braking moment pushing my body weight onto the bars through my increasingly tiring wrists. Eventually the road levels out and I find the group waiting for me in a layby. Amid cheesy smiles we have a brief but animated exchange of stories of near misses, impressive cornering and near perfect roads.

Onwards we go through the town of Berga following the L236 passing Stolberg to locate the B242. This 30 mile or so final blast along a road we now know to contain zero speed cameras is a real treat. I don't recall seeing another vehicle the entire time, but then maybe we just swept past them as if they weren't there. Whichever it was we all arrived back at the hotel thoroughly blown away by another cracking days riding.

After a shower we all met up for a drink pouring out our memories of the past couple of days to Foggy who seemed fairly impressed with our adventures. Foggy then tells us he is planning to take himself off for a ride tomorrow and we can tag along if we like. If we like! Man we're there, when do we go? Ever hungry Desperate D reminded us we hadn't eaten yet and asked if there was any chance of a pizza nearby as we fancied a change so Foggy recommended a place but warned they may not speak much English.

The Italian themed restaurant looked empty but rather smart as we five English trouped in and were met by a very welcoming chap. Typical Brit I tried "Englisch sprechen bitte?" which registered a smile and the response of "A little" in a thick German accent as he showed us to a table. Running out of German phrases I counted on my fingers "eins zwei drei vier fünf" before I attempted the most important one I could muster "fünf biere bitte". "Gross?" came the reply "Oh Ja".

So that was the sum total of my German but when I looked back to the table there were confused faces staring at the menu, all in German with no sub-titles. With further examination and little guess work even Kryten was able to decipher a four cheese pizza for his vegetarian pallet. It was all going so well until someone suggested he would quite like some cheesy garlic bread. We tried to explain this to our host and he desperately attempted to understand the complete nonsense being uttered by his dopey guests. After a while a spark of recognition crossed his face and we seemed to have pulled off a most unlikely piece of linguistic gymnastics as he headed off to translate our order in the kitchen. Well that wasn't so hard was it?

Presently our host appeared with the most enormous platter of miscellaneous cheese and biscuits and other stuff this side of a Tesco delicatessen counter placing it with some ceremony in the centre of the table. It looked fantastic and we accepted the challenge gleefully tucking in to the Wallace and Gromit mountain. It was hard to resist this tasty selection but then the pizzas began to arrive and they were like dustbin lids!

Needless to say that even after an hour of valiant chomping we all had to admit defeat and leave various sized portions uneaten, even Desperate D. With the very reasonable bill paid and a large danken to our host we struggled manfully back to the hotel. Foggy was greatly amused by our garlic bread tale since Germans don't have this delicacy as we sat for one last beer. Well one last beer for me but as I made my excuses and headed off to bed Festa was ordering another. As a postscript I Google translated garlic bread to German and got back "Knoblauchbrot" which I believe is German for plonker!

Wednesday – Ride-out heaven knows where (100miles? 5 hrs).

I've listened to the sound of rain falling overnight and am disappointed to see the wet woodland outside my window. Over breakfast the rain has stopped but Foggy suggests we wait a while for the roads to dry out a bit, it's a good plan. Time to enjoy a nice leisurely cup of tea, if only we could persuade it to crawl out of the pot! Oh well we'll have a trip down to the village and see what shops are open. I find just the thing to take home for my 6 year old in a near deserted town centre. A Harz T shirt which I hope will fit. We had nearly given up the idea of finding a café that was open and were making our way back when we found one. A very pleasant lady delivered tea and a variety of cake as we sat outside willing the roads to dry more quickly.

By late-morning the view from the hotel windows is far more promising and soon we are sat on the bikes warming the engines eagerly awaiting our last ride out. The familiar roads close by Bad

Grund are soon forgotten as Foggy leads us out into yet more uncharted countryside. I think Foggy has been as keen as the rest of us to get out this morning as the pace is a little hotter than our previous outing. Chippy and Kryten are tucked in close mimicking every twist that Foggy takes. I am less confident and the gap between us all seems to stretch out further each time. At every junction though we are reunited before the hare and the tortoise chase begins again.

All too soon that extra cup of tea at breakfast starts to work its way down and my attention starts to focus less on the bends and more on possible emergency stopping points. I gesture to Festa to come past me as I sense he is keen to be at the sharp end.

This leaves me clear to perform the necessary task of finding a suitable place to stop hoping to catch the group at the next junction, but frankly past caring by now. I must have had more than one extra cup and I am sooo pleased to have stopped (why does peeing in inconvenient places outdoors take longer?). Suitably relived and with concentration back on the road I start my way down-hill once more. Coming in the other direction is Kryten and he looks worried. When I arrive at the junction I can see why. Concern about my sudden disappearance had grown and Kryten was returning to check on me fearing the worst.

To add to the drama, while performing the slowest of 'U' turns Festa had toppled from his machine snapping the gear change leaver and footrest bracket, trapping himself under the bike in the process. Dam, I feel bad. If only I knew the hand signal for "I'm just stopping for a pee" none of this would have happened. Fortunately the only injuries were sustained by the bike and not the rider. Foggy takes command of the situation and many hands work to solve the problem of getting the bike to the repair shop. Festa rides the stricken 600 back to Bad Grund screaming away in second gear with his foot resting on the rear footrest. In Osterode some impromptu alloy welding is performed and Festa is back on the road. While the damage is sorted the rest of us sit outside a café with tea and cakes. We chose this venue instead of the temptingly titled 'Greasy Helmut's Brockwurst Van' which was parked close by the workshop.

Keen to not let the incident spoil the increasingly warm day Foggy leads us off onto some more of the areas delightfully tortured back roads. The sun is out, the sky is a clear blue and the roads are virtually car free, what could spoil all this? Recent road works that's what, bugger! Foggys' route recalculation had unfortunately led us right into the trap with little chance of escape. After we had diverted this way and that over bumpy little 'under repair' roads, stuck behind buses and lorries for a while we were well ready for a break at the petrol station. Foggy was full of apologies for the unforeseen events; somehow it just didn't seem to matter to any of us though. What mattered more was where we now found ourselves, on the outskirts of the dreaded Nordhausen, our nemesis with trams.

Foggys' explanation of the route through the town seemed simple enough. If we got lost we would meet up on the road back into the mountains. Traffic was dense and we had plenty of chance to refine our filtering technique but we managed to keep each other in sight for most of the time. At one point I was slightly un-nerved to find a large and impressive steam engine coming towards us. A Wikipedia search later reveals the Harzer Schmalspurbahnen or HSB company operates The Harz Narrow Gauge Railways with 1950s vintage 2-10-2 tank locomotives, this ones' destination was possibly the Brocken, the highest mountain in the region, I wished I'd brought my anorak.

It took a while but we eventually managed to break free from the constraints of the town back to the fresh open countryside. It felt great to be free to play once again on these superb mountain roads, the stable door was open and we were bolting. We were now benefiting from Foggy's knowledge of the area once again as he led us up and down some of the quieter side roads that make the region such a pleasure to ride in. As we pass through a village I notice a working guy wearing orange dungarees. When I start to think about it I have seen loads of blokes in dungarees while we've been here and wonder if it is a regional or national workers uniform, or maybe there's a lot of children's TV made here? (Her Tumble perhaps?) Anyway concentrate on the riding, after some time we travel down a more familiar road and stop at the old border café once more. It's a 'Magnum Moment'.

Although it is late in the afternoon the sun is very warm so leather jackets are quickly discarded as we look for some shade. Talk is of this being our last day and a return to reality and work is imminent. Then it strikes me, this is Foggys' job, it's what he does for a living. His place of work is not a factory or an office but his hotel and the mountains of the Harz. Lucky git!

It isn't long before the ice creams are devoured and it seems like a perfect opportunity for a photo session. As anyone who owns a camera I am sure will testify, it is unusual for a camera owner to appear on many photos taken with their camera. Today the lady from the café is cajoled into taking group photos of us all grinning away with Foggy in the middle using the numerous cameras thrust towards her.

Before heading back to the Hotel Foggy needs petrol and the place to get it is up the wiggly roads through the valley to the top of the hill. This is great but unfortunately we encounter one or two other vehicles along the way. As the road is very wiggly passing is not so straight forward. Local knowledge and skilled bike control mean such hazards are swiftly dealt with by Foggy with those at the front in hot pursuit. I am left foundering at the back waiting a clear opportunity. By the time I clear the last car everyone else has cleared off up the mountain.

Normally I am a fairly cautious rider, fancy bike, fancy gear but all show and no go. Now, however, with a clear dry road snaking up in front of me and no-one looking I can't resist winding things up a bit. I adopt my version of the racing crouch, slide my bum from one side to the other and stick out a knee towards every apex desperately hoping to feel it touch down. I wind open the throttle of the twin cylinder Aprilia beneath me pushing the needle further round the rev counter than I normally dare. The sound of big the torquey motor resonates back from the surrounding hillside as I hurtle towards the summit. This is brilliant fun and for a brief moment I am a possessed speed junkie, high on adrenaline, with the world flashing past my visor. Aprilisimo! The garage at the top appears far too soon and it's all over. Inside my helmet I am bursting with the excitement of it all. My bubble is popped when I realise that Foggy has managed to fill up with petrol while waiting for me and is now ready for the return journey!

I arrive back at the Hotel a little after everyone else, my normal cautious self has returned. The downhill trip could never have matched my uphill buzz and I didn't want to spoil things now. The group was positively glowing with excitement and, were it not for some newly arrived guests that needed his attention, I believe Foggy would have been carried into the hotel shoulder high. In the bar for the après ride beer we sing Foggys' praises to the new guys and envy their scheduled ride out tomorrow. We don't, however envy the three course meal they unwittingly accept and we dash off to get showered and changed before heading down to the restaurant at the bottom of the hill to complete a stunning few days.

After some time Kryten has a brief moment of enlightenment. "Where's that hotel we had tea and cake outside of earlier?" "You're sitting in it Kryten dude". Despite eating there for the last couple of nights he hadn't realised.

Thursday – Bad Grund to Europort (345miles 5hrs 45mins).

We gather outside in the sunshine chatting to the new guests admiring each-others bikes and recounting various biking tales. The question they want answered most is "Where is that restaurant you went to last night?" It would seem Foggys' 'sausage surprise' has few takers for second helpings!

Our departure is a prolonged affair this time; I don't think anyone wants to leave. We take time securing our possessions to the bikes, chatting to Foggy and his wife and taking more photographs but time has run out. One last glance back and we turn back up the hill and away from Bad Grund. All too soon we are dodging in and out of the autobahn traffic as we wing our way back to Europoort and the ferry. It's hot and sticky and it gets worse when we encounter heavy slow moving traffic in a town besieged by road improvement works. Filtering through an endless row of articulated lorries is a dangerous business that is no fun at all. Well maybe more fun than being trapped in a car in the same situation. At a petrol stop the decision is taken to leave the motorways at some point and stop at a 'proper' restaurant or café for something to eat. In the past time constraints have meant food was a fairly miserable event taken by the side of the motorway on a busy, noisy garage forecourt.

After some fairly hair raising Dutch motorway lane hopping and aggressive car dodging Chippy leads us off and into a reasonable looking place to eat. The sun is beating down in total contrast to our outward journey. We eventually settle outside under a large umbrella and order from a very plcasant waiter and waitress. I start to people watch and notice that the place is frequented mainly by flash business guys in dark suits with slicked back hair and shades. Most seem to be either talking loudly on mobile phones or tip-taping away on lap tops, even those in the company of others. Seems such antisocial behaviour is universal. Still, the food is good, well presented and reasonably priced when it arrives and it sure beats squatting in the squalor of a motorway service station.

The trip back to the ferry never seems to get any shorter. We seem to hit familiar roads and signs for 'Europoort' but I am always caught out by just how long it takes to actually get to the ferry. The last section involves a number of short dark tunnels out of which you then merge from one busy motorway to another before plunging into darkness once again. The sight of the huge canal that signals the closeness of the ferry is a great relief and we are soon past the helmet off helmet on passport check and on board.

Once the bikes are secured I am in less of a hurry and struggle with my gear up to the tiny cabin. Inside Festa is already in the shower while Kryten and I dilly about. Kryten is next up on the wash rota as I catch the blur of Festa striding manfully towards the bar. By the time I have moved everything round twice and eventually got showered and changed the ferry is on its way past the windmills. I join everyone else in the sparsely populated bar area and pay little attention to the mediocre 'entertainment' on offer in the background. All our talk is of the Harz Mountains and was it the best trip we've done? After a trip to the on-board shop for a last prezzie to take home and a couple more beers in the bar I am well ready to sleep in the shoe box cabin.

Friday - Home to Hull (40 miles 1 hour)

BING – BONG! "Guter Morgen die Herren und Damen" Wake with a start as I've slept like a log. We're nearly back to Hull and the ships tanoy system is in full flow telling us the time and trying to flog breakfasts. I just want to get off the boat and get back home now. Downstairs on the vehicle deck we lash everything onto the bikes for the last time and head out into the grey damp world that is Hull in the morning rush hour.

Filtering through this traffic seems much easier somehow, maybe it's all the practice we had yesterday. Over the Humber Bridge and we start to go our separate ways. I hurry back down the motorway and get to practice my filtering technique one last time as I enter Grimsby. I glance down at my bikes clock watching precious seconds tick by at traffic lights before drag racing off to the next set.
 If I am lucky I can just catch my son before he disappears into school for the day. I make it with a couple of minutes to spare and am rewarded with a big smile and questions about any possible presents that may have returned with me.

Back at work a week later the photographs begin to circulate and memories are being shared. Was this the best trip so far? Probably was. The Harz has more hairpins than a super-models handbag, more turns than a bad day auditioning for X- Factor and more bends than David Beckhams football career. OK, so I'm no Jeremy Clarkson with the clever analogies but if you enjoy riding a motorcycle you really ought to treat yourself and ride it in the Harz, Guten Tag!

Chapter 5.

Pyrenees Adventure. (10 Days).

I am fortunate enough to know an ex professional cyclist who also owns a house in France. In conversation one day we were discussing how he liked to ski from the house in winter and cycle in the summer months. He then proceeded to tell me of a route he once cycled called 'La Route des Cols'. This follows roads from the Atlantic to the Mediterranean over some 30 odd passes (cols) through the Pyrenees and is about 550 miles long. A lot of the roads within 'La Route' are used by the Tour d' France and include some famous mountain stages (if you know about such things). Apparently he and his friends managed this feat in five days.

I left his house with a map and some web addresses and began plotting. The boys seemed keen enough to give it a go, the only downside being the travel to the area. Brittany Ferries seemed to offer the quickest route at around 20 hours but this still meant at least 10 days away from home.

Sunday - Home to Plymouth (350 miles 7 hrs).

The trip starts by meeting outside Morrisons supermarket at silly in the morning o'clock. I don't remember shitting the bed but curiously I'm first to arrive. While waiting for the others I have chance to admire my latest stead. It's a Honda CB1300, a 'proper' bike many tell me, bought last year to replace my Aprilia RSV. The Aprilia was fantastic round Cadwell and performed magnificently in the Harz but we never really gelled around town or on the bumpy country lanes of Lincolnshire. The huge softly sprung CB is a dream in these areas and still a hoot around the track as I discovered. But not today. Today it stands fully laden with tank bag, Givi throw over panniers and a neat Givi roll bag my wife bought me for Christmas. It looks the part and I am almost looking forward to the 350 mile ride down to Plymouth. Then I ponder the wisdom of not fitting at least a handlebar fairing.

The sound of an approaching BMW overwhelms the early morning bird song and I can see Desperate Dan is surprised not to be the first here. Meticulous preparation means the deep blue BMW R1100S gleams beneath its lesser burden of tank bag and roll bag. Kryten is next arriving on his version of motorcycle nirvana. It's a different Suzuki SV650, blue this time, with various parts fitted to cosset its besotted and now excited owner. Uncle Festa is last onto the grid and shows little remorse as he believes the journey south will not require the amount of extra time insisted on by Kryten and Dan. Festas' ageing Kawasaki ZX6, wearing battle scars from previous European campaigns, is barely asked to carry a thing, just a tank bag and roll bag lashed to its' seat. I am questioned as to the duration I have packed for as it appears to be at least twice as long as Festa is planning. Kryten announces a very original approach. He has packed all his worst clothes and intends discarding them throughout the Pyrenees once worn. Oh, in case you were wondering, Chippy can't join us this year as work commitments mean he is on the other side of the world in China.

So the 'Long Way Down' begins (did someone else use that somewhere already?). The A46 soon gives way to the madness and boredom that is motorway riding. The M6 threads its way southwards and I sit waiting for signs that countdown first Exeter then Plymouth. The CB copes superbly but I am left with the distinct impression that a fairing of some kind would be a jolly good idea if there's ever a next time.

Plymouth is a bustling place but after a minor detour or two we successfully navigate our way to the Millbay dockside, err, with two and a half hours to spare, Festa was right. The midday sun is beating down and none of us fancies joining the queue to board the as yet to dock ferry. We set off in search of 'The Hoe' the place where Sir Francis Drake was told of the approaching Spanish Armada and calmly finished his game of bowls. Today, however, a somewhat different Armada fills the bay as a powerboat race meeting is in full flow. We park up and enjoy the sun drenched carnival atmosphere as, in-between race commentary; Heart Radio is played through the public address system.

Out at sea the boat shaped silhouette of the MV Pont-Aven grows larger by the minute and soon the racing is halted to allow our home for the next night to berth. On board and on the car deck our bikes are left to the tender mercies of the crew to be unceremoniously lashed down for the crossing. Once located our tiny four berth cabin is soon filled with discarded motorcycle attire as we all endeavour to slip into something cool and head out to the bar and the sunshine. We are confronted by Krytens first choice of 'disposable fashion' and it's not a good look. One must conclude he has a very deep wardrobe and has thrown little, if anything, away since the early '80s, bold yet frightening. Anyway, with our small piece of deck secured it's time to watch dear ol' Blighty slip away port side and enjoy the sight of condensate trickling down the sides of four long overdue glasses of Magners Pear cider (and a bag of nuts cos I was getting a bit peckish by then to).

Out came Krytens mobile phone, a sight we would become very familiar with by the end of this trip. For some time he was away in his own 'fastest finger first' text world saying bye-bye to his Mum, sisters, daughters, friends, postman, cat who knows. Once he re-joined the real world it was time to forage some food from the very busy café. Afterwards, around 6:30, we were a bit lost for things to do so took the mutual decision to go and have 'a bit of a nap' (a power nap) before going back to party the night away with the on-board entertainment. I woke up at around one in the morning and Festa and Kryten were still in bed. Only Dan had made it back to the bright lights for another couple of beers! (Must have been a long day).

Monday – Santander to Arette, France (225miles 4hrs 15mins).

The next morning dawn was breaking over the yard arm, what-ever the heck that nautical nonsense means. Well actually, for us, it wasn't. When you're cocooned in a cheap inner cabin on-board this kind of vessel there are no windows and there's no sensation of time until you reach out and jab a finger onto the light switch. This action revealed it was breakfast o'clock and I hadn't felt the ship move all night, a smooth crossing of the Bay of Biscay is possible!

We took advantage of the restaurant at the back (stern for those ex Matlows out there) of the boat (ship). The price was slightly higher than the rif-raf end but you paid your money and ate and drank as much as you liked, quite some challenge given we weren't due to dock until 12:30!

When the Spanish coastline began to grow larger we began to repack our gear and don the leathers that had been unceremoniously stowed under the bunks in the haste of the previous afternoon. When the port grew closer so did the frequency of the knocks on the door from the stewards trying to coax us out of the room so they could begin the cleaning process. Tannoy announcements informed all those on a 'mini cruise' returning to Plymouth that afternoon that they had basically 3 hours to enjoy the delights Santander had to offer before they had to be back on board and ready to sail. Why would anyone in their right mind do that?

Eventually we bowed to the relentless pressure and exchanged the sanctuary of the room for the tight labyrinth of corridors that lead to the garage deck where our bikes had spent the crossing. This was a busy place where bikers, lorry, bus and motor home drivers all competed to reach their vehicles. The bikes were very closely packed wheel to wheel and held down to a central metal wire by a strap ratchet tight enough to give a perfect 'C sharp' when twanged. Then, after what seemed like an eternity, light could be seen flooding in and that was the cue for the resulting free for all. Think of that Christmas favourite 'The Great Escape' where they are popping out of the tunnel under the glare of the search lights and you get the picture.

In the sunshine we regroup on the Spanish side of passport control and thrust ourselves into the insanity that is Santander lunch time traffic mixed with bewildered British holiday makers and battle scared lorry and coach drivers. Local mopeds buss about like annoying wasps after a bit of your jam sarnie in the summer but we are eventually spat out of the centre and heading off down the motorway. And what a motorway the A-8 turns into. There are some rather sharp bends and steep gradients to contend with as well as stunning views of sandy inviting bays to try to ignore as you pick a safe route onwards.

There are also the toll booths with their grasping arms poking out demanding a share of your nice fresh Euros. Top tip, have plenty of small Euros accessible as the paying gets quite frequent. Pay to use a section of motorway, pay to leave Spain, pay to enter France oh, and make sure you wipe your nose as you'll be paying through that too when you top up with fuel on the motorway (just like being at home then).

Once off the motorway the ride to our first Pyrenean hideaway becomes much more enjoyable. Dan has a sat-nav. and we follow deep into the countryside. Possibly deeper than we anticipated as the roads tend towards, well err, tracks. Gravel covers much of the surface in front and we half expected to see Euan and Charlie coming into view at one point. The track winds on higher and higher until we are brought to a standstill on several occasions by passing livestock, cows, sheep and a small herd of horses. It matters not a jot and adds to the sense of fun and adventure. Our bikes were really not made to be here, maybe we wouldn't have chosen this route had we known, but it was a giggle.

Heaven knows where we went but eventually we find some tarmac and a fuel stop. The guy in the garage tells us we are very close to Arette, the village in which our hotel is situated. It's about 7:30 when we disturb the tranquillity of its sleepy streets. Well I say tranquillity but soon an odd church bell begins to chime to let everyone know its 7:40, then 7:55 then 8:10. Over a couple of beers on the pavement outside our hosts ask if we would like an evening meal or would we be dining in the restaurant down the road, which is closed tonight. That kinda narrowed the choice down so we quickly changed and awaited the culinary delights of the Hotel / Bistro de L'Ours (hotel of the bear). Well despite the pictures of brown bears that bedecked the walls I formed the opinion that the Bear in question was not a furry Pyrenean beast but the contents of our plates! Maybe it was novelle cuisine?

Tuesday – Arette to Gavarnie (120miles 4 hrs).

At breakfast the next morning we share the dining room with a group of Dutch cyclists doing the coast to coast. They look lean and fit and probably ate at the hotel last night to. I am non-to well but rule out food poisoning as the cause. The gang is concerned and I am offered various remedies. Dan appears to carry a Mary Popins style medical bag and I add some of his pills to the chemical concoction already racing through my system. There's no chance of lying about feeling sorry for myself though so we pay up, mount up and ride off in search of some Pyrenean Cols.

The first of today's Cols is accessed by a long and winding road that leads (to your door?) upwards through the wooded hillside around the tiny village of Sainte Engrace. Col de Suscousse is the crown of the winter ski resort of Pierre Sainte Martin but there are few people about today as we pass through and head on down. The roads all seem narrow and in many places the surface can be unpredictable so this isn't the best start.

Things soon begin to change for the better as we crest an unassuming hill and find ourselves in a truly beautiful place. It's called the Col d'Marrie Blanc and a large area of meadow slopes sharply away to our right. What seems to be a large party of school children on a field trip are milling around some mini busses and wave as we pass by. There are cyclists at regular intervals and we pull over to take in the full splendour of the scene. As the sound of our engines fades away it is replaced by the sound of distant cow bells. In the warm sunshine we cast aside our crash helmets and leather jackets to enjoy the tranquillity of the vast vista laid out before us. After a while we watch as the school party heads down the slopes scattering the cattle and making the sound of bells more noticeable.

William Henry Davies wrote "What is this life if full of care we have no time to stand and stare?" Well by now we are most certainly not full of care but we can't stand and stare as sheep or cows any longer if we are to reach our destination. Remounted we head down the hillside and find the road much more to our liking. Some more spirited riding follows as the surface is clean and un-rutted. More cyclists are passed working hard towards the summit we are leaving behind in our increasingly confident decent.

The need for petrol is becoming an issue for the two smaller machines in group. The sat-nav. turned us away from the tarmac and led us up along some more challenging farm tracks before depositing us in a village where we take the opportunity for some liquid refreshment at a pavement cafe. I practice my dubious French on the lovely old lady owner and we receive some great tasting coffee in return (and directions to the toilet, always a handy phrase in any language).

After locating petrol we head out on a decent road that gets busier and busier. Somewhere we have taken a wrong turn and now are heading into the famous pilgrimage town of Lourdes. This is a hot and heaving town from which we gain no healing qualities whatsoever. The vision of a fort beckoned through gaps in buildings but we were in no mood to attempt a visit. From the peace of the Cols this place is filled with people and traffic and we are relieved to find the best thing to come out of Lourdes, the D821 back to the mountains!

Eventually we find the town of Soulom and detour upwards once more to find the 'Pont Espagne'. The Spanish Bridge is a man-made structure in an area of outstanding natural beauty. We follow the D920, known locally as the Route de Casacades the interweb tells us, and soon find out why. There is a small car park and we stop to have a wander. Two huge waterfalls collide here and it is an impressive sight and sound. The water looks so pure and cool that our jaded water bottles are emptied and then refilled from the fast flowing river. On such a long hot day and after the torment of Lourdes the taste of this water perhaps has healing qualities of its' own. So much so in fact that Kryten decides that Festa is baptized with a dash of the 'holy' liquid. A water fight ensues and both return thoroughly, well, err Baptized? Kryten takes the opportunity to get his shirt off and reveal his muscular physique to the passing busloads of Lourdes bound pensioners, not that he needs an excuse for 'tis the temple at which he worships.

This, however, is not the 'Pont' we have come to view and we continue upwards to the extraordinarily large, but relatively empty, car park. From here we strike out to view the bridge and after 5mins of upward toil it appears through the trees. A narrow metal bridge has been slung above a gorge through which a torrent of water roars.

From this bridge we get a view of the brick built structure that is the 'Pont Espagne'. It is well above our vantage point but not far away, barely visible through the mist and dappled sunlight. At the viewing area water from several powerful streams meet and mingle before rushing onwards beneath the bridge. The temple is once again revealed and a camera is thrust into Festas' unwilling hands. After some 'pumping up' images are captured that, frankly, err look a bit, well like the front page of a Gay magazine (I imagine). It's all a little un-nerving when you watch the reaction of our fellow tourists, three blokes dressed in leather photographing another half-dressed one (thank goodness he didn't bring the baby oil!).

We manage to persuade Kryten to get dressed and return to our bikes to begin the decent. Time has pressed on and we need to get to our hotel. The Hotel is located at the end of a long valley in a village called Gavarnie. It has an interesting welcome on its interweb page; "After having been around a lot, Sylvie, an indefatigable hiker, wanted to give her charming hotel a Nature & Mountain vocation". Well whatever that meant we struggled to find it until we heard a voice calling from above. It was the indefatigable hiker herself guiding us to the grassy car park at the rear of her hotel. Sylvie had the look of one who had indeed been around a lot and fixed us with a broad open mouth smile that didn't move. She waited patiently, smiling away while we found a space where our bikes wouldn't sink into the ground. Inside, after being asked to remove our shoes and leave them at the bottom of the stairs, we were shown to our rooms and the views from the windows were stunning. The huge natural wonder of the Cirque de'Gavarnie and its waterfalls formed the backdrop to the town made all the more spectacular by the elevated position of the hotel. But we were hungry and Sylvie recommended a restaurant that could be seen from the hotel.

We were seated in a glass sided room with a magnificent view of the Cirque and the setting sun. The young waiter spoke reasonable English and the menu was translated far enough for everyone to make a choice. Beer, wine and fine food ensued as the sun turned the sky red before bidding farewell behind the mountains. Cheap it most certainly was not, but as an end to a thoroughly enjoyable day it was just about perfect.

Wednesday – Walking day (8miles 5hrs).

After working out how to operate the blinds the view from the hotel room window the following day could not have been better, the shadows cast by the morning sun were slowly revealing the outline of the Cirque. The delightful sound of silence was broken only by the occasional sound of Monsieur or Madame collecting bread from the Boulongerie. Downstairs the hardy crack of dawn types were already fed, watered and ready to yomp. We had set aside today to leave the bikes behind and walk to see the waterfall. After breakfast we decided to ask the indefatigable hiker what would be a good route to take and Sylvie was very keen to show us. Maps arrived as did an ex-pat old timer dressed in plus fours complete with walking cane and rucksack looking like he was off to climb Everest with Edmund Hillary. With Edmund chipping in his ten-peneth a fairly gentle route was planned. Then Sylvie looked us up and down, fixing us with that strange smile/stare "You go dressed like this?" she asked. Now to be honest it hadn't really occurred to me to think too hard about what to wear, it was going to be sunny and warm after all. Only after Sylvies' question did I take a look at us, shorts, T shirts and trainers (in Krytens case from the early 1980s), sun cream and a bottle of water each…sorted!

After popping into the local shop for a bit of fruit we set off in the general direction our guide had pointed and soon after realized one or two minor details in our plan had been overlooked. Primarily we had no map and secondly none of us had really listened to what Sylvie had told us about the route. We developed a phrase that seemed to fit both our situation and the expression on Sylvies' face 'Stupid English'.

We found a path going upwards on the edge of the village and started to climb. As the path meandered on it presented us with several choices. After making these choices Kryten decided it would be quicker if we just headed directly up rather than backwards and forwards on the paths. This saw us tackling some more 'interesting' terrain and doubts were expressed as to the wisdom of this venture.

Kryten remained undaunted and eventually we emerged onto a narrow path we could once again follow. Each time we stopped to catch our breath the views became more and more beautiful. The village of Gavarnie was being left below and the full extent of the valley was becoming clearer. Onwards and upwards we forged on for over an hour before the ground began to level out and reveal our first objective, the refuge, a small stone built hut alongside which stood a party of well-equipped French folk surveying the spectacle.

Like a scene reminiscent of 'The Last of The Summer Wine' our small party of poorly dressed stupid English wandered over the rise to stand and admire some of nature's finest. Kryten decided that nature needed a little garnish at this point and so took off his shirt (again). This decision may have also been influenced by the female contingent in the French over sixties walking party gathered at the hut. One of the ladies approached us to warn of the dangers of 'z 'ot sun' but Kryten responded by smoothing sun cream over 'the temple' (eee, it makes one proud to be British). The lady then pointed to the snow on the rock face nearby. "The black dots you can see are sheep on the snow" she explained. Also from this point we were able to see La Brèche de Roland across the valley in the distance. This is an impressive natural gap, 40m across and 100m high, at an altitude of 2804m in the steep cliffs of the Cirque. It forms part of the border between France and Spain. Kryten remarked that although we were above the snow line at this point we were not above the fly and poo line as 'the temple' seemed to be attracting some unwanted attention from a persistent horse fly.

After a photo call it was time to move on. The French lady's' advice to Festa and Kryten to "Porter un chapeau" went unheeded as we boldly headed out across the meadow in the vague direction of the waterfall. Soon we came to a larger refuge that was surrounded by cows. Each had a large bell hung around its' neck, the animals every movement adding to the campanologists convention. From here our path headed down towards a small wooded area. Blimey crikey we actually seemed to be on the right track! Sylvie had told of the mystical 'Balcony Route' which started at the edge of a wood and here we were right on cue.

We soon discovered why this was named so as the trees gave way to a narrow ledge alongside steep rock, glorious views could be had back to Gavernie and across to La Brèche (and downwards to). We stumbled our way along the ledge and began to meet others stumbling towards us. The path took us under some parts of the imposing rock, over outcrops and back into woods again until the welcome sight of the Hôtel du Cirque began to filter through the trees. Here is where for six generations the adventurous types (and stupid English) meet the more traditional walking and donkey riding folks. When we arrived a large party of school children were having a group photo with the falls in the background. This seemed like a reasonable place to rest for a while before setting off towards our goal of the waterfall. Looking out at the huge circle of cliffs reminded me of the Coliseum in Rome.

As we admired the grandeur an older couple from the hotel approached us, they were both dressed like 'Man at Millets'. In their younger days, around the early 70's, it transpired they had ridden an old Triumph something or other to France from England stopping only, when various bits fell off, for repairs and modifications to be carried out by Mr. Millets. Sounded like a proper adventure and they were a very interesting couple to talk to as we all sat admiring the view.

Time to move on and as we did so we were met by the first of many streams. These were usually too wide to simply jump and were usually bordered by snow fall. One we encountered had a drift of 1.8 to 2m high and cool swiftly flowing water. As we carefully picked our way across on the slippery rocks a snowball fight ensued. Don't know about you but I have never had a snowball fight dressed in shorts and T shirt before so being hit square in the middle of my back with a ball of ice came as quite a shock.

At last Europe's' largest waterfall, La Grand Cascade, was getting nearer, larger, louder and wetter. The spray from its' tumbling waters, dropping nearly 1400 feet, drifted over us in an increasingly heavy cool mist. The pathway was now loose wet stones that were darkened by the waters and it was increasingly difficult to climb upwards as they slipped away from beneath our feet.

Kryten soldiered on and eventually came to rest on a rock to one side of the giant falls were we joined him. It was loud, it was wet, very wet but it was absolutely exhilarating! Looking back from here you could see other pilgrims trudging towards us, many had turned back, and the hotel had shrunk into the distance. Kryten announced that 'the temple should be cleansed beneath these sacred waters' and hurried off down to get underneath them. After many comical attempts it seemed temple cleansing would be put on hold as the strength of the water was greater than even his.

After standing on the snow drifts and photographing each other in front of the falls it was time to begin our soggy walk back to the hotel. Once out of the mist and back into the sunshine we began to dry off and the long walk back to the town was pleasant enough. I even had chance to practice a little scree running as the momentum and will to get back for some food over took my normally cautious self. Kryten was still merrily tripping along and we realized why he found things so easy. Throughout the day he had asked Festa to "just carry this or that for a moment" and hadn't reclaimed any of it.

After about an hour and a half we were back into town and soon realized that Gavernie is a tourist trap blessed with outstanding natural beauty. Unfortunately the town does not reflect this. Lots of touts had appeared trying to flog horse and donkey rides to the falls and from these creatures there is a considerable amount of 'produce' in the streets. This was why Madame Sylvie had insisted on the removal of outdoor footwear upon entering the hotel.

Weary bodies were soon washed and refreshed and we were back out looking to replace lost fluids. Just so happened it was 'Beer O'Clock' and we were to discover that this was quite an expensive time of day at €5 a pint. Then, with fluids suitably replaced and some more added just in case, we headed out to find something savoury for the by now wilting Dan. A pizza place was swiftly chosen and it appeared to be run by a jovial Colonel Sanders look-a-like who spoke no English. Festa decided he would like garlic with his but surprisingly the French for garlic isn't garlic. Luckily a helpful bi-lingual chap behind us did the translation and some superb tasting pizzas duly arrived, I topped mine off with some of the Colonels secret recipe chilli olive oil, fandabidosi! As the French say (probably).

Thursday – Gavernie to Ax-Les-Thermes (200miles 6 hrs).

Oh dear, someone has pinched the mountains overnight! I awake to the sight of grey mist shrouding the hilltops but it isn't easy getting out of bed this morning. Yesterdays' activities have reminded me that I am no longer in the first flush of youth (or second flush for that matter). Madame Sylvie's' very reasonable account settled and bikes once again burdened we set off retracing the single valley road that leads out of Gavarnie.

Soon we have to stop and don the wet gear as the rain is getting heavier. This is never a comfortable or elegant procedure as it is usually performed in haste by the side of the road. My choice of weather protection is a two piece affair with zips and Velcro which seems to stick to anywhere but where you need it to. Next comes a pair of dainty booties that will protect my expensive but distinctly un-waterproof boots. Finally I must try to put on my waterproof gloves. This is made more difficult by having wet hands making pushing the fingers all the way to the tips of the gloves hard work. More comical, however, is the sight of someone entering a one piece suit. The legs go in ok but getting a wet leather arm into that last arm hole is nigh-on impossible making the unfortunate would be wearer resemble a fledgling duck. Once in the gear one must then attempt to remount a soaking motorcycle with limited seat space (because of luggage) and even more restricted physical movement due to wet leather and plastic tending to stick to each other.

Remounted we continue our journey towards the first of todays' peaks, the Col de Tormalet. At 2,115 m / 6,939 ft it is the highest road in the central Pyrenees and is one of the most famous climbs on the Tour de France cycle race. Thankfully, as we begin to climb, the weather begins to improve and we are soon blessed with a drying surface on which to play. Being famous this is a popular piece of road and we have one or two vehicles to contend with, the largest and slowest being a huge lorry that was being tailed by a couple of motor-homes. Great time to be riding a bike as, after a little patience, we soon whistled past this mobile obstruction and made our way upwards. From here we encountered very little traffic as the lorry had probably held everyone back for a while.

Kryten bustled off ahead as the twists and turns of this mountain pass grew tighter. Careful forward observation became an essential part of the experience as the drops from the side of the road got ever more severe. The surface was littered with loose gravel and random sheep that would wander across your chosen line making deposits as they went (somehow I can't imagine the Tour de France guys having similar obstacles to negotiate). There was little opportunity to develop any kind of rhythm in such circumstances with the last couple of bends before the top being really tight hairpins.

At the summit we park up and prise ourselves out of our by now obsolete waterproofs. It's a busy place with many suitably exhilarated cyclists taking time to appreciate their achievement. There is a shop come café but it has the look of 'the local shop for local people' in the 'League of Gentlemen's' Royston Vasey. The most striking feature of the summit is a stainless steel statue of an early 1900s Tour rider called Octave Lapize gasping for air as he struggles to make the climb. Apparently one of the things he is famous for is looking at some Tour officials and yelling, "Vous êtes des assassins! Oui, des assassins!' (French for 'You are murderers! Yes, murderers!').

Apart from the excellent views I find the summit disappointing after all the hype and am soon ready to continue. Over the other side the road was much more appealing, better surfaced, less gravel and fewer sheep. The bends seem to make more sense and the views seem more spectacular. The road plunged us down through a village, through tunnels and under concrete carports set above the carriageway to prevent snow or rock fall blocking the route. Eventually at a garage we stop for petrol and regroup. Kryten, who normally claims to be 'riding well within himself' when part of the pack, is now well beside himself with glee (does he have schizophrenic tendencies one wonders?).

Fuel tanks replete we head onwards and once again upwards to the Col d'Aspin, another Tour favourite. Being so close to the Tormalet means this peak has far fewer people but also a far more spacious air to it. Far fewer people there may have been but the people had been replaced by cows. It was once again wise to check and adjust your intended line as a corner apex seemed to be the preferred option for the bovine inhabitants' deposits. At the top the, by now, obligatory photographs and mobile phone text checks followed before it was time to move on once more. Sometimes I find it frustrating that, having worked to discover such stunning scenery, time constraints mean we are not able to explore it more thoroughly. But then I remind myself that this is a touring trip for the pleasure of riding our bikes and the more we linger the later our arrival at our next stop will be.

The road down from the Col d'Aspin leads us through delightful forests and into the town of Arreau. We had had a blast for the last couple of hours and must have let it go to our heads as somewhere here the navigation went a bit tits-up. Playing follow the leader without paying much attention we started to head away from the mountains and into the foothills. Signs for a motorway and major town began to appear and we eventually ground to a halt for a consultation with Monsieur Michelin. Turns out we were well adrift of our intended route, but all was not lost as an alternative plan was soon drawn up. Off on the new route and we were soon lost again in a large crossroads town by the name of Montrejeau. Above our heads signs appeared to places we didn't want to go so I quickly pulled to the side of the road for another conference.

With an amazing stroke of good fortune we came to rest outside of a small office the human contents of which promptly spilled out onto the pavement to view the bikes. A young lady approached and, seeing our perplexed faces looking at a map, asked if she could be of assistance, she spoke perfect English. On the map I pointed out our intended destination of the D618 Fronsac to Sainte Girons road. The lady became very excited and asked how we knew of this road as it was a local favourite full of bends and Cols. "I wish I was coming with you, you'll love it" she said after giving a detailed explanation of the escape route from the town. With a swift "Merci Beacoup" we were back on track and soon turning onto our chosen path.

At Fronsac we re-joined the fun roads and as foretold the 40 miles of D618 did not disappoint. This is a glorious road with barely a straight line to be found. It snakes back and forth wriggling uphill and down through forest and field. As I ride I continually anticipate this can't go on, but it does and even the odd camper van and car fail to interrupt my juvenile pleasure. I am so taken with the whole experience that, having performed a slightly unwise overtaking manoeuvre and whistled past a couple of slow moving vehicles, I fail to spot where the road turns off and we end up in a small town scratching our heads once more. Time for a coffee in the pretty but busy town square. After consulting the map we discover we are in the town of Aspet and locate my navigational error at junction some five miles or so back. One of the great pleasures about such a journey is that none of this matters. Sure the rest of your mates take the piss a bit but that's all part of the fun. There's time to drink the coffee, relax, people watch and enjoy a little banter while reprogramming your on-board direction finder to the next destination.

Ten minutes later I've had a pee, locked and loaded myself back into the 'Captain Invincible' leather suit, wedged my head back into my extremely comfortable Arai helmet and we are back on the D618. Soon we emerge onto the summit of the Col' de Portet d' Aspet but we've only just restarted and so press on down the other side. All the while the D168 continues to thrill and delight, there are views and glimpses of views through woodland, there are small hamlets and isolated farms to fascinate us while all the time experiencing that deep down pleasure of riding a motorcycle with friends.

Fantastic though this is, more practical considerations begin to come to the fore, a quick glance down at the trip meter reveals we have travelled just over one hundred miles since our last fuel stop. As we are in rural France the chances of fuel are few and far between. The miles tick by and the two smaller bikes tanks begin to edge nearer and nearer to reserve. With each town that approaches springs new hope but in each town a local shakes their head or shrugs a shoulder. Things are becoming desperate as we climb up to the top of the Col de Port. From here we can make out the large town of Tarascon some distance away but the small bikes are running on vapour. Nothing for it but to head on down and hope. In the town there are no garages obvious and we pull off a roundabout to a small piece of waste land. Kryten and Festas' bikes are beyond their supposed 150 mile range and our destination town is too far away to attempt. Dan and I make one last attempt to trace the illusive fuel and I spy a signpost for a Super U. This French supermarket chain I remember also sells petrol from some outlets and as luck would have it this was one such place. I leave Dan filling up and return to guide the others. Once on the forecourt the attendant comes trotting up telling us to hurry as she will be closing in two minutes!! Phew!

With full tanks, and having breathed a collective sigh of relief, we soon enter the town of Ax-Les-Thermes, 200miles further on our journey. After abandoning the bikes a small search party seeks out the hotel on foot. This is a fairly common occurrence I've noticed. Most of the time it is fairly straight forward to navigate great distances, the tricky part usually comes right at the very end trying to pinpoint that final missing piece. With one way systems in many towns it can often be simpler to wander about on foot better orientating yourself from street names or landmarks.

The hotel is eventually located tucked a short distance away from the main thoroughfare. It is recognisable from the image I had downloaded from the internet, a creative piece of photography that failed to reveal the large electricity sub-station humming away directly opposite. Inside the building was pleasant enough and the proprietors were friendly and welcoming. As by now it was quite late, Monsieur Feuvier was busy in the kitchen so Madam Feuvier conducted the checking in. I took a deep breath and confidently delivered my stock French phrase about our booking. Rather mistakenly Madame leapt to the conclusion that I could parle Francais like a native and promptly began chattering away.

It would seem that my limited grasp of the language has improved somewhat in recent times as I understood some of what she was saying and was able to fumble a response in the right place. The difficulty came when she asked if we would like to eat in the hotel that evening. The group decision was inconclusive, Kryten wanted vegetarian and Dan wouldn't eat fish and my language skills couldn't cope so I just said "Oui" before my head went pop.

We were shown to our rooms and panic set in as we entered for there in front of us was a lone double bed, not a most welcome sight when one is due to spend two nights with a snoring farting roommate. Then relief as behind the door bunk beds are revealed. We dump our gear on the floor and Dan is first into the shower giving me time to rummage through my bags for my evening-ware. Dan emerges from the shower all fresh and clean so it's my turn. The shower is an interesting experience, I find, the doorway is so narrow that I have to apply soap to my middle age spread to squeeze into it.

Downstairs in the dinning-room it was beer o'clock and, as was now becoming traditional, the mobile phones were again in evidence. Electronic messages were flying back and forth as we awaited the arrival of whatever it was we had ordered. Over the mediocre meal the conversation is of the days' highlights, the magnificent views, the roads and the lack of petrol.

With the night still relatively young Dan is keen to explore this new town and seek out a purveyor of alcoholic refreshment. Kryten is deep into text talk and decides to remain tout seul. Festa, Dan and I venture forth to sample the bustling nightlife in this out of season ski resort. After about thirty minutes of aimless wandering we conclude that the town is closed on Thursdays and start back to the hotel. As we approach what appears to be an ornamental pool we notice several people sitting chatting with their feet dangling in the waters. Our curiosity draws us nearer and we see that this is a thermal pool and a place where people come to meet with friends. Soon we find ourselves sat alongside the pool, our shoes and socks off with the warm waters lapping at our calves. Looking towards the heavens the sky is clear and the stars are shining down on us. The sounds of peaceful chattering and warm water moving around our feet complete a blissful half an hour or so. But Dan is restless, time is moving on and no beer has been forthcoming. Across the square bright lights beckon through an open doorway and we are drawn in to the almost deserted bar for that all important nightcap.

On our return to the hotel Kryten had retired to bed with his precious mobile phone. In the room I check my phone and find a message from my wife informing me of the various goings on back home. When I look up from the message Dan is out like a light throwing up big loud Zs drowning out the sound of the power sub-station opposite.

Friday - Ax-Les-Thermes to Andorra plus detour (130miles 4hrs 30mins).

A somewhat more varied breakfast is soon dispatched before we locate the garage key master and release our bikes into the cloudy Pyrenean morning. A debate ensues as to whether waterproof riding gear will be required. Dan and I opt for the cautious approach and add this extra burden while Festa and Kryten laugh off the prospect of inclement weather with the casual 'It's only water' retort.

Our host town is conveniently situated on the N20 road that leads from France into the small landlocked principality of Andorra. Our plan is to ride through here and into Spain, a journey of around 50 miles or so, enjoy the highly rated biker road of the N152 to Ripoll, before returning through the mountains to our hotel.

Soon after we leave the outskirts of Ax les Thermes we begin the twists and turns that allow the road to follow the contours of the mountains that defend Andorra. Unfortunately this is a fairly busy road and progress becomes a rather ponderous affair as we seek to escape the endless stream of heavily laden vehicles grinding their way ever upwards. Major road works then bar our way and we are diverted skywards along a much narrower road. Far below the work to improve this artery can be seen cutting a swath through the once peaceful meadows. Eventually we pass through a customs post and enter the disappointingly shabby looking town of El Pas De La Casa clearly thriving on its' tax haven status like a spider with a web over a honey pot.

The roads' many bends get progressively more serious. It becomes difficult to focus on the direction the road is taking when ones eye is drawn to the prospect of a one way ticket to oblivion courtesy of an ill judged piece of motorcycle control. As we approach the summit an odd sight greets us. There are numerous petrol stations up here, very little else, just petrol stations. The attraction is immediately obvious when I read prices that make me realise just how much tax we pay for this blood stained commodity back home.

At the very top we park our bikes on a baron windswept gravel car park alongside a petrol station to admire the view. It's quite an aw-inspiring moment as our eyes survey the panorama before us. Out of the corner of my eye I catch sight of something large and brown taking to the air. We probably all experience the same thing as we collectively watch in slight disbelief. Not being a twitcher myself I am unsure of my facts at this point but, we are convinced that what we saw was an Eagle taking to the air with an effortless beat of its' huge wings. Silence fell over us all as we followed the great birds' flight path disappearing into the distant mountains. Not something you witness very often in the Lincolnshire Wolds. Once our eyes had given up scanning the horizon another unexpected vision replaced that of the Eagle. Slowly making their way up the pass came three open topped Rolls Royce Silver Shadows from the golden age of motoring circa 1920. A fine and impressive sight made more remarkable when you consider the tortuous route to where we were.

From here it was downhill all the way. The road was surprisingly uncluttered by now as most traffic only went as far as the petrol stations. Uncluttered the road may have been but the steep drops off the sides kept our minds fully occupied. Soon we entered another dull town and the traffic began to build up before grinding to a halt. After several minutes waiting in a queue engines were turned off and puzzled looks exchanged. Traffic had been halted, we concluded, due to an accident somewhere further along the route. Andorran police lazily went about their duties redirecting local traffic but it was becoming clear that this could be a long wait. As we traced the line of waiting vehicles winding its way far into the distant hillside the decision was made to head back the way we had just come as the congestion showed no signs of abating in the near future. This decision was hastened somewhat by the looming presence of a dirty great black cloud.

Our return may have been along the same route but this was by now an even more daunting prospect. The dirty great black cloud had overtaken us and bumped into the mountain we were trying to scale leaving it shrouded in a dense fog. Kryten, strangely for him, was leading at this point and tried waving us past so he could follow but we were having none of it, no one wanted to lead into something you couldn't see through! Slowly we crept over the mountain top and eventually arrived back at the customs post with the fog beginning to clear. Andorra had been a bit of an anti-climax and it felt good to be heading elsewhere.

Rather than return to Ax-Les-Thermes we turned right along the N320 climbing over the crest of the 1920m Col de Puymorens. From here on down the weather improved with every passing mile until we came to a halt in search of lunch on the outskirts of a small town called Enveitg. An inauspicious looking roadside café seemed to be popular so we ventured inside to investigate further. The place looked like a railway station snack bar on a wet Sunday afternoon but it did have an intriguing menu being cooked and served up by an odd looking multinational, multilingual couple. Dan was displaying the onset of malnutrition and was about to set about his leather jacket with a knife and fork when we decided to stay and eat.

While we waited outside in the glorious mid-day sunshine more bikers of various nationalities arrived. Among them was a small band of English folk from Manchester. They regaled us with tales of motorcycle based touring that beggared belief. It seems they had set off from Manchester and ridden to Dover then caught the ferry to Calais before spending the night in Reimes. The next day they set off and rode to Benidorm in Spain, a journey of around 1000miles at speeds regularly touching 120mph arriving at near midnight!

Pizzas and coffee were served up and we sat sheltered from the warm sunshine under parasols stretched out over the simple roadside bench tables. The proprietors may have been an odd Chinese / Turkish pairing but their pizzas tasted mighty fine.

We left the cafe slightly reluctantly and continued our journey along the D618 towards Mont Louis, a town I had visited on a family holiday a couple of years before. By now the dark skies that had dogged us since leaving Andorra were once again threatening above us. Retracing my family holiday route we headed along the D118, a very pretty road, towards the winter ski resort of Les Angles. Unfortunately a cloud managed to clip the top of a nearby mountain and began unburdening its' load. The road soon became awash and navigation almost impossible through the driving rain. Pretty and picturesque though I knew the road to be it offered no opportunity to shelter from the deluge. Luckily as we entered Les Angles I spied an apartment block with overhanging balconies beneath which we could just about park up. From here we would have had a fine view across the town to the lake if we could have seen anything through the rain. As the sound of gently 'pinging' engines died away it was replaced by the sound of gently bleeping mobiles as Kryten once again began reporting our situation to all and sundry back home.

It took well over an hour before the rain finally began to abate but the road had turned into a river. Dan and I eased ourselves into the waterproofs Festa and Kryten had insisted we wouldn't need and we all cast off into the by now light drizzle, well it's only water. The route I had looked forward to travelling on through the villages of Formigueres and Puyvalador was now a disappointing wet and unexpectedly bumpy trial and I was pleased to turn off onto the narrower D16. This took us up into a hilly and densely forested area which became drier and drier the further we travelled. By the time we reached the tiny village of Mijanes it was time to stop and repack the waterproofs as the sun had chased away the clouds. Kryten took the opportunity to head off on foot to investigate the ruins of a castle on top of the hill but returned to say it wasn't worth the climb.

We fired up the bikes once more and the sound reverberated off the walls of the buildings shattering the peace in this, until now, quiet place in front of the post office. We quickly left to let the locals enjoy their tranquillity and began to follow the signs directing us back to Ax-Les-Thermes. Before us lay an impressive mountain to the sides of which our path clung precariously. The road became steeper and narrower while the bends tightened into hairpins the higher we rode. We were on the Port de Pailheres pass, the second highest in the French Pyrenees used in the 2007 Tour d' France apparently, and made significantly more tricky by random encounters with horse and cow deposits.

At the rather barren summit we were treated to the most spectacular views from almost every conceivable angle. The area is notorious for being shrouded in mist and fog but for us, at this moment, we could see for miles. Far below the tortured ribbon of tarmac that had brought us to this delightful vista was clearly visible and I couldn't help but wonder who had come up with the notion that such a road was possible and had then convinced others to build it? The sign above the door to the small brick shelter informed us we were 2001m up, 17km from Querigut (from whence we came) and 19km from our hotel in Ax-les-Thermes. This high point had certainly become the highlight of a slightly, until now, disappointing day. For a brief moment or so cameras even replaced mobile phones, it was that good!

It was all downhill from here, bend followed bend followed bend as our glorious decent raced by with barely a hint of our fellow road users. We still had to exhibit a little caution along the way as on occasion there was clear evidence of the passing of large well fed livestock just on the line we wished to take. It was good to be riding with some pace on such a road at last after the frustrations of Andorra and the weather. At the top the narrow road had no defining edge just a gentle slope leading to a considerable drop. Further down the trees begin to return hiding the drops and defining the road, there is even the odd bit of Armco from time to time.

All too soon we arrived back on the outskirts of Ax-Les-Thermes heralded by the site of a Citroen 2CV hoisted aloft four piles of bricks with all wheels and various other essentials long since 'recycled'. We refuelled the bikes at a local supermarket and returned to the hotel for, as a swift glance at our watches revealed, it was now 'Beer O'Clock'. Quickly wedged in and out of the micro-shower, a change of clothes, several beers and we're off into town to uncover some typical French style cuisine. Humm, it's raining a bit. Pizza anyone?

Saturday - Ax-Les-Thermes to Argeles Plage   (120miles 3hrs 45mins).

Last nights' inclement weather has long since departed and been replaced by the far more welcoming sight of sunshine over the electricity sub-station. Breakfast set us up well for the day ahead and l'addition (the bill) wasn't too painful either. For me the hardest part is always transporting all of my gear from the hotel room to the bike. I try very hard to be organised so as to speed up the process but frequently fail for the sake of one overlooked item or another. Kryten normally rivals my stupidity but on this trip he is triumphant. The hardest choice he has to make is what to throw away, each discarded item helping make the repacking and reloading of his machine that little bit easier. He is still no match for the super cool Festa, however, who seems to pack little but always have the right thing to hand.

After the passage of some farting about time eventually I am ready and awkwardly encourage my right leg into the gap between tank bag and roll bag before making myself comfortable on the seat and poking the start button. We leave the hotel and head back into the hills and passes at the back of Ax-Les-Thermes. The route leads us over some unspectacular Cols before plummeting into the Gorges du Rebenty. We ride alongside the free flowing river that carved out this gorge over many thousands of years surrounded by woods of Beech, Fir and Oak through which, at various points, I spy a fisherman tempting the trout that fill these beautifully fresh sparkling waters. The air is cool and the roads more reliable as we weave our way with exhaust notes reverberating off the sides of the steep walls. Sometimes the cliffs form a canopy above our heads, sometimes we pass through short tunnels and at one point there seems to be an enormous boulder the road must detour around.

We leave the gorge to join the far more purposeful D117 soon passing through Axat and looking for our next side road escape route. After the tranquillity of the gorge road the pace of this road is a bit of a shock so in the grandly named town of Caudies-De-Fenouilledes I bring the group to a halt near a railway bridge. Helmets are removed to allow for some head scratching while pouring over the map. Dan and Kryten wander off to photograph the bridge while Festa wanders in the opposite direction to read a signpost.

 When we regroup I have found the road we need to take on the map, it runs near an old castle. Dan and Kryen point to an old castle they have been photographing through the archways of the bridge and Festa confirms we just missed the turn as we entered the town, I think that's probably teamwork.

The old castle, by the way, is the Chateau de Peyrepeteuse a large ruined Cathar fortress. The lower castle was built by the kings of Aragon in the 11th century on an 800m (2,600 ft) high crag and when the weather is clear you can see the Mediterranean Sea from it. Just thought you might want to know.

With the route now located we start to head upwards once more along a narrowing road towards the Col Del Mas. The road has a more rural, farming kind of feel to it. It's a bit like riding along some of the more remote lanes in the Lincolnshire Wolds, only much higher and steeper and warmer with sharper bends (I did say a BIT like). At times we emerge from the tree lined road to find a meadow bathed in sunshine with a Buzzard circling overhead. At other times there's a small hamlet (that's one or two houses not the cigar!) to pass through but only rarely do we meet another vehicle.

I get slightly more confident and begin to quicken the pace heaving the laden CB1300 through the turns like a fat bloke on skis. I find myself shuffling from one side of the seat to the other and flapping a knee out at times as well. My confidence is rewarded as the bike never gets out of shape and copes admirably even when I've miss-read the next piece of tarmac. It's hard not to love this kind of riding, dry twisting roads under a clear blue sky with little coming the other way. Concentration is the key to remaining upright though as these Pyrenean roads have a way of testing you with an unexpected sharp turn or well-placed pile of gravel just when you're taking a quick glance at the view.

By now my concentration was being taken up by an over filled bladder so it seemed like a good time to find a place to stop.
We came to rest on a wide bend in the road and when the engine noise died away it was replaced by the sound of silence.

There was barely a breath of wind, except from Festa, and the sun felt much warmer. From within the tightly packed luggage various forms of snacks and liquids emerged and we stood taking in the serenity of the landscape presented before us.

Back on the road once more and there is no let up to the constant direction changes this road makes; it's like a bike gymkhana and I am working harder in the increasingly warm sun. We are heading for a planned lunch break at a town called Ille sur Tet but it doesn't seem to be getting any closer. At some point the road changes to a far wider and better surfaced effort and as we continue our decent out of the mountains the road treats us to some stunning wide open views. Then, totally unexpectedly, we find ourselves looking at an extraordinary site. I Googled this on our return and find it to be called 'les orgues d'ille sur tet. Over thousands of years the Tet river eroded the clay and rock here to leave organ-pipe like shapes that stand up to 12 meters high. Now, however, the river takes a different course and only the numerous tourists erode the area. It's a fascinating sight but we don't really have the time to explore it as we must move on.

Above the rumble of the bikes engines I am convinced I can hear the rumble of Dan's' something savoury stomach so it is with some relief that we finally approach Ille sur Tet across a bridge over the river. The town looks old and has a large church in the middle. We finally come to rest close to the towns War Memorial. Above the plinth, inscribed with the names of the "Sons of Ille" who gave their lives for La France, Marianne flies through bomb filled clouds of war, her hair streaming out behind her, her mouth wide open, it's an impressive tribute.

Once settled we decide it would be nice to briefly visit the church before lunch and set off to find it. From the bridge it seemed like a huge structure but from the town it was a different tale. The streets were very narrow and most of the houses were three or four stories high giving the impression of a labyrinth. There were voices from somewhere but almost no people.

As we were about to give up a local looking fella appeared so I greeted him and bust forth with my bestest "Où se trouve l'église s'il vous plaît?" but this receives a completely blank expression and he walks away. Moments later he returns saying "l'église?" and points us round the next corner. On rounding the next corner we find the entrance and the main tower. Bloody Hell! There are huge cracks all over the thing and it looks to be in immediate danger of collapse. Maybe the visit is unwise so we retreat to find a café.

It's very hot now, too hot to be in motorcycle leathers and we all remark on it as we enjoy a 'Magnum moment'. Our intended route should take us back into the mountains once more before finally ending up at the town of Argeles Plage on the Mediterranean coast. General consensus seems to be that it's now too hot to enjoy anymore slow mountain tracks and the most favourable plan would be to strike out for the cooler coast and jump in the sea using the most direct route possible. Dan programmed the sat-nav. pointed his bike eastwards and off we went as fast as we could caper.

After the splendour and solitude of the rural roads the D612 had only one redeeming quality, it got us there quickly. Unfortunately, as it turned out, rather too quickly as we arrive to find our hotel doesn't open for about another 1½ hours. After some deliberation we ride our bikes round to a car park on the beach. It's very hot and soon Kryten, Festa and Dan strip down to beach attire hurriedly abandoning sticky leathers. Kryten is in his natural (should that be un-natural?) element, time to 'pump-up' the temple for the crowd. Bemused holiday makers are treated to a poor-man's version of 'The Full Monty' before Kryten leads the stampede to the sea. I sit in 35°c dressed in leather trousers and boots guarding the bikes and piles of hastily cast off gear. To be sure it's not a great look and as I attempt to look cool by draping myself casually over a wall I become aware that I too am the cause of some local amusement.

After my elated chums return from the sea we check into the dubious portals of the hotel, shower, change and head back to find a beach bar, oh yes...it's beer o'clock! The beach bar prices take your breath away faster than the heat from the sun, but we're on holiday so what can we do? Well get out the mobile phones seems de rigueur as I sit and compare Dan's' firmly prodding digits and Krytens' 'fastest finger first' techniques. Later, as we mooch about looking for somewhere to eat, I realise I am in my own personal holiday hell. It's 'Chav-ville sur Mer' and I am in the bar from a Star Wars movie! It's teaming with semi-pissed Brits, loud Agga-do music playing from naff souvenir shops lit by flashing neon lights, to quote Top Gears James May 'Oh Cock!'.

After dinner it is dark and we find an ice-cream shop. Among the many temptations is 'Red Bull' flavour, you just gotta try that, it really tastes like the stuff. Our wanderings draw us to the sounds of a Jazz / funk group playing in a bar. This seems slightly out of place for the area so we stop and listen for a while. Moving on through the freaks and weirdoes once more we follow our ears and are lead to a beach disco in full swing. This seemed an oddly civilized affair that had attracted many people with young children to dance the night away under a starlit sky.

Sunday Argeles Plage to Biarritz (320miles 6hrs 30mins).

Festa and I have enjoyed a deep sleep accompanied by the very welcome sound of the air conditioning unit. The breakfast room is bright enough with most of what you can expect from a budget continental hotel. For our return trip to the fashionable Atlantic surf town of Biarritz we planned to divide the journey up slightly. Firstly we would use the fairly direct D612 again to cut out a large corner before succumbing to the motorway for the final push to our destination.

First, however, there was the tricky game of 'Hunt the petrol on a Sunday in France' Yeh, you're right, we should have filled up yesterday but the smell of the sea lured us away. The petrol station was a bit of a bugger to find as it was located just around the corner from our hotel. This fact, however, did not become apparent until we had circumnavigated a large part of the town. Note to self, make sure we fill up on a Saturday evening when in France

On occasions we were able to crack on along some swift straight roads but at times we were frustrated by slow moving traffic and confusing road signs in major towns. As we approached the town of St. Girons we had travelled around 150 miles and know we may not make it to the motorway as fuel reserves were dangerously low. An elderly couple are treated to some 'Give us a clue' style mimes that basically involved pointing at petrol tanks and uttering the words 'fuel' or 'petrol' (L' essence s'il vous plaît for future reference). The couple shrugged their shoulders and shook their heads but eventually told us there was no fuel in town on a Sunday and Andorra was the nearest place, well I think that's what they said, probably. Strange then that, 500 metres up the road we locate a garage doing a steady trade in petrol sales, and now Magnums to.

The motorway has little to relieve the boredom except for a stop for fuel and the obligatory stops to collect toll tickets and pay up. As we approach the slightly unexpectedly large and busy towns of Bayon / Biarritz we get separated at a large roundabout. Out of sight of the group the sat-nav. sends Dan back the way we have just come while we continue straight on into some very busy rush hour traffic. There's only one thing to do, park up off the road and try to regroup.

On seeing the unfolding crises Kryten leaps from his machine and runs off to take some photographs of the view from the bridge we have just crossed. Festa and I are left to attempt to contact Dan, but it is vain. We both get the sound of a confused lady on our mobile phones and conclude we have missed some international code or something. Eventually Kryten and his camera return and he sends a text to Dan, there is no reply. After a 15 or 20 minute delay the decision is made that the sat-nav. will guide Dan to the hotel somehow and the sketchy map I have will do the job for us.

We begin to make our way deeper into the unknown until signs start appearing directing us to Biarritz. It's very busy and very hot but we eventually catch a view of the sea and gain heart. A quick consultation and we head along a narrow bustling coast road dodging much more suitably attired holiday makers until we come to rest in a square. The best thing to do now, we decide, is to leave one of us to look after the bikes while the other two try to pinpoint our location and the location of the hotel. Kryten immediately volunteers his security services and begins removing clothing and admiring the bikes we are parked near. Festa and I head off like two native tracker scouts and are soon met by Dan coming the other way on foot. Sat-nav. has led him to the door of the hotel which is only round the corner!

As it turns out finding the hotel was only the start of the challenge. Once the bikes had been unburdened and our rooms located it was time to find the place recommended by the guy on reception to leave them overnight. On the face of it the instructions sounded simple enough as the underground car park was only 2 or 3 hundred yards away. Complications arose the moment we entered the Biarritz one way system. The tight busy streets became a confusing maze. I was immediately separated from the group and missed a vital left turn. My only hope was to navigate blindly back to the hotel and try again. This was easier said than done as the one way system tightened its grip. Suddenly I found myself back in the square from earlier. Going in the opposite direction I saw the rest of the group and tried to catch up. As I rounded a corner they were coming back the other way until we all ended back at the hotel. Once more with feeling we set off and managed to keep together locating the underground car park entrance after two more laps of the one way system, phew!

Now we are ready to live the dream of swimming in the Med. one day and the Atlantic the next. It's a short walk to the beach and when we arrive we are distracted by a superbly situated bar, well it is beer o'clock. It has white linen covered basket furniture and overlooks the small bay. We are served by a very attractive lady (big boobs!) and as she brings the drinks to our table a band strikes up and starts to play Police songs wiz zee French accent. The sun is still warm, condensation runs seductively down the sides of the glasses, the view is great (barmaid and bay) could things be better? Well possibly, y'see the price of all this manifested as 8 Euros a pint! The steep cost was so outrageous it meant that we could only stay for another two pints.

Tough though it was to drag ourselves away there remained the little matter of the promised swim. The beach was, by now, just about empty as four slightly merry stupid English strutted down to the waters' edge.

It should come as no surprise to read that Kryten was the first to discard his clothes but this plunge, being our last, demanded a little extra. So, doing an absurd version of 'Hey Hey We're The Monkeys', in song and walk, we strutted our way towards the ocean running the last couple of yards and then screaming like girls at the temperature. Safety note: Alcohol and swimming do not mix. Don't try this at home. This stunt was carried out under controlled conditions by professional idiots. As if this wasn't daft enough Kryten suggested a spot of 'Tombstoning' (I understand this to mean lobbing oneself into unknown waters from height). Festa and Dan were up for it so they all swam to a jetty and duly took the plunge while I thrashed about in the shallows resisting Greenpeace's' efforts to repatriate me with a nearby pod of Orca.

All of these shenanigans helped us work up a decent appetite so once we got dried off we headed out to find somewhere suitable. Being a resort town there was a fair amount of venue choice but some of the window prices seemed so ridiculous we struggled to locate somewhere we could all agree on. After a while we gave up and went into the first place we passed, a Tapas Bar. Unfortunately the menu was considerably depleted due to our late arrival but we were at least offered something, even if we were unsure of what it was. Dan was, well desperate, and ordered what he thought would be a pie and chips. When the food arrived there was little but lettuce and tomato for Kryten, Festa and I had a sort of meat feast but Dan's' face was an absolute picture. The "pie" was little more than a 50mm finger bowl containing a small amount of lamb and veg. topped with puff pastry, and no chips! Dan poked the crust with his fork and asked the waitress if this was it. Rather indignantly she replied it was adding "It is very 'ot 'ear so we do not need to eat big lots" before turning on her heels and marching off.

It didn't take long before we were back on the streets looking to supplement the Tapas with something more substantial, and savoury. As luck would have it about 50m along we found a restaurant with a huge Paella pan on the go as well as offering Pizzas and Kebabs. The beer was a mere 5 Euros and the pizzas pacified even Dan's' insatiable appetite. We left the restaurant and walked back to the hotel in the warmth of a beautiful calm still evening spoilt only by the thought that tomorrow we must begin our journey home.

Monday – Biarritz to Santander (150miles 2hrs 45mins).

Breakfast in the hotel is the meagre affair of croissants and coffee taken in the uninspiring reception area. It is therefore not hard to draw ourselves away from the table for that last bit of packing, or discarding of 80s' clothing in Krytens' case. We have some time to spare and decide to take one last walk to the beach and to a small peninsular surrounded by the crystal clear blue waters of the Atlantic Ocean. As we return to the garage we walk down the out ramp and discover something rather interesting. The barrier stopping vehicles leaving only covers about three quarters of the road. A plan is immediately hatched to banish all thoughts of payment and turn into wild desperado bad ass bikers and well, err, kind of not pay (best €6 I never spent!). With the bikes once again laden up in the narrow street we head on up the hill catching only glimpses of the lovely town we are leaving in our rear view mirrors. I'm not a great fan of beach type holidays but I could have willingly spent a good few days more in this one.

The motorway draws us in and we fall into the inevitable clutches of the final cash drains that are the toll booths. We pay to join the motorway, to leave France and to enter Spain all within about five miles. Once clear, and with only lose shrapnel rattling around in our leathers, we blast off towards our Santander dockside rendezvous with the good ship Pont Aven. Crikey blimey crikey it's hot, seriously un-Britishly hot. We are travelling at around 80mph and it's still hot. It's like having someone aiming a hairdryer at you at close range. Only very occasionally as the road swoops down nearer a bay is there a small amount of cooler air rushing through my vented leathers.

It's not a massively long ride but the sight of Santander brings a sigh of relief. Traffic is moving slow and the filtering antics of the local moped population have to be seen to be believed. They rarely appear in your mirrors but apparently materialise on your front wheel before vanishing equally swiftly into the Malay. Then the entrance to the docks is directly in front of us and we have made it. It's actually quite a straight forward piece of navigation just complicated by the sheer volume of traffic and the intensity of the heat.

The wait to board seems endless as we stand in the full glare of the mid-afternoon sunshine. I suddenly remember to swill down a couple of sea-sickness pills, phew. We get talking to two custom chopper riders who look relatively cool. Their bikes were made in Doncaster and this is a trip the pair of them make every year. As we swap tales we discover that they are away for about a month and usually have no set ideas as to where they will go. Their approach is to ride at a relaxed 50 to 60 mph and pitch tents where they haul up. I am reminded that motorcycling has very many different variations in styles and motivation.

The wait continues, as does the people watching. We are drawn to the sight of a pedal cyclist slowly weaving through the patient ranks of vehicles. He is a skinny, slightly rough or weathered man with an even tan towing behind him one of those wheeled yellow child carriers. Eventually he stops beside another similarly dressed cyclist and a conversation ensues. As we rudely listen in we discover that one of the guys has been pedalling around Spain for some time. The child carrier contains, among other essential items, a diesel generator. The other guy has pedalled from Singapore! They try each other's bikes before pedalling off onto the boat.

At last we are allowed on to the ship and the scramble to remove essential items from the bikes for transport to the cabin begins. Our bikes are once again to be lashed down by the burly French crew of the Pont Aven. We are given an access card to remind us of how to get back down to the bikes; it reads D2, the mental health ward of my local hospital.

My companions are soon changed and raring to go, it's 'Beer o'clock' of course. I have waited patiently in a corner of the tiny room while bike clothing was discarded and sun-worshiping apparel donned. Despite over a week in the sole company of blokes I'm not yet comfortable being in close proximity to an undergarment clad male buttock. The door closes and it's me time. I have a long shower, change, rearrange and then sit on the bed with the air-conditioning filling the place with cool air. This has no reflection on the company of the good friends I have enjoyed but it's nice to just sit in peace for a short while sometimes.

I open the cabin door and return to the land of the lost and bewildered. There are countless suitcase burdened people still pushing past one another trying to locate that illusive accommodation hidden somewhere in the labyrinth of identical corridors. Out on deck I join the less bewildered ones watching the ship slip its moorings and glide out into the Bay of Biscay. The sun is still warm and I locate the trio sitting in low slung deck chairs drinking cider over ice the condensate slowly sliding down the sides of the glasses.

After dinner we try to watch tennis from Wimbledon but the picture keeps breaking up. We turn our attention to the cabaret but it's a poor show, as can be seen by the few in attendance. The decider came when the female chanteuse warbled out her version of Motorheads 'Ace of Spades' in a Country and Western style, honest, there was hardly a dry eye in the house. There is more fastest finger first mobile phone action so I wander off and end up on deck watching the sun being extinguished by the limitless ocean, it's vivid reds and oranges an almost perfect way to end the adventure.

Chapter 6.

Pining For The Fjords (11 Days).

I was sitting in the dentists' waiting room nervously awaiting my turn with Doc Cavity when I began casually flicking through the pages of a well-thumbed, once glossy, magazine. After watching the pages fly past my eyes glimpsed a picture of a twisty road. Turning back a few pages revealed a brief article extolling the virtues of motoring in Norway and a couple more fabulous photographs. The twisty road in question even had an evocative name 'The Trolls Staircase'. It turned out to be one of those rare occasions where my check-up ended with the words "Your teeth look ok, see you in six months" rather than the usual "You need a little work in there, see you next week". I was on a high and returned home to enter the words "Norway tourist information" into Google.

In the weeks that followed I became more and more convinced that this beautiful country would be the perfect destination for our next motorcycle tour. All the web-sites show Fjords, snowy mountains and smiley happy blond people. There are National Parks to explore, glaciers to walk on and Nasjonale Turistveg (National Tourist Routes) to ride along. The Norwegian Government have designated certain roads as Turistveg and are promoting these to visitors. Alongside these routes 'Art Installations' and viewpoints have been, err well, installed. It was time to run the idea up the flag pole to see if the troops would salute.

Mention Norway to most people and the response will probably feature, cruise ships, Fjords, Northern Lights and "Bloody Expensive". You may also hear they have zero tolerance of speed so you can only go 40 mph and if you're really lucky a rendition of Monty Pythons Norwegian Blue dead parrot sketch. Show some of the pictures of the roads and scenery the place has to offer and most of the negatives are quickly forgotten.

I began to place the various Turistveg on a map and then tried to join some of them up with some of the 'must see' highlights around the route. Next came the hotels, a nice selection to choose from and then the ferry.

Ah, bit of a problem there. You see, there are no direct ferries between the UK and Norway. For sure there used to be one from Newcastle to Bergen but it was withdrawn in 2008, the Harwich to Esbjerg in Denmark route closed in 2014. At the time of writing the only ferry options directly between the UK and Scandinavia are the DFDS-freight ferries from Immingham to either Brevik (Norway) or Gothenburg (Sweden). ...Bugger.

Our trip took place before the closure of the Harwich to Esbjerg in Denmark route. From Esbjerg we could ride up to Frederikshavn catch another ferry to Gothenburg before riding up into Norway. At this stage Dan decided he thought the whole venture too expensive and too ferry bound and so backed out. And then there were three! Such was the lure of the photographs we had seen and the promise of some truly exceptional roads we three 'wise' men elected to 'Go for it' (ironically three people fit into one hotel room, making the whole trip cheaper!).

Friday - Home to Harwich (170miles 4 hrs).

As is the case with such things the wait seemed endless but next we knew we were sat outside the petrol station rendezvous, not Morrisons this time, bikes laden with various trussed up baggage and we were off. This year's ride to the Harwich ferry terminal would take about four hours so our lunch time departure gave us plenty of time to settle into an unrushed journey south bound. The weather also played its' part by being kind enough to keep warm and dry. Our route took us through some beautiful Lincolnshire Wolds before we had to use some of the much busier routes towards Kings Lynn. The A17 was particularly busy following an accident but we used the filtering potential of our bikes to great effect gently caving past the miles of stationary traffic. Towards Thetford we chose to keep away from the 'A' roads and enjoyed good progress through the Norfolk countryside until the inevitable last few miles of bustling 'A' roads again into the port of Harwich.

Arriving with time to spare we stopped off at the conveniently placed Morrison's supermarket for some vital supplies to take on-board the anticipated expensive ferry. At passport control we experienced a full helmet off scrutinizing before shuffling forwards to await the call to board.

While waiting we encounter Britain's best dressed cyclist. A wiry well-spoken gent whose dress sense seemed to have been inspired by UK comedy series 'It ain't half hot mum' complete with calf length cream socks and open toed sandals (Jesus Boots we used to call 'em). In conversation he tells us he is to spend two weeks cycling around Denmark and we wish him well. Finally we are beckoned forth by a man in a florescent jacket and head over a bridge to board the ship persuaded by 'Lofty'. In the twilight bowels of the vehicle deck we find ourselves with another bike tying down system to work out before re-emerging back into the light of the accommodation labyrinth.

I find it hard to pack all of what I consider essential into my tank bag and therefore end up dragging tank bag, roll bag and crash helmet upstairs and along narrow corridors dressed in full leathers clearly not designed for such activity. This year I have managed to leave my soft luggage panniers attached to the bike, but they only contain changes of clothes and some footwear. Kryten and especially Festa have no such hang ups and perform the task with consummate ease bringing only what is needed for the sea voyage in neatly packed tank bags. The windowless cabin is fairly typical of our voyages so far but has the welcome addition of a firmly secured TV.

Motorcycle attire stowed away we make our way to the outside decks briefly stopping to experience the breath-taking price of a pint hand pulled by a less than cheery bar lady. Harwich and the rest of England are slowly being left behind as our ship cuts a stately path through the calm flat waters of the harbour. Following announcements made in impenetrable Scandinavian languages our captains thinly accented tones inform us that the ship is now in the open waters of the North Sea and all ships time will operate in Danish time, one hour ahead of UK, the adventure begins.

Our ship is the DFDS vessel Dana Sirena, built in 2002 she is capable of carrying 400 cars and 600 passengers but it soon becomes clear her main function is to carry containers. It is not possible to walk round far outside as there are only small isolated areas. The passenger part is located at the front, focsle, bow, pointy end and although fairly lively it appears small compared to our previous vessels. Looking back over the rear, stern bit the open decks reveal numerous multi-coloured containers.

We have soon experienced pretty much all the ship has to offer and sit watching the on board entertainment. This is a guy sat on a stool with a guitar. He seems like a seasoned pro and has some well-rehearsed witty lines that he delivers to a largely unresponsive audience. At the end of one song he asks if anyone has any songs they would like him to play. People either look at their shoes or go about their business as if nothing has happened. Kryten can't contain himself and asks if he knows Rudy by Kenny Rogers. Our guitar hero scratches his head and says he doesn't know that one as it is probably the Gay version of the song, he does know the correctly titled Ruby which he proceeds to play extremely well.

There's only so much banter one can enjoy with a jolly guitar fellow so we leave the public areas for the small screen football based entertainment on offer in our cabin. It's world cup time and some team I'm not bothered about is playing another team I don't care about, still Festa and Kryten seem amused by it. I fall gently to sleep and fail to catch the final score as I apparently drown out the TV with contented snoring.

Saturday – Esbjerg to Frederikshavn - Ferry to Gothenburg (210miles 3hrs 15mins).

I've no idea at what time I woke up but I do know our vessel is encountering a little swell. I lie, for a while, in the darkness of the windowless cabin trying to anticipate the next roll and then decide to search for the seasick pills, which makes me feel worse. To tell the truth the ship isn't really moving that much but neither is it sailing on a mill pond. Cruise hardened Kryten descends from the berth above mine and heads out for a turn on deck. Festa puts on some tunes but elects to stay in his bunk. None of us feels much like accepting the breakfast invitations we are by now receiving over the ships 'annoy'.

Eventually the rocking subsides as we enter the more sheltered waters leading to the port of Esbjerg. It's a cool, grey day with a very strong gusty wind that greets our mid-day arrival in Denmark. Passport control seems pretty much non-existent and we are soon riding into town looking for an art installation (proper cultured us lads yer know). Man Meets The Sea is a public sculpture by Sven Wiig Hansen. Created in 1995 entirely from white concrete it is comprised of four nine meter high male figures that sit rigidly facing the waves. Today they are joined on their windswept pedestal by three, somewhat shorter, individuals for their first brief photo opportunity of the trip.

There's not much else to see and the four blokes have little to offer in the way of conversation so we retrace our route back into town and join the E20 motorway. As with all motorways the E20 is a fairly dull affair, as is the E45 that takes us all the way north past Aalborg to our next ferry at Frederikshavn. It's a three or four hour motorway stint made more arduous by the constant buffeting of the wind and the ever present threat of rain but we make it in good time and join the queue to board with full fuel tanks.

Tonight's is a three hour crossing of Kattegat Bay (no I'd never heard of it either) to the Swedish port and city of Gothenburg. Tonight is also the night of the start of England's bid for World Cup glory as they play the US of A. We eventually find a seat that Kryten is happy with, i.e. directly in front of the huge screen TV, and the match kicks off, enough said.

From the deck of the ship Gothenburg looks like a nice place, even though it's now eleven o'clock at night and it's raining, it has a kind of welcoming glow. In this dark wet night we must attempt to find our hotel "a short easy two kilometre journey from the berth" the advert had said. I had taken the precaution of Googling the route and had a look with the street view. This made the fairly complicated route, on the wrong side of the road in the dark, easier to follow and we soon found the inviting lights of the hotel and the warm smile of its well-spoken receptionist. The small road that led down to the underground car park was wet and covered in leaves so we ended up a bit sideways at times, which has the effect of livening up proceedings somewhat.

Warm, dry and with a clean set of clothes on we sit in the bar and enjoy a well-earned glass of expensive Swedish beer until the wee small hours.

Sunday - Gothenburg to Lillehammer (300miles 5 hrs).

Breakfast time at last! Since we found the prices on board ship a bit steep we hadn't really eaten much since leaving home and now we could redress the balance. The breakfast room was light and airy with a modern Scandinavian feel. We made full use of our bed and breakfast accommodation, although we couldn't quite find the courage to try the grey fish dish thing. There was no hurry today, as it would be another motorway day, so we had another cup of tea before loading the bikes and heading into a sunny Gothenburg Sunday morning.

Today we are heading north once again to the Norwegian Winter Olympic town of Lillehammer. It's a day on the motorway that sees us leaving Sweden and entering Norway without ceremony. Further north we ride past the capital Oslo and on to the main E6 road where we begin to view some of the more pleasing scenery we are here to experience. The weather is much kinder than the wind and showers of yesterday which helps develop the feeling that the journey is over and the 'holiday' starts here.

It's around six o'clock when Lillehammer comes into view across a lake with the impressive backdrop of mountains and an Olympic ski slope. Our accommodation for the evening is the Stasjonen Hotel, really the local hostel, situated above the train and bus station making it fairly straightforward to locate. There are very few people around, just the hooded youth common in most European towns. Kryten is left to monitor the bikes as Festa and I seek out the reception, manned by a very young person, or, more likely, I'm getting old. The very few formalities completed we unload ourselves into the pleasant room and move our bikes to an area where we feel they will be ok. Tonight turns out to be the only place on the trip where we feel the need to lock them together, probably totally unfounded.

After a long day on the motorway the desire for a decent shower is a strong one and our room provides the perfect solution. Festas' IPod is employed to provide some suitable background ambience while the first bottle of his red wine stock is cracked open to celebrate our arrival in Norway.

Kryten meanwhile unveils a fine selection of gentlemen's grooming products, pills and potions and heads into the shower room first. Soon Festa and I share puzzled looks as all manner of strange sounds begin emanating from behind the bathroom door. We swiftly conclude that it is best we don't enquire as to the cause. Tonight will be our first hot evening meal since leaving the UK and we are all eager to get out and hit the town's restaurants. The young receptionist gives us a town map and few ideas before we head into a fairly deserted town.

The main street isn't far from the hostel but time is pressing on. It's our first experience of how light it stays at night when you begin to travel north and it means that some of the places we call in have finished serving food. Thankfully we do find a dubious looking place in the high street that turns out to be a very pleasant one once inside with a very accommodating waiter and a menu in English. The price? Beer and a Reindeer pizza £20 (five minutes in a country and Festa and I have already eaten Santa's' number one).

After the meal we took time to wander around some of the streets, pushing our noses against the window of a particularly excellent looking outdoor and cycling shop and, for me, eyeing a useful gift emporium for an expectant nine year old back home. There is a manmade civic style waterfall that leads us down to the cinema where it would appear the film has recently finished. Briefly the area seems busy, but curiously mainly with young ladies, probably a chick-flick we surmise before heading back to the hostel and more red wine. It still isn't really dark when we finally turn in just after midnight.

Monday – Lillehammer to Gjendeshiem (215miles 5hours 30mins).

The hostel breakfast the next morning has an unexpectedly large choice of tempting, and not so tempting morsels. The room is situated to give a view of the comings and goings of the railway station with a glimpse of the countryside possible from certain angles for good measure. A more relaxed start to the day sees us wander back into town for me to visit a souvenir shop and for Festa and Kryen to visit a designer label shop to purchase a smart bargain winter coat each in the sale.

We return to find our bikes still securely manacled together and are soon on our way. Our first stop is a quick back track down the E6 to a view point by the side of Lake Mjosa. We wait our turn while a coach party takes its photos before placing our bikes to give the lake, Lillehammer with its ski slope in the background and a sign saying 'Olympic City 1994' in the foreground. A camera is then thrust into the hands of a passing tourist and the moment captured.

Back on the road we soon turn off the busy E6 and on to the Rv255 heading for the Gudbrandsdal Valley and a high mountain pass evocatively called 'Peer Gynt Vagen' (the Peer Gynt road). This 60km long toll road (except for motorcycles) ranges from 1100m to 1500m above sea level and is only opened for the brief summer season from June. The roads leading up begin to narrow as we turn off one small road onto a smaller one passing by small villages and farms. Higher up the road surface deteriorates into nothing more than a loose gravel tack and I begin to wonder if I have missed a vital turn.

We stop in the seemingly deserted village of Skeibo. Krytens' brake fluid reservoir has lost a retaining bolt on the rugged road so a cable tie repair is carried out. Looking around at the houses we are struck by their construction. Mainly dark brown wood with white painted window frames but nearly all have grass roofs, presumably for insulation. As Kryten toils to fix his bike a lady appears wheeling a wheelbarrow. "Do you speak English?" I enquire. "Of course" came the smiling reply. "Please could you tell me where the Peer Gynt Vagen is" I continue. "You are on it, just keep going up the hill to the toll gate".

Looking up the hill the road surface got worse and seemed to be heading towards snow. Sure enough we soon encountered the toll gate that informed us we were entering onto the Peer Gynt Vagen (motorcycles free). Small pine trees lined the route as we rapidly gained height on a winding forest track. This was adventure biking like Euan and Charlie only without the proper bikes for the job. A CB1300, SV650 and ZX6R are certainly not the first choice of anyone attempting this kind of terrain and our main concern was the dreaded puncture.

We were not alone on this road though as we were passed by the odd 4 x 4 somewhat better suited to the conditions. Soon we came across one or two more 'normal' vehicles as we carefully picked our way higher and higher into and above the snow line. Eventually we came through a gap and found a view that stretched out for miles in front of us. We were so high now that the tree line had given way to low lying vegetation. In the far distance snow covered mountains formed an uneven horizon that gave way to grey clouds broken in places to allow sunlight to illuminate patches of the earth below. It was lunch time by now and we parked the bikes by the wall of cleared snow to take in the vast scene, breathe the clear mountain air and enjoy a well-earned drink and bite to eat.

Later Krytens 'natural break' turning the snow yellow was rudely interrupted by a snowball hurled from Festa and a brief snowball fight ensued. It was now time to return to the riding and commence the decent back to civilisation. 60km is quite some distance at a maximum speed of 30 to 40mph bouncing over a rutted loose surface but I think we were all a little disappointed when we eventually returned through another toll gate and onto a tarmac road. Amusingly one of the first signs we saw was one advising caution following some resurfacing work 'Loose Chippings'.

The Rv255 now plunged downwards through the villages of Skabu and Vinstra before returning us briefly to the clutches of the E6. Back tracking slightly we then took a turn left and onto the rv27 climbing back into the mountains of the Rondane National Park. Once again we climbed higher and higher on the narrow twisting roads that eventually levelled out to a huge plain in the centre of which lay a sparsely populated ski resort. It became increasingly cold here despite the sun breaking up the clouds so we couldn't hang around.

In front the narrow ribbon of road stretched out weaving its way between what looked like some very boggy areas towards a valley.

As we began the decent into the valley a natural break was taken by the side of a fast flowing clear river of melting snow. Further on we stopped at the first of the 'Installations' provided by the Norwegian Government to promote the Nasjonale Turistveg we were making such good use of.

The Sohlbergplassen viewpoint was designed by architect Carl-Viggo Hølmebakk and from it Rondane appears almost exactly as it was depicted in Harald Sohlberg's 1914 painting "Winter Night in the Mountains" (yep, you're right, I did Google that). We leave our bikes and walk out on the swerving concrete walkway through the trees to see Lake Atnsjoen in the foreground and the snowy mountains forming a perfect backdrop, a truly beautiful scene.

I had planned our days so that we travelled around 200miles each time. This meant that by now the 600cc machines were beginning to require fuel but there had been very few opportunities to replenish diminishing reserves. The rv27 road gently twisted us through woods, passing fast flowing rivers and skipping over open plains slowly descending all the way. As we approached the village of Folldal the decent was a more severe one but it led us to a much needed fuel oasis. Festa and Kryen were impressed to find that with our average speeds being kept so low their fuel consumptions had reduced dramatically and far greater MPGs had been achieved.

With time now pressing on we headed off to re-join the E6 once again, this time heading south towards the larger towns of Dombas and Douvre. The E6 is like one of our A class roads but it surprises us to find that we are constantly heading down hill, 40miles downhill it turns out. At one point we pass a low-slung tandem type bicycle heading up hill, how hard must that experience be and how well will that boy girl relationship survive?

At around five o'clock we stop for a brief rest as our destination does not seem to be getting any nearer. On the road again after a stretch and a drink we arrive in Otta and turn off to the rv15 towards Vågåmo. Once again the road leads us through pine woodlands and alongside lakes. At Vågåmo we head off upwards once again on the final Nasjonale Turistveg of the day, the rv51. By now it's getting past 6:00 and this beautiful mountain road just keeps on going leading us to question whether we will even find our destination.

After some anxious glances at the map we eventually turn off the rv51 at a signpost promising Gjendeshiem. It's a bit like going up someone's driveway as the road is narrow and twisty and almost seems to be in the river that runs so close to its edge. Over a small hill and then suddenly there it is, a dark grey wooden building surrounded by mountains and sat alongside a beautiful flat calm lake. The Gjendeshiem Hostel is the only thing there apart from a small building a bit further on next to the ferry. Inside we are told that we should hurry as food will only be served until 7pm.

Our room is quickly located and a quick change sees us entering the large dining hall at around 6:45. "Find a seat and I'll bring your plates" says the cheery waitress. We do as instructed and sit with a view of the lake but are soon asked to move as our places have been saved in amongst the other diners. In the middle of some long wooden tables seating 10 people either side we find some spare seats and bowls are handed to us. An older Norwegian couple opposite smile and pass over a large alloy bowl containing a grey lumpy looking liquid, "Fish soup, it's good, eat". It's as close to a scene from Oliver as I can imagine and our faces must have been an absolute picture! Festa nervously ladles half a spoon full out and passes the bowl to Kryten and me who do something similar. Slowly our spoons are lifted to our mouths and tongues dip reluctantly into the steaming liquid. Bloody hell this is good lets have some more! Heaven knows what was in it and I couldn't tell you what to ask for but you'd have to try it for yourself as I haven't the words to describe it only to repeat it was delicious.

Looking around our fellow diners and listening to their conversations it is obvious we are not the only English speakers here. Loud American voices dominate the tightly packed dinner guests as we begin to make our way back and forth to the buffet for the main course. After dinner we sit outside in the warm cloudless evening with a beer or two. We are joined by a Tasmanian medical researcher and his son along with a retired Swedish couple and their son. It's such a beautiful night that we resist the need for sleep partly because it is still so light but mainly because of the company, what a place! In conversation we discover that we are all here for the same reason, climbing the Besseggen Ridge, Norway's most famous walk and something of a rite of passage for Norwegians. Our Swedish friend points down the lake and informs us that the start of the walk is from the 'walley' in the distance.

We are also told that the ferry that we are relying on to take us along the lake to the start of the walk does not normally run this 'early' in the season. As it happens, the only day it will run is tomorrow leaving at 9am and then only because the American party has chartered it but we should be ok to join them. How lucky is that!?

Reluctantly we return to our bunk bedded room to get some sleep before the big day ahead. It's a very narrow basic room made entirely of wood, two sets of wooden bunks, a sink (ok so that wasn't wood) and a rail for your clothes. Everything creaks and groans as we move about. Showers are a coin operated affair located down the corridor, ladies in the first half of every hour gents in the second. The toilets are the other end of the corridor and give their location away by the aroma that emanates from within. I have to visit though as the fish soup is working its way through. I choose the last cubical on the left and am amazed at what is behind the door. The toilet has a large window with clear glass which I open and then sit gazing out over the lake to the surrounding mountains, sure did beat reading the newspaper.

Tuesday - Walking day (10½miles 7 hrs).

We haven't slept much overnight due to the constant patter of not so tiny feet attached to larger mouths in the corridor making their way to the scenic wc. This situation was compounded by the far more agreeable sight of the light in our window throughout the night as it barely got dark. We have to be up and about reasonably early so as not to miss the only boat of the day but also to stock up on vital breakfast and lunch. A great idea in Norway is the Matpakke. You have breakfast and then can make your lunch pack up from the buffet. Some hotels charge a small fee for this but our hostel included it in the price, excellent.

We join our fellow hikers and American tourists on the quayside and pass our rucksacks (converted tank bags in our case) up to the captain. With little ceremony the boat turns away from the quay and begins chugging across the lake to the distant 'walley' and the quayside at Memurubu. It's an exceptionally perfect day, sunshine in a cloudless sky and not a breath of wind means out little craft is the only thing disturbing the lake.

We are in the Jotunheimen National Park where around 35.000 hikers cross the Besseggen in the period mid-June - mid-September every year. The hike of around 10½miles should take us about seven hours, with its highest point at 1743 meters above sea level. We will be walking between the crystal clear Bessvatnet Lake at one side and the Gjendevannet Lake with its emerald-green glacial colour (Small particles from the Glacier float in the water which reflect against the sunlight to produce a strong green colour) at the other, so the brochures tell us.

The ferry docks at Memurubu after a forty minute trip and once it leaves our only way back is to complete the walk. We set off onwards and upwards and soon encounter a sign telling us we will be climbing over 1000 meters and advising that the weather can close in rapidly at times. The steep and lengthy climb means that our fellow trekkers are soon spread out as some find the going tougher than others. One young couple is dressed in training shoes and the girl seems not as keen as her partner to attempt the walk. Fit Mr. Kryten is off at a gallop, IPod plugged into his ears he is 'in the zone' and Festa is not far behind while I toil on at a much slower pace. I have taken the advice of wearing an extra layer in case of inclement weather and have brought along my waterproof bike gear just in case. As I climb I realize that I may have over done it somewhat as it is very warm and I am pouring with perspiration.

After about an hour or so of constantly climbing the path begins to level off and we can stop to admire the stunning views. An old German gentleman bids us good-day as he passes by walking with two sticks at a steady but controlled pace. Despite what the brochures say Gjendevannet Lake far below us now is not green today but a stunning blue reflecting the colour of the cloudless sky above and the surrounding snow covered peaks. There are no trees here as we are too high up just small patches of moss and tough grass clinging on to life between the rocks.

The path undulates onwards and steadily upwards as we make our way to 'the ridge'. There are one or two false dawns along the way and some interesting variations on what constitutes a path. At one point we follow a lake side before the path narrows to cross over its outfall which is a waterfall. At another we cross a snow covered slope with heaven knows what consequences should we fall. Further on still we drop down to the shore of the 'crystal clear Bessvatnet lake' only it isn't crystal clear today as it remains frozen over. The route is a slightly worrying one as it involves us treading in the deep snow footprints of those who have gone before with the added peril that, should the snow give way, we would slip 20 meters or so into said frozen lake.

Finally we arrive at the base of the Besseggen Ridge, an un-nerving sight for one such as I. It appears to climb very sharply upwards with red 'Ts' to guide the adventurous hiker on. After a brief rest to admire the view and catch our breath we commence the accent. I have climbed Helvelyn in the Lake District via the Striding Edge route a couple of times but that is nothing compared to this. The red Ts zig zag a route over the rocks. Each zig to the right leads me towards a precipitous 1300ft drop down to the Gjendevannet Lake and each zag to the left a lesser drop to the frozen Bessvatnet Lake. I cling to the rock face with every sinew in my hands and toes although I speculate that my arse cheeks might give better grip at this moment! At one point I glance up to see Kryten and Festa looking down to check on me but they are soon off again.

It's a long way up but the path does eventually begin to level and I can begin to release my grip on the rock and stand unaided. Festa and Kryten have been waiting a while when I eventually join them and we push on over the very rocky final slope to the enormous cairn at the summit, 5717ft above sea level.

Standing on top of the cairn the views are spectacular over half of the Jotunheimen. There are mountains, lakes, rivers and waterfalls all around and below us and we take time to drink in the vista we have worked so hard to see. I can make out one road, the one we came here on, in the distance but there is little or no other sign of manmade structures. It's an extraordinary place, quiet, peaceful and stunningly beautiful. I may even go so far as saying I haven't seen anything to compare with this since.

After loitering for as long as we could and deciding on which was the correct path we begin our decent which starts by crossing a snow field. Kryten and Festa plough on ahead wrapped in their IPod enclosed worlds. I lag behind and enjoy the silence broken only by the sound of my feet compacting the snow beneath them. At times I fall back into the snow as I lose my footing but this adds to the enjoyment. I decide to share the moment and as I have no-one to talk to on top of this mountain I ring my wife on my mobile phone, aint technology wonderful!

The path winds its way down the mountain and at one point comes close to a ridge. Festa and Kryten look over the edge and report seeing the hostel below, I take their word for it. At one point I enjoy a little faster run down the path as we begin to drop out of the snow line and on to the loose rocks. There are small waterfalls by the sides of the path formed from melting snow and we fill our water bottles with the fresh, cool, fabulously tasting pure water.

For the last mile or so the hostel comes into view but seems to take an age to get any closer. By the time we are on the final stone staircase to the road in front my legs are just about collapsing and the flat surface is a very welcome feeling. It has taken us around seven glorious hours to complete this amazing walk and we have arrived just in time for a well-earned beer before dinner.

There are fewer guests tonight as the American party has departed and all the talk is of the walk. Our Swedish friends tell us that the lady is in fact Norwegian and has completed the walk for the first time, making her 'more Norwegian' than her father who has never completed it.

After dinner we chat away with my limbs slowly ceasing up until the young couple in the training shoes finally make it back. Kryten engages them in conversation and reports that they are too late back for dinner and are having a meal of crisps and chocolate bars. We decide that getting some sleep might now be a grand idea and so, with my increasingly humorous walk, we head off to the creaking wooden cupboard that is our bedroom, what a day, what an absolutely fabulous day!

Wednesday – Gjendeshiem to Geiranger (170miles 5hrs 15mins).

Slept like some Norwegian wood and my legs are as stiff as some to. When I try to move around I kind of have to aim at where I want to go then lean forward until, almost falling, I head off in that direction. Anyway, with breakfast over, a Matpakke in our tank bags and the bill paid we head off back along the rv51 towards Vågåmo. Our first major concern is finding fuel as the 600s are running a little low. The rv51 is another Nasjonale Turistveg lined with trees it pitches and turns its way alongside a beautiful calm lake with stunning reflexions. In an attempt to conserve dwindling fuel on a seemingly endless road Festa and Kryten elect to turn off their motors and coast. Their silent running isn't holding them back though as the Turistveg is mainly downhill and quite steep in places until it delivers them giggling, like someone who has farted in a lift and stepped out, to a filling station at Vågåmo. From here we take a small mountain road back to the E6 that turns out to be a good choice as it has recently been resurfaced and provides a little extra entertainment to start the day.

Any entertainment is then put on hold as we travel another 60miles north leaving the E6 eventually to join the E156 towards Andalsnes. For a while after the village of Lesja we travel alongside a vast open flat plain, bordered by distant mountains with a central river weaving its way majestically through. There are signs to warn of Moose crossing but despite some piercing glances into surrounding woodland unfortunately I see no evidence of them. Much of the road contains long boring straights but we resist the temptation to open up the bikes too much to get this bit out of the way.

Eventually though our patience is rewarded as the road becomes enveloped by increasingly high mountains on either side, we are entering the Romsdal Valley. The cliffs tower above almost overpowering us with their imposing size as we progress through this narrow foreboding landscape to come to rest in the viewing area of what draws people here. It's the Troll Wall, Trollveggen, the tallest vertical rock face in Europe, 1100 meters from the base to the summit at its tallest. At its steepest, the summit overhangs the base by nearly fifty meters making it a firm favourite in the criminally insane world of Base Jumpers. We sit in the shadow of this monster cliff and begin to consume the contents of our Matpakke. Clouds bump the sharp rocks that form the jagged horizon above us and we realise that the tiny vegetation that clings to the rock are in fact trees as it is so difficult to gain perspective.

Back on the road and it is a short ride to our next turn left onto the rv63, another Nasjonale Turistveg. The 6km road is a narrow one through meadows it seems at times and we are now behind the Troll Wall heading along the Isterdalen valley. Soon we stop at a car park with many others as we are all here to view the same thing, the Trollstigen, the Trolls Staircase, the road from the magazine in the dentists' waiting room that inspired this trip. This engineering wonder lifts the road out of the valley by way of a steep 9% incline and eleven hairpin bends. About half way up a bridge carries the road over the powerful Stigfossen waterfall before it emerges at the ubiquitous gift emporium.

We try to pick our moment to begin the climb so as to avoid the numerous motor homes and tourist coaches that labour their way back and forth coughing diesel fumes into this stunning place. Once that time comes we accelerate up to the first twist and begin the ascent. We do not have to wait long to encounter the first motor home coming the other way. The male drivers white knuckles desperately grasp the steering wheel while he receives 'advice' from his frantic lady passenger. We don't have to travel much further before the drop off the edge of the road becomes a perilous one. Over the bridge that marks the half way point with the Stigfossen crashing close beneath we hardly dare stop to admire the view.

Concentration is the key as we set ourselves for the next tight right hand bend only to discover a large lorry has claimed most of the road. Squeeze past and at the next bend we encounter running melt water making turning that little bit more hazardous. Throttle, brake and clutch control are critical to maintain just the right momentum to safely negotiate each steep hairpin bend. Too little power will result in the bike stalling and possibly rolling backwards, you really don't want that, too much power could easily find you slipping off on the cold wet tarmac, you don't want that either.

As we round the final bend building work comes into view and the road degrades to a loose gravel track bounded by hazard tape and a hap-hazard traffic control system. We find a parking spot for our bikes then make our way towards the viewpoint foretold in the brochures for the area. Unfortunately, when we eventually negotiate the wooden walkway, access to the viewpoint is barred as workmen toil to renew the pathway. Another viewpoint does provide a glimpse of what will be a fine vantage point so we photograph each other here before returning to the gift shop area. I leave with a small ceramic Troll and a plastic Norse helmet complete with horns feeling pleased that I have presents for the significant small person back home. The Troll finds a home easily within my tank bag but the helmet must reside atop my tail luggage.

Troll and helmet secured I swing my right leg back between tank and luggage and we re-join the road past the construction site that will be the impressive new visitor centre sometime soon. The rv63 now begins its descent to meet the Storfjord at Linge and is joined by the Valldøla River draining melting snow water. I nearly miss another tourist viewpoint that comes upon us much quicker than I was expecting. Gudbrandsjuvet is a 5 meter narrow and 20–25 meter high ravine through which the Valldøla River forces itself. The waters have formed a complex of deep potholes and intricate formations. To view all this an architect designed bridge made of what appears to be rusty metal bounces you to the main platform of 25mm steel sheets, cantilevered like a precarious walkway around the cliff. When we cross another bridge to look back the whole structure looks rather flimsy and I can't help but marvel at those who conceive and build such things.

Back on the bikes and after a short ride we are soon entering the town of Linge from where we board a ferry to cross the Fjord. On board we are treated to fine views along the Fjord and of the 'V' shaped valley that frames our destination town of Eidsdalen. I watch the sister ferry leave and glide past us before the 15 minute crossing ends and we roll onto the quayside for a bite to eat, a rest and a photo opportunity. Our bikes are posed to give a view of the Fjord and the approaching ferry and we set the self-timers to capture the moment.

Our companion rv63 road leaves Eidsdalen and starts a steady climb upwards heading towards the cruise ship hotspot town of Geiranger. It's late in the afternoon now and we have had a full day of amazing sights but when we crest the hill the beauty of the Geiranger Fjord starts to come into view. Excitedly we grab a photo or two as opportunities present themselves through the roadside trees and undergrowth. We are on the 'Eagles Highway' so called because it soars like an eagle above the Fjord, and it's a catchy name, and as we round another of its eleven hairpin bends the Norwegian Government have obligingly commissioned a suitably precarious viewing platform. As the only level ground appears to be on the platform we park up and move to the edge to admire the stupendous view. The severe sides of Geiranger Fjord plummet down to the flat calm water some distance below us, a tiny red dot can just be made out to be a canoeist helping to give some perception of scale. The small town of Geiranger at the end of the fjord occupies the left side of our view and is framed by snow covered mountains. Parked up, seemingly in the town its self, is a large cruise ship preparing to leave, its tenders returning coach loads of travellers from sharing the sights with us today.

It's the sort of view you could stare at for hours but after many photos we must find our hotel somewhere just off this road. We pass it as it comes upon us unexpectedly quickly and is set into the hillside of the Eagles Highway. From where we park the bikes the hotel appears to be a single storey but a sign directs us to reception via a lift which goes downwards. Our room is on the fifth floor and we are completely unprepared for the view that greets us as the door swings open. We have an outstanding view over the Fjord and a balcony from which to admire it. The cruise ship sounds its horn to leave and soon it glides past our room now considerably larger than it appeared from our lofty vantage point earlier.

Unpacked, showered and changed we head upstairs to the bar, it's beer o'clock and we have decided that we should treat ourselves to a couple of drinks and a meal in the hotel. Unfortunately the hotel has other ideas and there's no one about to serve up the anticipated beverages. Undaunted we decide to walk the half mile or so into the main town. It's a cool pleasant evening and the walk along the road alongside the Fjord allows us to enjoy the scenery further.

With the cruise ship gone most of the people seem to have vanished too as the town appears almost deserted. We take each other's photo alongside a large fibreglass Troll and have a wander around the quayside before trying to find somewhere to eat. There is little choice as most places are shut so we end up in another pizza place where I choose the less than authentic dish of Reindeer Pizza again which is really quite nice.

Thursday - Geiranger to Dragsvik (165miles 4hrs 45mins).

Breakfast is taken with the superb view of the Fjord through the floor to ceiling glass panels that form the outer walls of the restaurant. We make quick work of breakfast before we jump on the bikes for the brief trip back into town. We have decided that a 2 hour boat trip around Geiranger Fjord is too good an opportunity to pass up so we leave the luggage with the helpful hotel guy. Freed from its' great burden the CB1300 feels alive once more and the brief jaunt to the quayside is a real pleasure. We park the bikes and arrive with moments to spare as we are last to board the boat as it casts off onto the Fjord full of happy tourists.

We pass a newly arrived cruise ship and then see our hotel hiding beneath the twisted profile of the Eagles Highway. A little further on and we pass the impressive Seven Sisters waterfalls with the single waterfall across the Fjord, The Suitor. The story goes that he was turned down by all the seven sisters, and consequently began drinking. This is symbolized by the bottle shape at the foot of the fall, where it splits into two falls. More stories are told over the ships multi lingual PA. Absurdly inaccessible farms are pointed out pitched high above us and a tale of ladders being hauled up when the tax man came knocking is recalled. At another precarious ex dwelling young children used to play tethered to the farmhouse to prevent them falling over the edge.

Another huge cruise liner is making its way through the narrow Fjord and our vessel is dwarfed. Our captain then heads directly to the side of the Fjord to where a small jetty awaits. The boat is not tied up but two people scramble ashore and are seemingly abandoned at the foot of a huge cliff. Looking back I could just about make out a faint footpath leading to some old buildings half way up the steep sides but could not imagine why anyone would undertake such a journey.

As we return to Geiranger the second cruise ship is moored alongside the road leading to our hotel and is beginning to disgorge its passengers to the attendant quayside coaches. It's quite a chaotic site that greets us once we are reunited with the bikes but I imagine one that is easier to deal with on two wheels rather than four. At the hotel our luggage is heaved back into position before we head on back through town and begin our accent away from this beautiful place. An opportunity to survey the scene from a lofty vantage point presents its self and we can't resist one last look. It's another of the Norwegian Governments' purpose build seemingly impossible platforms clinging to the side of a rocky outcrop high above a ravine. After a short time admiring the views, and as we are about to depart, a well-spoken retired gentleman engages us in conversation having seen the GB plates on the bikes, not a common sight in these parts. Turns out he is cruising in the Fjords but he is on the Queen Mary 2. He tells us she was due to berth in Greianger but with two other ships already berthed there she was diverted to a town called Olden on Utvikfjorden. As luck would have it this was on our intended route so we thanked him for the information and set off onwards and upwards.

The weather began to close in a little the higher we climbed and we started to encounter snow by the side of the road. We abandoned thoughts of riding up the Dalsnibba Mountain to its popular viewpoint as the fog shrouded its summit and continued upwards until our road emerged alongside a large frozen blue coloured lake. It was distinctly chilly now with the mist hiding the detail rather than blotting out the view completely when we spotted a large bird above the road and pulled over to do a little twitching. There were a couple of motor homes where we stopped and a Dutch guy joined us by the roadside. Between us we concluded this large bird was an Eagle before we lost sight of it in the mist.

Our journey continued upwards until we dropped down onto a large open plain area with little to see in any direction for miles. Just before the town of Grotli another choice was possible, ride through a tunnel under the mountain or take the scenic Fylkesvei 258 Turistveg

over it to Videsaeter, Turisveg it had to be. All started well but the Turistveg soon turned from tarmac to gravel, still, no worries, we've done some 'adventure biking' already this trip
.

Onwards we bounced passing the occasional motor home coming in the other direction and even a family having a picnic by the lake in the increasingly cold and misty great outdoors. The route continued on with a slight but noticeably upward trend. The mist then began to thicken into what could be safely described as, well, err. fog. To add to the increasing sense of foreboding the road began to be bordered by snow and streams with some nasty little drops should a bend be miss-judged. As if this wasn't enough my, until now, clear Arai visor was misting up inside and out and I could barely see my front tyre. We were crawling along, picking a precarious route between gravel and rocks on the road and drops off it. I was leading and in the end just had to stop to relieve the tension.

All around was the sound of running water. Over the wall at the side of the road a wide river raced by viewable only through the holes that had collapsed in its frozen surface, we were high up somewhere but heaven knows where. This adventure biking was becoming a little too adventurous and I asked Kryten and Festa if it might be prudent to turn back. After some debate we realized we had come too far to turn back and made the decision to press on. I pressed the start button and eased the CB gingerly into the gloom, the headlights of the SV and ZX following in my mirrors. The fog was a pea-souper and the road surface kept wrestling with me for control of the bike when suddenly in the gloom the road appeared to end abruptly in a black void....SH# @# #T!!! I had expectations of plummeting to some freezing watery end only to be found later in the year as the snow and ice receded.

But wait, I was still travelling forward and I was alive, what was going on? The answer was that we had traversed the perilous Turistveg and had re-joined civilization on the other side of the mountain heralded by this beautiful piece of black smooth tarmac. There was even a summer café, closed of course, but we knew we had survived. Not long after that we dropped below the fog and found ourselves twisting down more hairpin bends, over another waterfall and into the deserted valley floor. The road followed the path of a fast flowing river and as the road began another sharp decent we passed another viewpoint for the Videfossen waterfall as the river to hurled its' self-down the valley.

Our adventure route lead us down to join the original rv15 road at the exit to the tunnel we could have taken to get us to this point, but we would have missed so much (ok so I wouldn't now be wearing soiled under garments but at least I was warm). A few miles further on and at the village of Hjelle we are treated to a stunning view, should that read 'another' stunning view. Surrounded by mountains that could have been drawn by a child the stunningly beautiful Lake Strynevatnet (I think) was as flat calm as a flat calm mill pond, its surface providing a perfect mirror image of the truly majestic scenery encircling it.

Images captured we hug the shores of this lake for a mile or two more until we reach its outlet and follow the river down to Stryn on the shore of Utvikfjorden. Round one more bend and the stately silhouette of the Queen Mary 2 comes into view across the Fjord. For once we are on a comparatively busy road (for Norway) and it has started to rain so we make fairly quick progress around the waters until we come to rest alongside this mammoth vessel. Due to the immediate depth of the Fjord it is as though she is parked in a car park alongside a busy street. We park the bikes and head back across the bustling main road to try to get a better view. We can't get far enough back to capture an image in one shot. I take out my video camera and pan along the ship but even then her enormous height means I still can't fit her all in.

She is barriered off to protect her from such riffraff as us and has a check point where those fortunate enough to be sailing with her are beginning to filter back on board. The rain is now fairly steady and we still have a way to go so we head back to the bikes. A posh gent seeing the GB plates approaches "I say, have you chaps come far?" (Think Stephen Fry in the First World War Black Adder series). We explain that we have travelled from Geiranger but he is getting wet "Oh, right ho, just orf for a spot of afternoon tea now, good luck". He's off and he's not the only one getting a soaking.

Our route now heads along the rv60 around the side of the Fjord on what should have been a delightful afternoon run. Unfortunately major road repairs were underway and we once again had some 'adventure biking' to enjoy. The adventure seemed to last for a very long time as we picked our way around the mountain to our left and Fjord to our right. I was looking to find a café for a rest but there was hardly a dwelling to be found. Then, as the rain began to ease we rolled into Utvik and spied a small and hospitable looking place. Locals sat smoking under the shelter of the covered entrance to the café come post office come deli and whatever else. Coffee and cake provided a warm and welcome break giving us time to consult the map and take stock of where we were.

From Utvik our route took us upwards once again dropping us down to Byrkjelo for fuel and then on to Skei before turning to run alongside the Jolstravatnet lake on the rv5. We had accepted that our two hour jolly on the Geiranger Fjord would have a knock on effect but we hadn't foreseen the heavy rain which had now begun to fall. As we turned onto our final Turistveg of the day our thoughts where only on getting to the hotel and getting dry. The Turistveg had other ideas as it wanted to show us all the delights this part of Norway had to offer. At one point we came across a sign proclaiming 10k of downhill bends, normally manna from heaven but now more of endurance. Brief teasing glimpses of what could be amazing scenery could be seen through the rare break in the clouds and mist but our attention had to be focused on spotting the large bumps and potholes in the road. I stopped near a raging shallow waterfall but we had lost any desire to investigate. Finally the village of Dragsvik was signposted a couple of kilometres away and soon we saw our hotel beckoning these three no-so-wise men.

At reception a pool of water started to form at my feet (from the rain water! I may be aging rapidly but I still retain a certain amount of bladder control thank you). Posters on the walls showed happy blond people frolicking in sun kissed Fjords but now I think about it we haven't seen too many blond folk so far. I followed the guy up several flights of stairs to the room where he apologized for there being no lift. I wasn't prepared for the accommodation we had been assigned though. It was a huge two bed roomed apartment with its' own kitchen and a view over the Fjord. I returned to the bikes and poured water out of my luggage covers before hauling it all up stairs.

After showers and dry clothing it was beer o'clock and time to organize dinner.

"Have you booked?" asked the waitress. It was a bit reminiscent of a scene from Faulty Towers as the restaurant was virtually empty. She managed to accommodate us somehow and we enjoyed a meal before retiring to the TV area to watch some blistering world cup action with some fellow guests who eyed us Brits with a little trepidation. So blistering was the footy that I decided to head back to the room to try to dry out some of my gear. Clothes adorned every available hanging place and small puddles had formed. I took a hair drier to my boots and patiently sat blasting hot air inside the sodden footwear. It wasn't long before Festa and Kryten returned and all of the apartment's heat sources were turned to maximum. We finished the evening sipping red wine amidst gently steaming clothing. Outside the rain had finally abated leaving us a dimly lit view of the Fjord at gone midnight. It's been a funny old day.

Friday – Dragsvik to Aurland loop (125miles 4hrs 15mins).

The drying process had gone well overnight and the new day that dawned was heralded by a rainbow in the hallway. Breakfast was pleasant, Matpakke all round and the bill, including the previous evenings meal and drinks, was surprisingly reasonable. Outside the weather was much improved and after securing the dried out luggage to the bikes we revved up and sped out of the car park....300m to the ferry quay.

There weren't too many vehicles on board and we were soon heading out across Sognefjord heading for the tiny village of Vangsnes. Looking back towards our hotel in Dragsvik was almost surreal, the beautiful turquoise water of the Fjord was being churned white by the ferry's' eager motors. In the ever diminishing background cloud shadows slowly moved along to reveal green wooded hills leading to white topped mountains appearing out of the clouds.

Once ashore we took the narrow rv13 road alongside the Fjord for a while until turning away from water and into more mountainous terrain at Vikoyn. Unfortunately it started to rain here which meant a stop for me to perform the dance of the waterproofs over leathers while Kryten and Festa looked on smugly clad in their all-weather fabric gear. We pressed onwards and upwards until the road began to level off and the rain began to ease. The rv13 Myrkdalsvegen road now treats us to some unexpectedly lovely scenery along its' mountainous route. We ride alongside lakes and streams as the road ducks in and out of short tunnels cut through looming rock.

We finally part company with the scenic Myrkdalsvegen in the town of Vinje at its' junction with the far more purposeful E16 that brings traffic from Bergen. The pace is now slightly less relaxed as we share the road with lorries and cars requiring a little adjustment back to reality after peace and near solitude of the mountain roads. I am searching for a left turn onto another recommended road, the Stalhiemskleiva and almost miss it while concentrating on the traffic. We turn back to the tiny junction with what appear to be warning signs about the road being one way but decide to press on. The road is quite narrow, not an issue on a bike really, but not even the 1:18 hill sign prepares you for the vision that awaits around one corner.

The road suddenly turns sharply to the right and falls rapidly out of view as it cascades downwards through a series of tight hairpins to the floor of a valley, and we are a fair way up. A tiny wall marks out the edge of the road from the disaster that may befall anyone who gets anything a bit wrong. If you are familiar with the Hard Knot Pass in the Lake District then this is as close to that as I can imagine. We pull over to the side of the road to admire the view, steady the nerves and take a photograph or two. What a view! The steeply sloped sides of the valley are grey rock with only small areas of green where life has managed to gain a tentative hold. Below a river hurries its way through with the main road mimicking its twists and turns. In the distance more snowy peaks and the ever improving sky.

Photographs taken we tuck cameras back into the shelter of the tank bags, slip our hands back inside gloves and are just about to release the brakes to begin our decent when we are passed by a coach. It's laden with German tourists all peering anxiously out of the windows as the driver skilfully steers a perilous path, at times with the front few feet of one side of the coach hanging over the wall. Once past us we can see how such a ludicrous machine is capable of such a route, it has a rear wheel steering mechanism that allows it to get round these bends (that and the almost audible prayers of the party on the coach).

We leave our take off for a little while to give the coach chance to get out of the way but soon catch it up again as it inches its way around another bend. I feel as if I am performing a handstand or a rolling stoppie (I wish) as I ease the brakes on and occasionally off trying to be a little braver at each bend and trying not to look too closely at the drop!

Finally we are all safely down and after a short while we re-join the main road that has tunnelled its way through the mountain. I read later that the Stalhiemskleiva used to be the only way through the valley and that horse drawn wagons were used. I just can't imagine how it would be possible for that road to have been driven in both directions.

From here we had to follow the main highway once again towards the town of Flam and on towards our overnight stay in the town of Aurland. The landscape meant that we were regularly plunged into the darkness of tunnels, allowed brief glimpses of sky before being shepherded into darkness again.

By the time we reach Aurland it's around dinner time so we park the bikes and look for somewhere to eat. Nearby we spy a 'café pub' and are just admiring the authentic interior décor when the landlord appears and informs us that he doesn't open until evening and chucks us out. After some shuffling around we conclude that the only way we will eat is to visit the supermarket and duly sit by the bikes with a sandwich and a bottle of pop.

The culinary delight dispatched we ride back out of town for what promises to be an entertaining afternoons ride. It starts on the edge of town in the Aurland to Laerdal tunnel, not in its self particularly thrilling but at 14.9 miles this is the longest tunnel in the world. It's so long in fact that it has four areas throughout its length where full sized articulated lorries can turn round. These areas provide relief from the monotony of the tunnel by being lit in various subdued colours but after 20mins we are pleased to be emerging into daylight once more.

The anoraks among you may wish to know that Norway is a rather prolific builder of tunnels, one web-site lists over 1100 of them.In 2016 the Norwegian Coastal Administration, announced it was to build the worlds' first ship tunnel to enable cruise liners and freight ships to take an underground shortcut through the Stad peninsula thus avoiding the prevailing winds and rough waters of the Stadhavet Sea, a notorious stretch of water. In 2011 plans were even produced to construct the worlds' first submerged floating tunnel beneath the Sognefjord. I think we have established that Norwegians like tunnels as do those who have 'sporty' exhaust cans, so let's move on.

Out of the tunnel a left turn takes us onto the rv5 before we join our next Turistveg, the 243 Aurlandsfjellet known as 'The Snowy Road' 40 miles long and only open for a couple of months a year. As we journey up the Erdalen Valley the road starts a steady climb to the plateau to some 1300 meters up. Here we meet the snow and the cold the narrow sliver of dark tarmac undulating before us, dry and completely free of snow like a carpet freshly rolled out for our delight. At one point the snow at the side of the road is very deep and we stop to take photos. Crikey it's properly cold without the gloves on, strangely not too bad while riding, but without the gloves brrrr. Further down the road a coach passes by before we see a large party of people walking, two things sprung to mind, did they ask to be dropped off for a walk in the snow or did someone upset the driver? We don't stop to enquire but press on across a barren plateau, a desolate landscape of snow and rocks with the occasional sprig of grass.

It's quite some ride to experience until the plateau ends and the road begins its journey down to Aurlandsfjorden with some sharp hairpins and long ramp like straights. Lower down the road reaches the final surprise of the day at the Stegastein Viewpoint. With the car park being on such a steep hill it's not easy to find somewhere to leave the bikes without the nagging fear they will topple over. Once we convince ourselves the bikes are safe we walk a short distance down towards a right hand bend passing a very smart modern structure that turns out to be the toilet block but there are few clues as to what to expect from this viewpoint. A few paces more and this jaw-dropping structure is slowly revealed.

The Stegastein Viewpoint was designed and built by Canadian Todd Saunders and Norwegian Tommie Wihelmsen, architects who won the first prize in a Norwegian touristveg competition. Opened in 2006 it is a 33m long walkway of solid pine that curves round and down to be anchored to the rock face 650 meters above the town of Aurland.

Fearless Festa is the first onto the narrow structure with Kryten not far behind. I take time to 'consider my options' before taking a deep breath and heading out over the abyss. It's a stable structure with solid looking walls either side, until you reach the very end. Here the platform falls away to return to the cliff face below leaving only a glass panel to prevent disaster. I edge closer and peer through the glass at the tiny town way below my feet. Then I look around in awe of the incredible view my bravery has rewarded me with. It's stunning, it's almost as if I am a bird in flight with the Fjord held tightly in place by its steep sides and the snow-capped mountains all around. It's a lot to take in, peaceful and quiet the only sound is the wind and our footsteps as we shuffle back and forth trying to absorb this, ok, let's use the word 'awesome' (though not in the Radio One sense where everything and everyone is 'awesome'), yes a truly awesome sight.

It's hard to tear ones-self away from such beauty but we must return to the bikes and finish our journey back to town and our hotel. The road is narrow and twisty all the way down through the tree line and then housing to the hotel. From the hotel car park we look back upwards to see the now tiny view point balanced precariously on the skyline. Inside at reception we are greeted by the first attractive blond young lady we have seen. When she stands up to show us to our room I have to admit to being taken aback somewhat as she was over six feet tall and just seemed to keep rising as if in slow motion from her seat (I felt a bit like Dudley Moore in the film 10).

Ahem, yes, well the room was pleasant enough, tucked away at the back of the hotel. We organised an evening meal and then enquired if 'The Football' could be on the lobby TV tonight. I think we were all a bit surprised when we were shown the 'TV lounge'. There was a huge cinema sized screen in a darkened room. Kryten and Festa made themselves comfy with some other residents and some smuggled supermarket beer to watch England take on the might of...err Algeria while I went off for a wander about the fairly deserted town.

I eventually end up on a man-made beach at the side of the Fjord looking back at the viewpoint once again. As my eyes slowly drifted back downwards I noticed how many proud Norwegian flags were waving in the breeze and how most of the houses were constructed of painted wood with white window frames. Tomorrow will be our last in this beautiful country as we head to catch our ferry in the countries capital Oslo, and I just wanted to stand and stare to retain as much of the atmosphere as I could.

Saturday – Aurland to Oslo (200miles 4hrs 30mins).

Last night, while Festa and Kryten agonised over another woeful England football performance, I had taken the rare opportunity to unpack and repack my luggage ready for a speedy get away today. I say rare, as sharing what at times can be a fairly confined space with two others on such a trip presents few chances to regroup with such abandon without someone needing to squeeze by.

The day is cool but dry and party sunny as we line our bikes up for departure. A quick nod to each other that all is well and we press down on the gear levers, ease out the clutch and begin to roll away back through town. Our route follows, as so many others do here, a free running river for the first couple of miles before the inevitable climb begins out of the valley. There are tantalising views to be had all the way to the top but we pass up one or two opportunities to stop and admire them as they seem almost common place by now, oh look another huge waterfall or a Fjord view that stretches out for miles, it's that kind of place.

There are tunnels aplenty to and I soon get braver in them. It's sunny now so the transition from light to dark can be dramatic. Once inside though I discover the childish thrill of acceleration and the sensation of speed that can be had. These tunnels are all lit and speed makes it appear like you are in the Delorian from 'Back to the Future' or sat with Will Smith and Tommy Lee Jones in 'Men in Black'..Yaaahoooo!!! Festa doesn't share Kryten and my exuberance as he sports a dark visor on his crash helmet and has to lift it in the tunnels to see, and that's a bit chilly he explains later.

Sometimes on our trips the roads back to port can be dull back streets or tedious motorways, but not today, oh no, not in Norway. The road across the plateau is another fabulously clean clear one with few others to share it with. Then, once all that was over, the return to earth was a superb one with a much gentler gradient and some joyfully swept curves on smooth tarmac. We stopped for fuel with big grins on our faces at this unexpectedly excellent road. Here we took the opportunity to lubricate our chains for the first time as I think we had forgotten basic maintenance in the euphoria of each new day's adventure.

As lunch time came and Oslo got ever closer the peaceful roads began to give way to some busier ones as we joined up with the many others heading towards the Capital City. We had been looking, in vain so far, for somewhere pleasant to eat, maybe in a village or something we had thought. But now, almost in desperation, I pulled into a motorway style garage with a sign offering food expecting to buy a pre packed sandwich and a bag of crisps again. The sign to food lead us behind and away from the garage to a low dark looking building with a grass covered roof. Outside were parked two or three dark coloured Harley style machines and I think we almost turned away as the place transmitted a slightly foreboding first impression. Inside was completely different. The bright and airy decor was matched by an extremely pleasant waitress who explained the meal / drink ordering process. We could top up our coffee as much as we liked and stay as long as we liked. And we definitely liked! The food was nice, the atmosphere pleasing and the endless coffee meant that more numerous natural breaks were almost guaranteed all the way from here to Oslo.

It couldn't last, and on our approach to Oslo the threatened rain came to spoil the last few miles. Our final fuel stop was at a very busy and grotty motorway garage before we managed to navigate our way onto the quay side to wait for the ferry, which was late, but at least it had stopped raining and it could not dampen our spirits at another wonderful day in this beautiful country.

On board the Stena Saga (how old does that make me feel?) we head to the shop to buy red wine and crisps for the night then start to wander about. There's World Cup Football action to be had somewhere and Kryten and Festa are keen to find it. We are directed to a fairly small room with a bar where lots of similarly minded folk are gathered around the relatively small screen. As our ship slips its moorings for its' overnight crossing back to Frederikshavn in Denmark the match kicks off to the ooohs and arrhs of the assembled fans. Then it strikes me, Denmark are playing Cameroon. Cameroon play in green, we are on a ship bound for Denmark and I have chosen this night to wear my smart green top. I have little interest in football and as Cameroon go on the offensive I decide to abandon Festa and Kryten, who were by now firmly at the front.

Out on deck it's another beautiful evening as the ship picks its way between the many green and pleasant islands that nestle serenely in the 17km long Oslofjorden. After watching Oslos skyline slowly disappear I make my way to the front of the ship to enjoy the unfolding splendour and notice we are being guided out not by tugs but by two armed launches of the Norwegian Coast Guard. What a totally incredible way to leave behind this awesome (yep, it has to be that word again) country and the memories it gifted me.

Sunday – Frederikshavn to Esbjerg (240miles 4hrs 45mins).

The Stena Saga docked on time at 07:30 and we are soon on our way into the grey but dry Danish morning. I was looking forward to this day as, on the maps I had seen, we should enjoy some fabulous views riding the Marguerite Scenic route alongside lakes and the sea on our 240mile return to Esbjerg and the ferry home. But first there was the hour or so of E45 motorway to dispatch before we turned onto the more rural route.

The motorway passed by fairly quickly and we joined the number 11 road towards Thisted. This was much quieter, long straight and flat with little to obstruct the views across the countryside. After what seemed like an age I was beginning to question my navigational skills when the turn onto the number 513 Lemvik road was signed.

This 'scenic' route was becoming extremely tedious with almost nothing to see and not a bend in sight. We stopped at a fuel station with a café in the middle of absolutely nowhere but it was shut. A group of around twenty odd shaped cyclists passed by all dressed in yellow but I can't imagine where they were going to or from whence they came. We continued further until on a rare bend we spied a tatty garage selling fuel. Curiously its owner also sold chocolate bars, crisps, drinks and, ahem, ladies bedroom toys, but let's move on shall we.

On and on the road went straight as an arrow. At one point I was doing 90 mph to ease the boredom but was getting no sensation of speed as there was nothing but distant sand dunes to gauge speed by. Then, like an oasis in a desert of tedious, we came across the tiny seaside town of Sondevik (think Mablethorpe on the east coast). A narrow road brimming with pedestrians lead to the rapidly filling car park which mercifully had an inviting looking restaurant opposite. From its large windows we could keep an eye on the bikes and from our table we enjoyed a veritable feast supplied by a very jolly Danish lady, oh bliss at last.

It wasn't easy remounting for the final push to the ferry and we had plenty of time but we decided to press on. The scenery did not improve and the journey could have been a right off until, by chance, we spotted a motorcycle dealership. Steen's Motorcycles sat on the outside of a trading estate looking like many others would do in the UK. Once inside it put every dealership I have ever been in to shame. They had everything from scooters to Ducati superbikes, there was clothing of all fabrics sizes and colours, boots, helmets and other bike related merchandise like DVDs and posters alongside what appeared to be a very well equipped workshop.

We spent a very pleasant hour or so here and could have easily melted our credit cards had we room to store our purchases. As we were leaving a group of bikers appeared who turned out to be from the UK. One of their number had picked up a puncture in the UK and had only just made the ferry. Once in Denmark the bike had been picked up by a relative and brought to Steens for repair. Steens were closing but readily agreed to carry out the work. In conversation they also told of a rough crossing of the North Sea on the very ship we were heading off to board. Their descriptions of holding on to bunks while the ship rolled had me turning green at the thought, but there was no backing out now.

It was windy at the dockside as we sat patiently waiting permission to board. The BMW owners club kept us amused though with their his 'n' hers matching apparel and an impromptu sing-along from the stereo of one of the bikes (stereo?) bringing back a touch of the Dunkirk spirit. Once at last on board we were also joined by the Danish Jaguar owners club and their impressive array of rolling stock. There was little time to admire them though as we feverishly set about lashing the bikes down against the impending high seas.

As the DFDS Dana Sirena headed out of Esbjerg I wasn't too unhappy to see topographically challenged Denmark slowly disappear. I could see the statues of 'Man Staring at the Sea' and now I understood what they were thinking "Take us with you it's a bit dull here" Out on deck the ship seemed to be threading the needle between a myriad of small fishing vessels as it headed out from the calm of the harbour and into the unforgiving clutches of the North Sea. In truth however it wasn't as bad as I had anticipated it would be. Still that didn't stop me preparing for the worst. I took my seasick pills, left my coat handy for the dash to the deck, got a sick bag ready and resolved to go to bed in my clothes. As an extra precaution, and to ensure any 'produce' was little more interesting, I had a couple of glasses of red wine.

Monday - Harwich to Grimsby (170miles 3hr 30mins).

Well it wasn't the best nights' sleep I've ever had but the crossing was nothing like as bad as had been predicted, or the nautical blood that courses through my veins is beginning to kick in at last (Grandad was a trawler skipper and Great Grandad was a Danish Butter Boat Captain, ahoy there shipmates). I had no need to get up in the night and was only vaguely aware of Festas blissful snoring. Kryten had been up at the sparrows fart, been on deck and was now encouraging me to do the same. We were not due to dock until mid-day so I did venture out to view the North Sea and realise just how little swell there actually was.

Dear old Blighty began to appear as a thin darkened outline on the horizon that gradually grew larger as we neared the safety of Harwich Harbour. Our thoughts, oddly enough, were on Morrison's supermarket. Cobblers to paying the inflated prices on board ship we were heading for the culinary masterpiece that is the all-day big breakfast experience of a British retail outlet. I was starving having not wished to eat too much before the sea crossing and it was now lunch time, very few full English breakfasts have ever tasted so good. And so that was it for another year, replete we set off for the three or so hour ride back home eager to recount our Norwegian tales to anyone who would listen.

Chapter 7.

Bikes, Boats, Trains and Alps (8 Days)

I'd missed out one of the trips the boys had been on, partly because I felt guilty about being away from my family and partly because I was fed up with motorway miles. The year in question saw everyone troop off to the Alps involving a two day ride each way. Ever since their return they had been banging on about how wonderful the area was and how much I'd love it if I went. There had to be an easier way to get there.

A quick Google search revealed nothing helpful but a prolonged delve into the mysterious virtual world of Google uncovered the possibility of letting the train take the strain. I had stumbled across a web-site called 'Seat Sixty One dot com' (Seat 69 being a wholly different web-site) which was packed full of European Motorial companies and routes, one in particular shone out almost caressing my bloodshot eyes, DB AutoZug. Of the routes that this German company ran one seemed almost perfect, Düsseldorf to Bozan in Italy. Düsseldorf you may have heard of but Bozan? A swift consultation with Google maps revealed a bull's eye. Bozan is but a stones' throw from what had been described by Jeremy Clarkson and the Top Gear boys as "motoring perfection", the road from Davos to Stelvio, the Flüelapass. It was the very same area our boys had visited in my absence and was now within a more reasonable journey time.

The discussion period with my fellow travellers was brief and positive. The only downside seemed to be the prices. We would be staying in Davos in Switzerland to facilitate good access to various recommended passes and roads, a country however, well known for its steep hills and even steeper prices. Undaunted we booked a reasonable (for Davos) hotel, the Hull ferry and the overnight train. You have to justify the expense to yourself, then book, then forget the cost and enjoy. All that was sorted when I received an email from the hotel saying building work would be ongoing during our stay so we could cancel or take the chance for a two thirds reduction in price. We opted to take the chance and the reduction reasoning that we would be gone from dawn to dusk most of our stay.

Thursday – Home to Hull (40miles 1 hour).

So, after an endless wait, the evening was now upon us. It hadn't all gone to plan in those final weeks as I had the misfortune of getting a puncture in my rear Bridgestone. It was repaired but, do I trust the repair to take me through the Alps? No was the answer so more expense was required to give me peace of mind for the journey. We were heading off to the playground of the rich and famous, where Prince Charles and the boys hang during the winter months, where Top Gear TV royalty have smoked exotic car tyres, but first, Morrisons Supermarket on the outskirts of Grimsby for petrol.

Kryten now sits proudly astride his new Suzuki V-Strom, resplendent in its orange paintwork, complete with Givi top box and heated grips, having drooled over a similar bike in Demark on our previous trip. Festa too had been busily digging deep into his pockets and had managed to part company with the only machine to have been with us on every European tour thus far. His mean green Kawasaki ZX600 Ninja finally being superseded by the much praised made in England Triumph Street Triple, still in green though. Unlike Kryten however, the hard luggage hadn't quite materialised by the date of our departure so a hastily packed rucksack had been pressed into service upon his shoulders supplemented by the trusty tank bag of old. For me the faithful Honda CB1300 had been laden with all my essential items that once again spilled over into panniers bungee-chorded to its ample rear making the poor bike look like a tramps shopping trolley. The big naked bike has never once complained about this annual abuse and always inspires total confidence that it will get me anywhere I wish to go.

Ok then, turn the keys, light up the dash boards and with a quick nod to each other, a twist of the throttle and this years' odyssey begins. The last couple of trips have seen us depart these shores from Plymouth and Harwich so the short breezy crossing of the magnificent Humber Bridge to Hull is a welcome return to our local passage to the European mainland. Once dockside in Hull we join the back of an unusually large gathering of motorcycles. It's Assen weekend we discover and when we finally, and I do mean finally as we are the very last ones in the queue, roll up to the harassed P&O lady she informs us that we will be joining 300 other bikers on our crossing tonight.

After being held back for some time we eventually cross the gang plank to the Pride of Hulls car deck and begin the familiar lashing down of our bikes, a task made slightly more tricky due to 300 others having got to the ropes before us. Unlike previous years though, this time I am determined to leave as much as possible on my bike and have cajoled my evening wear into my tank bag along with all of the important documentation. Festa has all his worldly goods strapped to his back but Kryten goes to great lengths to demonstrate the convenience his top box affords him.

The route to the cabin was a far less fraught one and once we had slipped into something more comfortable it was time to, well, it was 'Beer O'clock'. In the bar area there was plenty of evidence of our fellow Assen bound bikers. Many seemed to have packed so lightly that bike leathers were their only clothing. Given Assens' notoriety for inclement weather this would seem a bold or maybe fool hardy move, then again maybe that's just poncey me requiring more home comforts the older I get. The ships entertainment was missable so after a couple of cool ones and a mooch around the on board shop there was just time to watch the darkened shores of home slip past the windows before donning the Wee Willey Winkey hats and plunging the cabin into darkness.

Friday – Europort to Düsseldorf (160miles 3 hrs).

"Goede morgen dame's en heren" The familiar tones of the ships' wakeup call penetrated the gloom alerting us to our imminent arrival in Dutch waters and offering breakfast. We had previously decided to miss the breakfast on board and had naively planned to partake our morning meal in Leiden, a small local town a mere hour or so from the ferry terminal. I had calculated that our 160mile ride to Düsseldorf would take no more than around two and a half hours down the motorways so a leisurely breakfast would be in order.

Suited, booted and clear of customs we were soon out on Dutch tarmac riding alongside a familiar waterway before joining the motorway. I had printed off directions for each day of the trip for each of us but after thirty or forty minutes of confident riding doubts began to creep ever more forcefully into my mind. Surely we should have turned off by now? Maybe the next junction then? Bugger, I was lost and needed to stop and consult. Problem was I had no map to consult as the route looked so straight forward sat at home on the computer.

After a very frustrating 40 minutes or so we eventually navigated back to a small petrol station by the side of the motorway to ask for directions, now, who amongst us speaks Dutch then? Mercifully one of the ladies was pushed forward by her colleagues and was a little surprised at our destination which turned out to be quite a complicated route but just that little further down the motorway than we had gone.

My rose tinted planning had us leaving the ferry without having eaten breakfast, riding some quiet back roads and partaking of some local Dutch fayre in a picturesque village within about an hour. I was wrong on just about every count. The motorway mix-up had cost us time and the roads towards my chosen town were very busy meaning we didn't arrive until around 10:30. According to the internet guides "Lovely Leiden is a refreshing, vibrant town, patterned with canals and attractive old buildings. It also has a claim to fame as it's Rembrandt's birthplace". Marvellous, but that's not the feeling we got as we hunted for a parking space in the middle of this busy town.

Finally abandoning our bikes next to some others on an island in the middle of the road we ventured into a sandwich shop to purchase breakfast and across the road found a seat on which to eat it. "No eat here!" came an angry voice from the owner of the bar (that was closed). We moved to another area, bought a coffee and watched the world go by. Now I know it's a cliché but blimey there's a lot of bicycles here and lots of thought has gone into where they can be safely ridden! Odd shaped ones to my eye though, back home there are a lot of mountain bikes but here they sit high up on big wheeled, wide bared things.

This makes the ladies look elegant but the blokes look ever so slightly, err, well, oh never mind, don't wish to be all non-PC.

.Heaven knows what they are like to pedal into a headwind though.

The sun shone on "Lovely Leiden" but I wasn't sad to be leaving. Back on board the CB1300 I pushed the starter, rolled forward and dropped off the kerb to join the traffic heading out of town to the motorway. It was about 11:45 and we had about 3 hours to cover the 150 miles to the motorail station in Düsseldorf. I had planned to call into Arnham on route but black clouds were gathering ominously in the distance. I pulled into a rest area and, after a brief discussion with my fabric clad accomplices, wriggled my way into my waterproof two piece over suit, swapped my summer gloves for waterproof ones and covered my summer boots with a pair of less than stylish overshoes. With the threat of rain and the very real possibility of us getting lost the Arnham detour was unanimously cancelled and we set off to re-join the Autobahn.

Very soon the brief pit stop proved invaluable as the heavens opened. We have a phrase for it in the UK "Raining cats and dogs". The French have a phrase more apt for these conditions "Il a plu comme une vache qui pisse" translated "It rained like a pissing cow!" I remember passing an articulated lorry, spray flying in all directions, and as I glanced underneath it seemed to be floating on a 25 to 50mm sea of water. A glance down at the speedo revealed I was travelling at an alarming 90mph just to keep up with traffic. In these conditions any slip over rain suit would struggle to keep out all of the wet stuff and so it proved with mine. For a cheap suit it was doing well but then that dreadful cold feeling began to gather a pace around the honeymoon suite and the misery was complete.

Motorways, rain and motorcycles are not a great combination so it was with great relief that on our approach to Düsseldorf the rain had eased off. This didn't stop me taking a wrong turn though and we ended up outside some deserted stadium or other with no idea where Düsseldorf was. We did manage to establish that it wasn't in the vast car park though. After some shoulder shrugging and pointing we rode around a bit more until we happened upon several policemen at what appeared to be a check point.

"Sprechen Sie Englisch bitte?" I offered. "Nein" Undeterred I asked "Could you tell us the way to the station?" With a puzzled look he replied "Vich Von?" Now that was a bloody good question. "DB AutoZug?" I asked. What followed was a detailed description of how to get to, well somewhere. I nodded and said "Ja" a lot before ending with a "Danka" when it looked like he'd finished.

"Which way then?" asked the lads. "I haven't a soddin' clue" I replied "But he seemed to point up that way a lot so we'd best try there". Heaven knows where we went after that, probably a complete circuit of Düsseldorf, but I eventually recognised a road number which led us to the centre of town. Quite a busy centre as it turned out and not one with any indication as to where the station may be. We pulled over and Festa disappeared into a telephone retailers emerging some considerable time later having located an English speaking local. "We're just round the comer from the station" he grinned and promptly led us to the rail oasis.

Now I don't know what your mental image of a busy German international motor rail terminal might be but mine was of a large, well signed, very efficient modern affair with smartly dressed staff on hand to whisk the traveller smoothly onwards. I was wrong. The terminal is down a small, one way, side-street to the rear of a budget hotel. The car park is tiny, the check-in no more than a shed and the corporate image could do with a bit of a makeover "Sprechen Sie Englisch bitte?" I asked as I handed over the paperwork. "Nein" was all the conversation we managed before being given some small webbing things and ushered through to join the queue. Being sure to join the correct queue is vital as the wrong one means your bike going to Verona and you are going to Bozan, which would be far from a satisfactory outcome.

The loading staff were a little more cheerful but the vehicle carrying wagon is something else. It's a double decked affair, like an open car transporter, where the bikes go on the lower deck. It's not until you ride through the carriages that you realise how slippery the surface is, how low the roof is and how much you have to duck down to avoid bashing your head/helmet (BMW GS riders beware!), it's a race style crouch at three miles per hour.

One is directed to a space then ordered to leave the bike to be locked and loaded by the efficient staff. It's a tight and fairly fraught affair and I never did find out what the webbing was for but I did return to collect my key which was still in the ignition.

With the bikes safely on board we traipsed round with our gear to wait on another platform for the accommodation coaches to be coupled up before squeezing into our compartment. Those old enough to remember the corridor trains of years' long since passed would find something very familiar about the layout. A sliding door opened to bench seats facing each other. There was enough seating for six but one can only imagine what these six, with luggage, would have to do to manage to sleep in such a space. For the three of us though this wasn't too much an issue and we were soon changed out of our biking gear ready for tea, which unfortunately we hadn't brought. No worries, we had shortbread, biscuits and Festas' red wine with musical accompaniment from an IPod, sorted! As we settled into improvised provisions a man appeared at the door, a bit like the shop keeper in Mr Benn. In excellent English he introduced himself as our steward for the journey and took our orders for breakfast, things were looking up.

The train rattled its way along and followed the Rhine for some distance with some fine views of boats and castles before it became increasingly dark and time to assemble the beds. The linen was clean and smart but the seats that were now beds were a bit on the small and uncomfortable side. Down the corridor there was one toilet and two tiny sinks, Orient Express this clearly wasn't but it was whisking us towards Italy while we slept and thus keeping us off those tedious motorways.

Saturday – Bozan to Davos (180miles 6hrs 45mins).

At around 06:30 the smart, helpful AutoZug steward appeared at the door to wake us and returned 15 minutes later with breakfast. A boxed continental style offering was taken with orange juice and tea while out of the window views of the Italian Alps drifted by, how jolly civilized.

By 07:30 we had finished breakfast, got dressed brushed our teeth and the train was slowing down for our approach to Bolzano (or Bozan depending on your map). After a little shunting we rode off the train and into the brilliant warm Italian sunshine that sure as hell beat thrashing down the motorways in the rain! Festa and I left Kryten to guard the bikes (and catch some rays) while we headed off on foot to try to get our bearings. Directly outside the station was a ski lift and information centre which proved very useful for this endeavour.

After persuading Kryten to put down his phone we made our way onto the Italian roads heading roughly in the direction we needed to go and looking to find petrol. Maybe the train journey had been too relaxing but I certainly wasn't ready for my first Italian roundabout or the following roads or anything else for that matter. My senses seemed to be overwhelmed with information and decision making became more a piece of nervous guesswork. A petrol station was located and I had to ask if someone else fancied trying to find the escape route out of town before my head imploded. Once more Festa stepped boldly forward clearly unaware of the old army phrase 'Never volunteer for anything'.

After a couple of minor adjustments we broke free from the town heading out along the ss42 into beautiful Italian countryside. So beautiful in fact that we failed to notice the ss42 was no longer the ss42 but the sp14 a pleasant enough road but in completely the wrong direction. Eventually realising our mistake we turned off and into a very quiet little village where we parked in the main square. The sun was hot but there was a very inviting fountain from which we drank the sweet cool water. I had seen a map on a wall as we entered the village so went to consult it while Festa and Kryten bought fruit from the village shop.

We could have stayed longer but we had to move on. The lost ss42 was located back towards Bolzano disguised as the 'Passo Mendel'. We should have guessed as some of the numerous bikes we had followed out of town headed up this way. What followed next was our introduction to Italian Saturday afternoon motoring entertainment.

As we climbed the road got steeper and the bends got tighter, the traffic got heavier and the madness began. Motor homes and cars laboured ever upwards where they encountered motor homes and cars coming downwards. All of these vehicles had to make sure that they did not hit any Lycra clad masochist cyclists that were grinding their way up, or indeed hurtling downward at breakneck speeds.

Now add a narrowing road and insane fellow bikers into the frame and you may begin to appreciate why my eyeballs were sticking to the inside of my visor! Then, just when I was about coping with all this, two black GSXR 1000s raced past us swerving and dodging the melee like players in a computer game. Imagine, if you can, being at Cadwell Park where, for a laugh, the marshals had decided to run two races simultaneously but in different directions and with any vehicle contestants could lay their hands on. Then, there they were again, this time heading back down at a similar speed, the two black GSXRs. I expected body bags to be amongst the many gift items available from the retail outlets we came to rest by at the top of the hill in Ruffrè-Mendola. There were bikes everywhere here so it seemed like a good time to park up and find a coffee, phew!

Soon we were back on the bikes again and, after a brief roadside stop to avoid the €2 Toilette fee, we continued our journey along the now far less insane ss42. The road eventually seemed to level out as it ran through a wide open plateau west towards the town of Cles. From here the north bound road offers glimpses of Lago Santa Giustina (an artificial lake built between 1943 and 1951 to collect water from the river Noce that is then employed to make electricity) before heading west again and climbing again. In places the road narrows and undulates as it clings to the side of a densely forested valley but always we are climbing.

A sign alerts us to the start of Passo del Tonale and what appears to be a deserted out of season ski town. It's a little eerie riding through the streets lined with empty chalets and very few people and it doesn't get any better as we pass the last building only to be confronted by a large dark angel standing atop a stern grey building. This turns out to be a memorial constructed to commemorate soldiers killed in both world wars.

On a brighter note, research uncovers that in the 1930s Italian ski jumper Bruno Da Col was the first to exceed the magic 100m here earning him a date with Mr Mussolini and a shiny gold medal.

(Eddie the Eagles best was 119.5m in 1998). We park up here for a short while to have a look around the memorial but there is little else to keep us so we ride over the 1883m crest and downhill out of town. It was warm in the afternoon sunshine and this high road twisted and turned through pretty villages and woodlands offering more glimpses of deep valleys as it took us towards our next target of Bormio, the gateway to the Stelvio Pass.

The Stelvio Pass (Passo dello Stelvio), is one of the highest Alpine Passes in Europe at 2758m and boasts 60 hairpin bends, 48 of them on the northern side numbered with stones. TopGear famously named it "The worlds' best driving road" calling it "A road that would satisfy every "petrol head's" driving fantasies". The original road was built between 1820 and 1825 by the Austrian Empire to connect the former Austrian province of Lombardia with the rest of Austria (Potted history lesson over).

Once through Bormio the road began to climb more steeply, the straight bits between bends got shorter and the edge of the road began to be marked more by low walls than grass verges. I was excited to finally be here and looking forward to the challenge. In hindsight maybe we should have expected the road to be busy given it was a Saturday afternoon but I'd allowed myself to think we would somehow have the place to ourselves. With so many people on such a narrow twisty road progress never really felt 'joined up'. The surface wasn't the best either, again what could we expect given its exposure to such extreme elements. Most of my concentration was on the road and its other users so maybe I missed the beauty of the scenery somewhere along the way to. As we climbed we left the tree line behind and the weather seemed to turn colder and cloudier as the scenery became increasingly grey and rocky.

It was almost a relief to arrive at the top and, to be honest, a bit of a let-down. I feel sure that the cold had dampened my mood but the sight of all the tat shops and expensive cafes here at the summit left me feeling distinctly underwhelmed. Sure we got off the bikes and wandered around a bit hoping to catch a view or something interesting but there was, as the saying goes 'Nothing to see here'. More in desperation than anything else I found myself inside a cycle clothing shop purchasing a vastly overpriced 'Cima Coppi' cycling top for my son before returning to the bikes to mount up for the long decent.

The climb up had been a disappointment but the decent began to restore my faith that this had been a reasonable thing to do. There seemed to be slightly less traffic and the ride seemed to flow better. I had to be mindful of the momentum a fully laden CB1300 could pick up between hairpins and the constant braking began to make my wrists ache but it was beginning to be fun again, although "Best in the world??" Naarr, not even close.

We were now heading for Glorenza where we would then turn onto the ss41 which would lead us over the Italian boarder into Switzerland. This was a far more agreeable road, better surfaced and with sweeping curves rather than harsh hairpins. We still had another 80 or so miles to go and the weather wasn't helping much but with a Swiss National Park to ride through I couldn't complain.

Finally though I had to stop to practice the dance of the wet gear over leather (a bit like traditional Morris dancing when you get your foot stuck in the leg hole - but without the pigs' bladder and bells). I was getting cold and the clouds were again getting darker. At Zernez we headed north briefly before turning onto the 28 and the Flüelapass. A promising start soon began to give way to mist and then rain as we climbed ever higher. Festas Triumph forged a necessarily cautious path cutting its way through the foggy bends closely followed by a more subdued Kryten on the V-Strom. Bringing up the rear I was intensely following two dim red lights when I noticed a single white light in my mirrors. I was expecting some local to come roaring past us leaving us in a wake of swirling mist. Not this guy though, I think he was just pleased to be letting someone else do the path-finding work and happy to tag along.

Eventually the road levelled out and we crested the top without stopping to admire the view, as there wasn't one to be had. I was feeling much colder now, quite tired and was looking forward to getting to the hotel. The lower down we got the more the mist and fog began to clear until eventually and at last we rolled up in a lay-by on the outskirts of Davos. The ghost rider that had followed us pulled up alongside. He was a lone German on a ZZR600 and spoke no English but using international sign language it was clear he was just as cold as I was feeling.

We consulted the maps I had and with only minor navigational errors found the Edelweiss Hotel in a secluded location a little way back from the high street. Inside there was a very warm welcome from the manager who, to our great relief, spoke excellent English. He told us of a decent restaurant a brief walk away and left us to find our rooms. As we would be based here for a few nights all of the gear came off the bikes and soon we were showered, changed and heading into town. The restaurant was called 'Hankies' and was every bit as good as we were told. For us the now ubiquitous pizza washed down with a glass or two of continental lager ended what had been a mixed, but totally enjoyable, first day in the Alps.

Sunday – Davos – Liechtenstein – Austria (200miles 5hrs 30mins).

I awoke from a very sound sleep; it was nice to be in a bed that wasn't moving! Festa and I were sharing a room while Kryten had the room above us to himself, the patter of tiny feet echoing across our ceiling. Outside the day had dawned bright and warm and I took a little time to admire the mountain views from the small balcony outside the room. Downstairs the comprehensive breakfast buffet was housed in a light airy wood clad room with a high ceiling, lovely views and two busy waitresses trying to understand our request for more than one tea bag in the pot.

Today we would start by heading out via Klosters (yes that posh ski place) and into the tiny principality of Liechtenstein (known as a principality as it is a constitutional monarchy headed by a prince, oh, you already knew that, sorry) and its capital Vaduz before heading into Austria and back into Switzerland. Suited and booted I swung my leg over the big Honda looking forward to a day in the Alpine sunshine. Festa and I waited patiently while Kryten, well did what Kryten does, only he could tell you what that is.

Once on the move it felt great to be unburdened from luggage and the riding seemed effortless. We soon turned away from the main road out of town and onto smaller roads that led through small villages that were surrounded by lush fields. At one point a bright red train trundled past us its colour outstandingly vivid in this predominantly green landscape. On a hill in the distance stood a castle that I just had to stop and photograph. A little further on we stopped to admire a beautifully tricked up Triumph 1050 Triple that was eclipsed only by the sight of a stunning looking lady dressed in tight fitting Lycra pedalling a bicycle.

Anyway, back to the plot, the day was hotting up in more ways than one which may account for our missing a turn in the busy centre of Vaduz. I think we were conscious of not wanting to join an Austrian motorway as there is a fee to pay for their use and a hefty fine for those without the sticker. To get our bearings we pulled up in the shade of a local Job Centre and while Festa and I deliberated over directions Kryten caught up on some mobile phone fastest finger first texting. Texting complete we were back on the right route and following a red Ferrari through this tax haven, the mid-day sun beating down on us.

Eventually we left the town behind and returned to the countryside and then into the Montafon valley in south Vorarlberg, Austria on the B188 Silvretta Bundesstrasse. Now we're talking beautiful with a capital B and almost overwhelming sights all along the valley floor. Tree covered mountains rose steeply either side, the roads contortions mimicking the contours of the sparkling river that it ran alongside. In the meadows people laboured with hand held scythes (like in Poldark for any ladies reading this) whilst in the blue skies above us soaring birds were joined by free spirited humans dangling beneath the canopies of their brightly coloured hang gliders. The only thing to do was to stop and really enjoy the whole experience. In a village there was a white walled church its neat clock tower topped with a dark green dome. Kryten was once more experiencing the 'joy of text' as he stood under the branches of a tree sheltering from the heat of the sun. Meanwhile, Festa and I took a closer look at some of the local buildings and peered into the windows of shops and cafes.

Further along the valley we were greeted by something quite unexpected, a barrier and toll booth and not a cheap one either, €10 each for a bike. We nearly turned back but that would have been a huge mistake for this turned out to be the Silvretta Hochalpenstrasse, a scenic mountain road that ascends to the Silvretta Reservoir and the 2032m Bielerhöhe Pass. What a road it turned out to be too! The surface was smooth and virtually devoid of traffic, the bends numerous, varied and rewarding, the views outstanding all the way past a huge dam wall to another stopping point alongside the amazing, almost un-natural, blues of the Vermunt and Silvretta Reservoirs. (Later research reveals that the majority of the peaks here are elevated above three thousand meters and are surrounded by glaciers from which minerals are deposited leading to the area being known as the "Blue Silvretta").

Photo opportunity (and joy of text) over we head onwards and upwards and meet what must have been a Porsche owners club rally coming the other way with some fine examples of the marques been driven, shall we say, 'enthusiastically'. Eventually we hit the level ground of the Bielerhöhe Saddle with its rather more busy parking area and tourist traps but we don't bother stopping. The road winds on and begins its decent into another superb valley that is an absolute joy to ride along in the warm afternoon sunshine. I think that if we had had the time we would have loved to turn round and repeat the experience all over again, much more like the best driving road...in the world!

At the end of the valley we had to re-join the real world for a while as we made our way to the triple border town of Nauders where Festa and Kryten had stayed on a previous trip. For such a major road the entrance to the town was a surprise for me as it was defended by two tight bends' that pushed the road up into the main street. It was a nice town but exceptionally busy when we arrived with some kind of sporting activity in full swing so we pulled into a road that had been closed off for a scratch of our heads. There was a big cycle race in progress and as luck would have it the race was being held on the very road I had selected as our onward route. A fine choice Kryten and Festa assured me as they had ridden it previously but unfortunately it wasn't to be ridden by us today.

We retraced our steps down the tight bends out of town and re-joined the busy 27 road all the way to Susch where we were able to turn off and have another crack at the 28 Flüelapass. What a difference a day made! Now it had been warm and sunny all day and the road was dry with excellent visibility and grip. It felt good to be chucking the bikes from left to right through these mountain bends over the top with its views before returning us down into Davos once more.

Back at the hotel the 'joy of text' was at fever pitch as Kryten was expecting to meet up with Lady Barbie Kryten and her sister Sindy tonight as our paths crossed. I should mention here that both Barbie and Sindy are both capable motorcyclists and were on their own grand European tour. Kryten was like a six year old waiting for Christmas constantly checking his watch and phone while we descended into town to find a place to eat.

Soon after eating we made our way back and sat in the hotel garden playing cards and drinking Festas red wine all the time listening for slay-bells, sorry, motorcycle engines. "Did you hear something then? Sounded like a bike didn't it?" "NO!" Came the chorused duet "Come and sit down, she'll be coming round the mountain when she comes Kryten". Soon we had to move inside though and sit in the foyer so we could maintain a vigil of the approach to the hotel. I was a little concerned myself as I had given the girls directions and it was getting late.

At last the unmistakable sound of approaching bikes sent Kryten over the edge. "They're here" he announced like an expectant father before dashing off outside to meet n greet his girls. Not long after he returned with two weary ladies who he introduced as the fabled Barbie and Sindy before dutifully carrying their bags to the lift and offering advice as to how to operate the mystical mechanical device. "We need a shower and we're starving" they said as the lift disappeared upwards. There was nothing left for Festa and I to do except finish the wine.

In far less time than it normally takes Kryten to achieve a state of readiness Barbie and Sindy return with Kryten firmly locked in attentive gentleman mode. We make our way back down into town with the girls recounting their journey and Kryten hanging on every word. For such a big town there seemed to be very few bars to choose from so we settled for the first one we found and entered a place that would not look too out of place as a saloon bar in a Wild West movie, small with wooden floors and furnishings of a practical nature. There are few people inside to eye up the strangers but the natives seem friendly enough as we order drinks and enquire about food. Unfortunately food serving had finished but Barbie and Sindy were happy to just be sat back with a drink.

As if by magic the shop keeper appeared, well not quite, but a young guy looking for all the world like Robert Downey Jr. as Charlie Chaplin had joined us and offered the girls some food from his table. He was a remarkably friendly and humorous chap who told us, in excellent English, he was home from college and asked about our visit to his home town while the girls tucked in. We swapped stories and drank beer until it was time to give in and acknowledge we were all too tired to continue.

Monday – Walking Day (12miles 6 hrs).

Another gloriously sunny day was unveiled by the opening of the curtains and the conversation over breakfast was of the day we would be having away from the bikes. Our trips into Europe have been constantly evolving and we now look forward to a day walking. In a way these days bring us much closer to the areas we are in. If you consider a sliding scale then speeding through on a train or coach could be followed by a visit by car and, after that, I always feel far more in touch when I am on the bike. The walking just goes that 'one step' further, one step closer to the surroundings.

I had taken the precaution of purchasing a map and we enlisted the help of the hotel manager to point us in the direction of a good walk. After some debate we settled on a path and the manager gave us each a pass to use on public transport should we need to return this way. We set off, as instructed, in the direction of Hankies, the restaurant we knew from our first night, but soon eyed up a funicular on the opposite side of the valley. A quick consultation with the map suggested an excellent walk could be had from the top of this railway with the plus that we didn't have to walk up the first bit. As luck would have it we arrived at the station with a couple of minutes to spare and discovered that the passes we had provided free use of the train.

All aboard the Parsenn Funicular for the rather steep climb and the views of Davos that very soon got quite spectacular out of the glass-sided cabins. So much so that Barbie became a little alarmed at our rapid gain in height. Stepping out onto the mountain in the sunshine the air felt clean and the sounds of busy Davos far below were barely audible. As always at the start of any walk it is best to spend a little time orientating yourself so you head off in the right direction, which is what we did. The main clue here was that we were one third of the way up a mountain and we wanted to get to the top, so 'up' seemed the best course of action.

As it turned out, up and up and up seemed to be the order of the day with several 'false dawns' along the way as "nearly at the top" turned into "it'll be just over the next ridge". To our left a large pointy mountain rose in the distance that reminded me of the front of an Alpen muesli box from my childhood (quite some time ago). A thought occurred that I had now eaten Swiss Muesli in Switzerland at breakfast this morning, I was living the dream!

Anyway, we kept on climbing until we began to draw level with the snow line and then a café came into view, it was as far up as a minimalistically attired group of biker-hikers could reasonably go and a damn good place to take in the stunning views. Davos had long since disappeared below us but over the ridge a lush green valley stretched out before us and in the distance snow-capped mountains reached into the clear blue sky forming a jagged horizon. We photographed each other standing on a rock then enlisted a passer-by to frame all of us in one last picture. It was very peaceful here on top of the world, the sort of silence that only isolation far from the modern world can bring. No need to shout above the noise of traffic or chatter to make ones-self heard.

With all the photographs captured we realised that it was still only about eleven thirty so we took out the maps to see what else may be possible. After some discussion it was decided that an interesting route around a ridge could take us all the way to Klosters (where Charlie, Cam & the boys hang in the winter) from where we 'should' be able to catch a train back to Davos.

The first part of the route took us around some most unusual rock formations on a pathway bounded by metal rope handrails and at times passing through covered wooden walkways. The views from this path and down the valley remained breath-taking, far below we could hear the sound of cow bells and just manage to pick out the small heard grazing the lush green pastures. Up ahead we could see a winter ski lift winding house and cafe area but it didn't seem to get any closer for quite some time. The terrain was rough shingle and rocks and became quite steep just as a group on mountain bikes came hurtling by.

The café was closed when we finally made it up so I had to make do with a quick drink from the rucksack. The area was a meeting point for numerous marked footpaths with a way marker that resembled a totem pole busily directing the hardy hiker along his chosen path. Our chosen path went through a covering of left over snow as it began its decent away from the café and into the small valley that channelled melt water to a small stream. Further down Kryten and Festa spied a rock jutting out over a steep drop and spent time photographing each other balancing on it. Among the Alpine flora above us we spotted our only sighting of a shy Marmot before it hurried away.

Over a ridge we got our first glimpse of Klosters far below. It was a bit like the first satellite image you get from Google before you zoom in to see what your house looks like from above. With the town below, mountains in front and blue skies above this was the perfect place to rest, eat and take more pictures and, as luck would have it, someone else had clearly thought the same as there was even a bench to sit on. Soon we were off again following the excellent signage that guided us along dusty farm tracks, through meadows and alongside bubbling streams.

As we scrambled down a grassy bank we were brought to a halt by the ever increasing sound of approaching cow bells. The herd was being shepherded by one man and his dog. Festa became the centre of attention for many of the curious bovines as he stood at the side of the track with nowhere to run, quite amusing from the safety of my perch. The collie came up to check us out but was far too busy to be petted and was soon back on duty ushering the herd to the milking shed. The passage of the herd along the track made our immediate progress a little more tricky as we needed to exhibit far more foot placement precision.

Onwards and downwards we trod until we eventually reached the tree line, I don't think I'd appreciated just how far up we had been. The trees provided shelter from the sun but blocked the views, only allowing brief moments that were framed by the sturdy trunks of the surrounding pines. In a clearing stood another winter sports café where we imagined we might have another "Magnum Moment" but it too was closed. Kloisters still seemed a long way away, in fact like Obi-Wan McGregor & his mate this was turning out to be "The Long Way Down".

Much as I had enjoyed the walk I was pleased to be finally setting foot on the concrete of platform one at Kloisters station. It had been a seemingly endless trek to reach here and I think we were all relieved to be studying the timetable now and well ready for a large cool drink, though not with the large cool price tag that accompanied it! It seemed we had about an hour or so before the next train so we sat outside the hotel opposite the station taking in the atmosphere and winding down. I had thoughts of home in mind and set off to explore any of the gift emporiums I could find. Unfortunately I was out of luck as I hadn't realised the time was now after 6pm and most businesses were closed.

Bang on time our bright red Swiss train pulled into the station and we joined the many commuters for our journey back to Davos. It was a fairly short ride passing some lovely scenery but I was pleased that we hadn't had to make the journey on foot as we had once discussed on our walk down the mountain. Off the train the walk back to the hotel was a chance to stretch my increasingly stiff legs before I was able to enjoy a most welcome shower and change of clothes.

We all met up in the hotel lobby and asked the manager where would be a good place to eat "local" dishes. Ever helpful he pointed us in the direction of a small restaurant about 20mins walk away and off we went. Inside was indeed small with probably six tables and two diners but it had the rustic feel of a good place to eat. Things, however, went downhill from there on. The manager seemed a little stand offish, maybe he didn't appreciate riffraff English, he showed us to a table, turned his nose up at our request for beer, wasn't impressed with Sindy and Barbie's choice of wine and then requested that we pay in cash.

At this point, and in hindsight, we should have made excuses to go to the cash machine and never return…but we didn't. We dutifully went out to the nearby machine and returned with cash. The "Speciality Fondue" I shared with Sindy and Barbie turned out to be no more than a bucket of melted cheese with bread and onions to dip in, and the price? How about around £90! The wine and beers a similar outrageous figure and with Festa and Kryten under whelmed with their offerings the whole evening had turned out to be a most expensive lesson. Oh, yes I admit I am a tight arsed English peasant on holiday in one of the most expensive countries in the world but in my defence we had experienced a far more pleasant meal at Hankies on our first night so a reasonable price was possible and the locals could be pleasant. Rant over and after a quick night cap of red wine bought for a very reasonable price in a nearby supermarket it was time for bed.

Tuesday – Davos to Verzasca Dam tour (250miles 8 hours)

Most of the talk over breakfast was of todays' destination, the Verzasca Dam (or Contra Dam apparently) in Switzerland. For those of you who don't know this was the dam used for the opening scene in the 1995 James Bond film Golden Eye where a guy escapes by jumping off on a bungee rope (The stunt was performed by British stuntman Wayne Michaels by the way). These days the dam owners, realising the income potential, have rented a platform out so anyone daft enough can do it. Festa and Kryten had both decided that they would be joining the insanity as, in their words, "It would be rude not to have a go while we're there". As for me, well I took the view that jumping 220 m (720 ft) into oblivion with nothing more than an elastic band attached to your feet was crazy; but I was happy to film them.

Outside the sun was kind once again and all five bikes were soon heading through the light Davos traffic as far as a gift shop where I had requested we stop. I bought a T shirt and an "original" Swiss army knife for my son which meant I no longer needed to worry about what gift to take home with me. Back at the bikes the others waited patiently while I loaded my prize purchases and then we were off for real.

It's a rather ambitious day I had planned which commenced with us heading south out of Davos on the 417, similar to an English A road with a similar amount of traffic but very different surroundings. Entering Thusis we turn south again to join the E43 motorway (later research revealed this stretch of motorway to be a toll road. The toll is collected by selling motorway stickers called "Vignette". One really ought to purchase these prior to travelling as anybody who doesn't have a valid sticker will be fined by the police if caught. Ignorance of the law is no defence, but 'tis also bliss).

The motorway whisks us 30 or so miles to where we exit onto the far more attractive route 13 just before the motorway disappears into a tunnel that goes as far as the actual village of San Bernardino, (Traffic flow was much facilitated when in 1967, the San Bernardino road tunnel was completed, since then vehicle traffic on the pass has been reduced, benefiting those taking the time to avoid the tunnel and enjoy the ride).

Route 13 is a far more pleasing affair and starts by winding its way through a couple of small hamlets before beginning its' climb. Festa is up ahead and is beginning to pull away so I decide to break ranks and try to follow. Easier said than done as Festa has always been that bit quicker than I and now armed with the quick turning Street Triple he is even more difficult to stay near. At times I approach one of the numerous hairpins and catch a glimpse of lime green flashing by on the road above me. The CB1300 is no slouch and has plenty of grunt once upright but its size and weight coupled with its timid rider mean it is no match for the Triumph. Most of the time it is just the sound of the Triples exhaust reverberating off the surrounding rock that lets me know Festa is still going for it somewhere up ahead. As we climb higher the road bursts out from the trees onto clear open bends its smooth clean surface urging us to use our bikes as they were intended. The pitch is less steep now and the emphasis seems to be to twist and turn between the sparking pools and polished glacial rocks that line the route over this high moorland landscape.

As the road begins to level out it emerges onto a plateau surrounded by pointy hills and snowy remnants (this pass road is only open during the summer). Ahead the unkempt looking San Bernardino Pass Cafe comes into view and I pull up alongside Festa who is already removing his helmet to enjoy the warmth of the sunshine and the clear blue sky. Soon the sound of approaching motorcycles fills the air as Sindy, Barbie and Kryten all join us. Kryten soon removes as much clothing as is decent in order to share a "My body is a temple" moment with the rest of the world.

Anyway, the BBCs 'Top Gear' lists this as another one of the best driving roads "In The World" and with bends like these and a surface to match it is easy to see why. In front of us a flag sporting a white cross on a red background moves lazily in the breeze that glides over the impressive and beautiful lake / Lago Moesola. At the lake side we photograph each other alongside the sign that informs us we are now 2066m (6778ft) above sea level. At this altitude, with very few vehicles and with snow and water around there is that delightful silence once again that's impossible to find in busy towns and cities. The sound of voices in numerous tongues can be heard unpolluted by background noise except for the sound of footsteps as people begin some of the walks that radiate from here.

After chomping on a piece of fruit and a sip of water this brief pause is over and we begin the decent. If the road up was good the road down the other side was even better. The surface was unbelievably smooth with predictable curves and beautiful views for miles (if you dared to look). Festa was off once again, like a Scotsman chasing a fiver on a windy day, but my confidence was creeping up too and the CB was urging me on. There were only a couple of cars in our way so they were soon dispatched and couldn't spoil the pleasure of this magnificent road. When we were all reassembled in a car park at the base of the climb there were smiles all round.

It would have been great to turn around and do it all again but Kryten and Festa had a date with a bungee cord about 60miles away so we re-joined the A13/E13 heading south. It was around midday now and the sun seemed to be gaining heat with every mile that passed. The traffic wasn't too bad but the hour or so it took until we could leave the motorway behind seemed to last forever. Almost in desperation we pulled into an anonymous estate close to the road and found an oasis in the form of an air conditioned McDonalds. Cool milkshakes rarely tasted this good!

We passed through a far flatter plain area with few redeeming features before finally locating the town of Gordola on the northern shores of Lago Maggiore. Here we found signs for the Verzasca Dam and began to climb the narrow road that leads up to it. As we climb we begin to glimpse the huge manmade structure through the trees and from viewpoints dotted along the route. We also view just how steep some of the sides are that our road is clinging onto before we eventually arrive at the dam car park. I say car park but it seems more like a bit of a lay-by with an awkward slope that made the safe positioning of a motorcycle on its side stand a tricky one. We were by no means alone here as it seems we are not the only ones to have seen the James Bond film so we pay the entrance fee and begin to follow the short service road onto the dam.

Anoraks on, here are some very interesting facts about the dam. It is a concrete slender arch dam with a height of 220 m (one of the tallest in Europe) and crest length of 380 m. It is 25 m wide at its base and 7 m wide at its crest (the road upon which we are standing). The dam creates Lago di Vogorno which has a 105,000,000 m3 capacity and supports a 105 MW hydroelectric power station. It was constructed between 1961 and 1965 but starting shortly after its reservoir was filled, a series of earthquakes related to its water load occurred until 1971, hope you were making notes as there will be a test at the end of this piece.

The first thing you notice as you walk along the approach road is the long graceful sweep of the off-white concrete that forms the top (or 'crest' as we now know it to be). Soon a viewing area is available and I stand peering over the edge trying to see to the river at the bottom of the valley without out opening my eyes coz I fear heights. It's an awesome sight and I can't begin to imagine what forces are pushing against this slender structure. Walking along the 7 meter wide top (crest!) of the dam seems strange too as on one side there is a 220m drop to the rocky valley floor and on the other the blue tinged waters of a large reservoir stretch out to the far hills and beyond.

In the middle stands a small kiosk, like a burger van, above which is draped a banner with the legend "James Bond – Goldeneye – Are You Ready?" Personally I think I should read "James Bond – Goldeneye – Are You Stupid?" but that's only my opinion and not one that is shared by those currently being incarcerated in what passes for safety equipment, a harness and some webbing to bind your feet. Festa and Kryten approach the kiosk and enquire if there is space and time for two more fools. There is...BUT... being an idiot costs money, €200 each to be precise! Plan B is quickly adopted, watch other fools.

The first fellow is helped onto the gallows / scaffold that jut out over the precipitous drop and is hooked onto the bungee cord before standing, unconcerned, on the very edge waving to his friends. Being the first jump of the afternoon a small crowd has gathered and join in chanting the 5-4-3-2-1 countdown. Playing to the crowd and with a loud Aaaarrrrhhh! the lunatic hurls himself forward and begins a rapid plummet earthwards. At the same time his feet leave the platform an audible intake of collective breath can be heard followed by Scheisse! – Merde! – Merda! – Shit! In hushed international tones as we all wait for the elastic to stop expanding and start to halt the guys fall. It does of course and this is greeted by a small round of relieved applause as we watch the tiny helpless human boinging up and down the side of the dam.

We watch another idiot have a go before returning to the bikes via a brief visit to the gift emporium. It's not great putting on biker gear in such heat and so it is a relief when we retrace our route back down-hill into Gordola then on to join the A2 / E35 motorway further south. Feeling pleased with the way the day had so far progressed what followed next was what can politely be described as a "navigational error" for although we were to head back along the shores of Lake Como I had not intended to visit the town of Como it's-self.

My intended route was via Lugano to the lakeside but we ended up hopelessly lost. I decided we could get back on track by heading over the hills on a small country lane that looked like it crossed the border from Switzerland into Italy somewhere along its route. Unfortunately it just got narrower and when we stopped to ask we were told "Is not possible go to Italy this road" proving once and for all that despite the well-known saying, all roads do not lead to Rome!

We turned around and headed back down-hill unsure of what direction to take next. After what seemed like an age we eventually ended up in a very busy and very hot Como looking for fuel and a way out. As luck would have it we stumbled upon a petrol station and filled up, well most of us did. I filled up and got back on my bike, helmet on and ready to go but Kryten was still in the shop. I waited in the heat but still he stayed in the shop talking to the cashier. Turns out Kryten had filled his 22 litre tank with 40litres of fuel according to the pump dial but the pump had been pumping air. What followed was Krytens basic Italian v disbelieving Italian cashier. This was abandoned at half time when Kryten brought out a substitute in the form of his phone with English – Italian / Italian – English web pages and the matter was eventually resolved.

Time was pressing on and with full tanks we blundered out of Como onto the ss340 that runs alongside the beautiful lake. Well the lake maybe beautiful and we did manage some tantalising glimpses of it, but the road most definitely is not. Ill-tempered drivers barging past on this narrow congested road coupled with the heat and noise made this a long, dangerous and very disappointing part of the journey. So it was with great relief all round when we could leave this nasty road behind us and head for the hills once more.

The ss36 is also known as the Splugen Pass was not greatly praised when I researched the route earlier in the year. Maybe it was just the relief of being away from the mayhem of Como but we found this road superb. We joined it in Dubino on the Italian side and it snaked and twisted 35miles over to its' 2113m Swiss boarder summit and onwards to the town of Splugen. Festa was off like a rat up a, well, high Alpine pass and I was keen to follow but soon lost sight as the roads numerous hairpins took their toll. Kryten, ever the gentleman, shepherded Sindy and Barbie somewhere behind me as we all made our way upwards. This is not an easy road as at times it disappears into dim tunnels or narrow galleries with wet uneven surfaces and the occasional hairpin bend hidden away. There are places where the tunnels are stacked on top of each other joined by tight bends, it all makes for a very challenging technical ride. As I climb the weather seems to be grey and cloudy and I pass through a couple of grim looking villages before riding around the shore of Lago di Montespluga, pass through the village of Montespluga and arrive at a bleak border checkpoint that seems deserted.

The checkpoint is just about as high as the pass goes and I soon begin to descend into a more open meadow like area. In the distance I catch my first sight of Festa and hear the faint sound of the triples 675cc motor as it propels him through the valley. The lowering evening sun begins to reappear and I gather a pace relishing the more open and predictable nature of the road as it leaves the barren summit and weaves into the trees. Splugen is now right below me and with a few more twists and turns I spy Festa, helmet already removed, drinking from the cool fountain at the side of the road. I remove my Arai and we are soon joined by Kryten, Barbie and Sindy all of us with a tale to tell.

By now it was getting late, very late and all we wanted to do was return to Davos as quickly as possible. After leaving the motorway the 417 road that seemed quite pleasing on the way out seemed endless as the light began to fade ever more rapidly. As we passed through the various villages' lights were flickering into life as townsfolk prepared for the evening. By the time we arrived the lights of Davos were shining brightly as we made our through the town finally parking up in the welcoming arms of the Hotel.

We were all tired and most of all hungry and thirsty so there was barely time to dump the bike gear, don the smart but casual and head back into town on foot. Oh dear, when we got there the cupboard was bare as most places were already closed. Fortunately there was a choice of one Pizza takeaway from which we then sat outside and ate. There was a better choice of bars so we settled for the one that seemed the liveliest. It had a rustic wooden floor large wood tables and a Europop soundtrack. The clientele were clearly a trendy bunch but the barman kept me entertained the most for he was the campest male I think I have ever seen. So much so I checked if we had strayed inadvertently into the 'Blue Oyster Club!'

Wednesday – Davos to Col du Bussang (200miles 4 hrs).

At our last breakfast in our Davos hotel I sit looking out of the tall glass windows that form most of one side of the room. Outside in the distance are mountains bathed in early morning sunlight and below us in the car park wait our bikes, lightly covered in condensation from the previous cool night air. Some of the conversation centres around the need for a Vignette to use the Swiss motorways as it seems Sindy and Barbie have purchased these already. But we must say goodbye to our glamorous companions today as they head off to continue their tour in Germany.

When we check out we ask the hotel owner about the Vignette and he smiles and says that it is very unlikely anyone will check. The most likely place would be at a border crossing but they are so busy that to check for Vignettes would cause chaos. This is good news and it was followed by more when we were handed the very reasonable bill for our stay. Outside I have plenty of time to faff about loading up my bike as Kryten was saying his fond farewells to Barbie and Sindy. Festa, of course, who had loaded up the Triumph and was ready for the off almost as soon as we stood next to our bikes, could only watch and wonder as I applied bin liners and bungee cords to my throw-over luggage.

Eventually, having poked a leg through the gap between tank bag and throw-over, I sit astride my bike alongside Festa awaiting an acknowledgement from Kryten that he is ready. After watching Sindy and Barbie depart we get the nod from the orange VStrom rider and head out of Davos, back along the 417 to Thusis where we briefly join the E43 motorway. At Tamins we turn off and begin our journey along the far more picturesque route 19.

Route 19 has a fairly steady beginning through anonymous towns and villages but, being in the Alps, it soon has to proceed over a pass or two. The first notable one is the 2044m Oberalp Pass which we reach after about two and a half hours steady riding. The road sweeps back and forth as it gains height and at times is protected by avalanche shelters which it shares on occasion with the railway line that carries the famous Glacier Express. There are some tight hairpins along the way and some unforgiving looking rock faces that match the changing mood of the sky above us. Over the top we pass the Oberalpsee lake before we descend through yet more bends made trickier by recent rainfall and passing a speeding cyclist or two on our way into the town of Andermatt.

Andermatt is in The Valley of the Bears and they are present in carvings and paintings all over the town. It has cobbled streets that seem fairly new and clean but more importantly a roadside petrol station where we decide to fill up and take a breather. It's a curious little petrol station as it has just two pumps almost on the pavement and is attended by what seems to be Grandma and Grandad who live in the shop.

Back on the bikes and as we leave town the road opens up across the valley floor before it begins to climb once more. Then, all of a sudden, right in front of me Festa appears to break violently half way round a hairpin bend and nearly falls off. He pushes the bike to the side of the road where Kryten and I join him to see what has occurred. Turns out that with such tight turns Festas bulging tank bag had come into contact with the handlebar mounted kill switch stopping the bike dead.

Route 19 at this point is also known as the 2436m high Furka Pass and was used as a location in the 1964 James Bond classic film Goldfinger. (Bonds Aston Martin DB5 chases a Ford Mustang driven by Tilly Masterson). We follow Bonds progress for a short while and turn the sharp hairpin past the famous Hotel Belverdere (also from the film) heading down some gut-churningly steep and narrow bits on the way to the village of Gletsch. This is glacier land and from here the Glacier du Rhone can be reached on foot, but not by us today. Outside the hotel people sit chilling with a drink but we still have a long way to go and have been advised by Sindy and Barbie that we could be in for a long day.

It's a steep climb out of Gletsch as we are now heading up the 2165m Grimsel Pass with, to our left, the ominously titled Lake Totensee or 'Lake of the Dead' (which got its name 'during the Napoleonic wars when, we are told, soldiers of Duke Berchtold V of Zähringen were driven into the lake by the people of Valais). There are several grey green lakes and reservoirs with hydroelectric plants next to imposing dams and high voltage power lines dotted about this very dramatic landscape. Festa and Kryten seem to be relishing the challenge of damp hairpins, rock and traffic amidst the increasingly misty and snow covered backdrop as I begin to lose touch with my more cautionary riding style (I can't help looking over the edge of some of the roads and thinking how high up we are!).

Our eventual decent out of the mist comes as a relief for me as I am getting a bit cold and damp and not really enjoying the relentless twisting and turning. It's beginning to rain on and off now but we are progressing well through a much greener environment so my spirits are lifting. They are lifted more as we drop down further and catch sight of the beautiful lake Sarnen through the trees, a sight that has Kryten reaching for his camera. I follow Festa who has chosen not to stop as he needs to find a public convenience and we park up in the town of Schsein while we await Kryten. Back together again we discuss the passage of time, our progress so far, the increasingly poor weather and the distance that remains to be covered. It's decided that we should forgo the green and pleasant route I had planned and opt for the 'Let's get there' approach.

With this option dialled in we join the Swiss motorway system for the next couple of hours hoping that no-one is checking for Vignettes today. As we approach Basel I begin to understand what the hotel manager had said about the chaos that would be created if border control were to stop and check, it's chaos already. Maybe to be fair it was around 4pm by now so the rush hour was beginning but I hated this bit. Trying to follow Festa and Kryten filtering through the masses of traffic I got squeezed out between a lorry and a Porsche and lost sight of my companions. I began to lose confidence in my ability to thread the bulky CB1300 through the eye of the overwhelming traffic storm and resigned myself to catching the boys up further on.

At the border between Switzerland and France I was lost in a sea of vehicles trying to make sure that I at least got the right turnings onto the right motorway to get me away from this bloody awful misery. Then, as the traffic began to disperse, I spied Festa and Kryten patiently awaiting my emergence from the mayhem. It was time for a rest and we soon found a service station for fuel, food and drinks. After hearing my tail of filtering woe Mr T look-a-like Kryten advised me to "Get some nuts" which I duly did in the form of a much needed Snickers bar. None of us felt inclined to pay the €2 to pee charge so we followed everyone else to the convenient wooded area to the rear of the carpark.

We still had around sixty miles or so to cover to our destination of the 'Biker Hotel' we had stayed in on one of our earlier trips. The hotel at Col du Bussang in the Vosges had been affectionately referred to as 'Marks place' ever since and we were looking forward to reacquainting ourselves with the multilingual proprietor. So we set off on the motorway again briefly before turning off and heading across country through Aspach and up to Thann. As we drew ever closer to the end of our day the weather turned from grey to damp to wet to chucking it down, the light got dimmer, the traffic got busier and the whole experience became an unpleasant endurance to the finish.

The sight of the hotel entrance came after following a crawling lorry up a steep wet hill and wasn't a moment too soon. Dripping wet we made our way into the welcoming light and warmth to be greeted by Mark and shown to a drying area in an underground dungeon then finally our room. Now maybe I had worn my best pair of rose tinted spectacles on our previous visit but this room seemed sparse and cold. The long awaited shower was disappointing but we had no time to worry about such things as beer and dinner were waiting.

Dry at last and in warm clothing we made our way to the restaurant and soon dispatched the beers we had been mentally promising ourselves ever since the Basal hell. We order copious amounts of tap water to replace lost fluids from a long hard day and soon polish off the basic food that is delivered. Once the plates are cleared away we settle down to complete the evening with a game of cards and ask Mark for some more tap water. "I only serve tap water with the meal" he replied "You will have to buy water from now" WTF? We had another beer each and a pleasant game of cards but began comparing our previous experience of the hotel with the current version. Maybe one should never revisit past good times as they may not live up to the memories?

Thursday - Col du Bussang to Bouillon (215miles 6 hrs).

Maybe last nights' water incident had left a bitter taste but I was keen to leave the Col du Bussang behind this morning and the meagre bread and jam breakfast did little to change my mind.

Todays' route would see us start by retracing a road we had ridden on our first visit, the D431 Route de Cretes (Crest Road). The ridge road promises spectacular views of bucolic countryside, lakes and valleys, forests filled with pine and silver birch and high rounded peaks (Ballons).The weather was much improved from that that greeted our arrival and the sun was even managing brief appearances from behind the clouds.

Climbing out of a slight dip we leave the hotel behind and head back towards Cernay on the N66. We then leave this busy road behind exchanging it for the pleasant D431 which soon begins to climb the highest Ballon, imaginatively entitled "Le Grand Ballon". The road weaves back and forth through cool pine woodlands occasionally skirting a meadow as we climb towards the 1423m summit. As we crest the Ballon we pass The Alps View Cafe I remember stopping at on our previous trip. Incidentally, a walk that leads from here to the very top reveals a monument to the 'Blue Devils' who kept the Ballon in French hands during WW1 and a large radar station perched on high (1423m) from which magnificent panoramic views as far as the Alps can be had.

Today, however, we ride straight past the cafe as we are now high up on the ridge road and with the hillside rolling away either side of us extended vistas can be had. Also, as it is still relatively early, we pretty much have the road to ourselves and are able to crack the throttle open that little bit more boldly. The road surface is decent (although later Kryten begs to differ with that statement) and the bends are often open and sweeping with no nasty surprises meaning we are making good time as we sweep between the trees and over the crests of Col de la Schlucht and La Bonhomme before descending into the town of Sainte Marie aux Mines in search of petrol.

It is close to mid-day now and the sun has chased away any

malingering clouds leaving a very warm day as we pick our way through the narrow streets before good luck succeeds good judgement and we stumble across a supermarché with l'essence. Taking off our helmets at a leisurely pace relieved at finding this place we are greeted by the lady in the kiosk shouting "vite" "vite". We oblige by filling up as 'vite-ly?' as possible and discover that as soon as we have paid up the shutters go down, the lady darts across the forecourt and it's lunch time. Festa and Kryten head off hunter gathering inside the large supermarché while I do my best to find a shady spot away from the glare of the sunshine to 'guard' the bikes.

All seems peaceful here as we partake our own version of luncheon upon the garage forecourt watching the residents of this small French town go about their daily routines. From here and for the next three hours or so we must work our way northwards using the motorway system so we are in no great hurry to leave. Along with talk of the ride over the Ballons we discuss how we might find our way out of the town as we have no real idea of how we arrived at this spot. On the way in we were looking for petrol and navigated the one way system with only that in mind. Retracing our steps was not an option so looking for signs to the D459 the right way out of town might be tricky. Back on the bikes and riding through the narrow streets once more we soon arrive at a roundabout with signs pointing to the D459 and before long we are back out winding our way up hill away from the town far quicker than anticipated.

The pleasant D459 soon came to an abrupt end as we joined the N59 motorway at Luneville (Looney-Ville) and began our northward journey via Nancy and Metz. We were expecting to be confronted by the grabbing hands of the péage system along the way but somehow our route avoided these pick-pockets making the 80miles or so far less expensive. At Longwy we leave the N52 at last and cross over the border into Belgium on much more agreeable local roads. Unfortunately these agreeable local roads had far less agreeable local road works in place at numerous points along our intended route meaning we almost appeared to be sneaking up on our destination by zig-zagging wildly.

After an extended excursion around some rural Belgium countryside we join a wide open dual carriageway through the lush green trees of the Ardennes forests and begin to make 'good progress' once more. Turn left off this road and after a couple of bends the sign for Bouillon, our overnight halt, appears followed shortly after by the sight of the castle perched prominently on the rock above the town. We are in the Walloon Region of Belgium (although it sounds more Australian to me) and the town sits snugly in a sharp kink of the Semois River.

Having been to Bouillon on our very first trip we found the hotel without much fuss and parked up alongside the river. It would be wrong to claim that we rough it on any of our trips but after last nights' disappointment the 4star Hotel de la Poste was the lap of luxury and a complete contrast. From the brochure it appears the hotel has been on the go since 1730 and it is claimed that one or two prominent folk have popped in through the years, most notable of which was one Emperor Napoleon 3rd in 1870. The lobby / reception area had a marble floor, a charming receptionist and a very agreeable dog (a Belgium Airedale Terrier I think). We enquired about the safety of the bikes parked in the street and were told that there were no problems with thieves here, how refreshing.

Suitably impressed, showered and changed we discover that it is exactly 'Beer o'clock' and head out into the late afternoon sunshine. Now it must be stressed that Bouillon is a very pleasant town but buzzin' it aint! We cross the bridge and spend some time wandering until we finally 'plump' for La Pergola with its raised decking, views of the river and the castle on the hill beyond. Our host is a very talkative chap but asks why we come to Bouillon as, in his opinion "it's crap and boring". We disagree and point out one or two of the highlights but he is unconvinced, still the long cool beers are most welcome. When I go to pay inside the bar I am engaged in an intense conversation about, of all things, English beer glasses when his supplier turns up. An animated exchange in French ensues, the way that continental types do, waving of arms and hand gestures, until the supplier turns to me and utters something in French. "It's no good talking to him" says the proprietor "He can't speak French you idiot" to which I reply with a smile "Je comprends un petit Français" and they both look at me open mouthed which allows me to finally settle the bill and escape.

Time to find some food and we are determined not to eat Pizza which seems to be our staple diet when on these trips. Most places are shut but we manage to locate La Chine (Chinese) and venture inside. Now if you have ever seen Auf Wiedersehen Pet where the boys go for an Indian in Germany you may know where I am coming from when I say that for a second or two I am confused when confronted by a Chinese lady speaking French. Stupid I know, but it just took a little longer than normal for my little brain to compute and send the signal to my mouth to ask for a table for three in French.

The meal we eventually managed to order from the Chinese menu written in French only (the lady spoke no English and ever polite Krytens attempts to inform her he is vegetarian and didn't want meat were classic) was exceptionally nice. While we ate the Chinese lady spent the time watching mum and dad swift (or swallow) supplying their young in a nest above the restaurant entrance. We bid the lady au revoir and return to the graceful ambiance of Hotel de la Poste for a final nightcap or two and a game of cards set against an illuminated river backdrop to while the evening away, très agréable!

Friday – Bouillon to Europort (250miles – 5hrs 45mins).

So this is the last day and we have plenty of time to take it easy this morning as we are just a few hours away from the ferry. The breakfast room in this hotel is a whole world away from the bread and jam of Bussang. There is a large expanse of glass affording magnificent views of the sunlit river and the tables have white linen tablecloths with precisely arranged cutlery. The choice of food available from several buffet style tables is a joy but the largest smile was reserved for the Champagne, Bucks Fizz that we toasted another thoroughly enjoyable trip with, how decadent is that? With time to spare we are allowed to leave our gear in a large conference room before heading off for a tour of the town. It's a brilliant warm morning and we follow the course of the river as it sweeps around the back of the castle. We return through the tunnel that goes beneath the castle and then walk higher up to gain some superb views of the town and its river. Festa and Kryten go in search of cheap fags but leave empty handed before we end up sitting in the sunshine outside the cafe opposite our hotel. We must soon depart but while paying the bill we notice the cafe also sells boxes of one of Belgium's' most famous products, chocolate, so purchase several to take back home as gifts.

Back in the hotels conference room there is a welcome cool breeze as we wrestle our way into motorcycle attire. Kryten has one last act to perform, the ritual disposal of an unwanted 1980s style T shirt which gets tucked away behind some chairs for puzzled cleaners to find. Suited and booted we pat the dog and bid our hostess goodbye before loading the bikes and heading out of town.

We top up with fuel and, for a short while, the roads still have a rural feel about them before we are obliged to join the soulless motorway system that speeds us through the mayhem of high speed lane swapping to the ferry terminal in Rotterdam and the comparative sanctuary of The Pride of Hull.

As the ferry glides us away from Holland we make a slight break with tradition and head to the top deck for beer and cards. The convivial atmosphere is complemented by an attractive lady playing the piano across the room from us and the boys even let me win a game, result!

Chapter 8.

ALPS Revisited - The Wiggo Tour. (10 Days).

This years' tour sees us return to the Alps once more only this time we start in the far south of France. It seems like a good choice as so far northern Europe has been wet, windy and cold since early April and it's now July.

Kryten and Festa have kept faith with their bikes from last years' trip, Krytens 650 VStrom and Festas 675 Street Triple having proved themselves' well capable of Alpine tomfoolery. Like many middle aged men though I have traded in my faithful old girl (CB1300) for a younger, slimmer and more feisty model in the shape of Suzuki's' GSR 750 "naked streetfighter" in mean looking black. Like all young things I felt obliged to heap gifts upon her in the form of a replacement Leo Vince end can (the original item is pretty hideous) and numerous other unnecessary bling trinkets.

Also new for this years' tour is the addition of a "proper" top-box to each of our machines. Kryten started the trend when his new pride-n-joy came complete with a full set of hard luggage last year. Festa and I envied the super-efficient way the top-box worked in stark contrast to the cloth bag, bin liner and bungee hooks I had persevered with. Festa had chosen the "thrifty" approach though and managed to cobble together a rack and top-box with a homemade base plate. I had gone for the all singing all dancing Givi V46 and even had the dealer fit it for me at the bikes first service (think Jeremy Clarkson's' practical prowess on Top Gear and you're close to mine!).

Other changes? Well Festa had talked much about acquiring a new textile riding suit but decided the one he was given with his first bike twelve years ago would do for one more trip; it may even fit him one day. Kryten, though, was sporting a fine new Arai Chaser helmet which apparently fits so well and is so comfortable I may have to revise his name as there are no more humorous marks pressed into his scalp.

Being a nerdy type I had decided to purchase a bike mountable bullet type video camera to record some of our journey, and there in lays a tale. Y' see it mounted on the handlebars ok so I decided a rear facing shot would be ticker-T-boo to. The best place for this seemed to be using a fixing for the new Givi base plate but this meant removing said plate. It was a fairly straight forward task and the end result proved pleasingly successful, provided I took the time to ensure the camera was the right way up. As the departure day drew closer I began to assemble various things and store them in the top-box which was now in the bedroom. This years' packing was going to be so easy and trauma free!

Thursday – Home to Hull (40miles 1 hour).

Departure day duly arrived and I set about neatly packing my stuff into the vast 46ltr chasm I had recently purchased. It all went well for a while until I remembered my size 11 walking shoes, the maps, the paperwork and my bag full of gadgets. The more I shuffled stuff around the worse it seemed to get and time ticked relentlessly by. After several items had been jettisoned the lid could only be closed without the walking shoes which I had resolved to carry in a bin liner, which also contained my wet suit, bungee corded to the back seat.

Time was now an issue, I had all day to pack and now I was sweating like the Battersea Dogs Home postman. I heaved the bulging top-box to the waiting bike and hoisted it onto the rack only to discover it didn't fit! I was perplexed, how could it not fit? The sun beat down on me as I tried many times but it wouldn't go. My wife appeared to bid me farewell as she had to go and in passing remarked "Have you got it on the wrong way round?" I was stunned by my own stupidity and for a while could only stand motionless staring at what had become so bleedin' obvious. The race was then on to turn the rack and my day around which I completed in amazingly quick time but which left me panicking to get to the meeting point by the deadline.

As I approached I could see an agitated Kryten begin to put on his helmet while cool as you like Festa waited for my explanation. Kryten had finished work at lunch time and gone home to pack his previously prepared items while Festa claims to have left all preparation and packing until he left work at 4pm (it was now 6pm). Mind you, most of Festas packing consisted of bottles of red wine!

I led the way towards the ferry terminal in Hull, all the time cursing my stupidity while trying to concentrate on riding my bike safely. On the Humber Bridge another first, bikes no longer have to pay! At the ferry terminal however my mind was completely scrambled as at the last roundabout I led us first to a dead end, then to the lorry terminal and another lap of the roundabout before finally choosing the correct exit to get us to the ferry. This time, after a quick passport check, we were ushered straight up the gang plank and on board. I turned the engine off with a great sigh of relief but with the niggling suspicion I had forgotten something.

Festa had no sooner dismounted than he had lashed his bike down and departed for the cabin while Kryten waited patiently for me to gather myself together enough to follow Festas lead. After negotiating the labyrinth of corridors and miscellaneous confused passengers Kryten and I finally joined an already changed Festa in the cabin only to see him wave goodbye as he headed to the refreshment centre on deck 9. Through the large round windows of the Irish Bar we watched the ship slip past the Humber light house and into the North Sea as the night began to close in around us.

Friday – Europort to Dusseldorf (170miles 5hrs 30mins)

The wake up calls began crackling through the tannoy system advising all that the Breakfast Buffet was now being served in the Four Seasons buffet Restaurant. It's an offer we have long since decided we can refuse due to its' excessive price and elbows first 'bun-fight' ambience, so we turn over and go back to sleep waiting for the next announcement. I eventually stir, dress in bike gear and wonder up to investigate what the day has in store for us. It's a disappointing dull grey industrial skyline that greets me and I soon return to the cabin to gather together all my things ready for the push 'n' shove down to the vehicle deck.

I faff about, Kryten Faffs about and this is quite normal for us but the sight of Festas puzzled expression and his repeated visits to his tank bag are new. He leaves the cabin and goes to the vehicle deck but returns still puzzled. "I can't find my passport" he explained. The search begins in earnest as the announcements for disembarkation become more frequent and crew begin knocking on the cabin door. "Have you double checked your tank bag?" asks Kryten, a man, like myself, well used to losing things only to find them where we left them. "Yep" affirms Festa as he leaves the cabin once more to try customer services to see if it has been handed in. Nope, not there either so I accompany him for another check around the bikes on a by now empty vehicle deck, nothing.

Festa returns to the cabin while the ships' crew try to speed up our departure. We are going nowhere without a passport though and I am relieved when Festa and Kryten return having finally found the missing item, erhem, exactly where Festa had put it before charging up the gang plank last night, safely in his tank bags zip up pocket! With great relief all round we finally wave goodbye to the crew that had begun to surround us and head out onto European tarmac to begin our trip. We don't get far though as it begins to rain and I decide I have to halt proceedings just after passport control to struggle into my wet suit.

I had spent a long time with Google mapping out our trip and had planned a route to keep us away from the motorway system allowing us to enjoy some Dutch countryside and a visit to the 'Bridge too Far' town of Arnhem. Luckily I had also taken the precaution of mapping out a motorway route to the motor rail terminal in Dusseldorf and this is what we chose to do given the faltering start and unhelpful weather. 'Let's just be sure we make the train on time' was the feeling and after an unplanned visit into Westervoort south of Arnhem we duly arrived in Dusseldorf. Ok, so due to a navigational error on my behalf we arrived at a Mercedes garage somewhere in the city but we were close to the station we felt.

It was now Krytens time in the navigational spotlight as he produced his sat-nav. from within the confines of his top box. After some coaxing the system managed to recognise some part of our destination address, possibly, but as it had started to rain I decided to rely on my memory of the route from Google and have another go. So after a complex 'U' turn we were back on the right road heading through the centre of Dusseldorf where we eventually started to see signs for DB AutoZug with the comforting symbol of a car on a train to confirm this as our route.

In the narrow street that leads to the station we joined a queue of miscellaneous vehicles all waiting to check in. We soon discovered that there were two trains due to depart at roughly similar times and the expected German efficiency appeared to be somewhat lacking. Employees in florescent bibs carrying clipboards were harassed by frustrated motorists all longing to board the train and shelter from the now warm afternoon sunshine, but few could speak German. During the wait Festa and Kryten went off to hunter gather water for the trip which they sourced from a grotty shop just around the corner at half the cost of similar stuff on the train.

After making it through check in and another wait in another queue we were eventually called forward to begin the slightly scary ride along the lower deck of the train. I say scary as the roof is very low and very solid, couple this with attempting to burry your head into your tank bag whilst trying to maintain good bike control over an undulating smooth and slippery floor and you can maybe understand my relief at finally seeing my bike clamped securely in place by the hunchbacks of NotreZug. All that is left now is to remove the tank bag (containing tonight's' stunning evening wear), and alight the train without contacting the metal beams of the ceiling and rendering myself unconscious.

After an endless walk along platform 7B our carriage awaits but, as we approach, the doors are slammed shut and the train begins to move. There is an amount of confusion and even panic among some of our fellow travellers until staff move to explain that the process of coupling people coaches to vehicle coaches is in progress. Eventually we are able to board and arrive at our allotted compartment only to discover someone has beaten us to it. We double check and soon confirm we have the correct compartment but are to share it with another couple of German bikers as the train is full tonight. This could be a very cosy evening!

Our travelling companions politely excuse themselves and head off to the buffet / bar while we try to store our gear and slip into something more comfortable for the evening. That achieved we then locate the table and proceed to burden it with all manner of food and drink items. When I say we, I refer to Kryten and Festa for my contribution is a pathetic bag of nuts and some shortbread. I have no idea from where Festa produced so much but must assume he has acquired a Marry Poppins style bag. Festas further contribution was a seemingly endless supply of homemade red wine.

Now came one of the great pleasures of international travel, the return of our travelling companions. We were half way through eating when they introduced themselves as Dominic, an anaesthetist, and Emanuella a lawyer both of whom spoke exceptionally good English. They accepted our invitation to join us and produced provisions of their own to share while eagerly accepting Festas offer of a red wine supply. Outside the window the Rhine and its castles passed by while inside the conversation flowed almost as easily as the wine. As the evening wore on it became clear that Emanuella was an accomplished consumer of alcohol, trading glass for glass with our own champion consumer Festa. Dominic was quieter now, in fact I think the anaesthetist had probably anaesthetised himself, but still able to raise a smile or a word or two until time had to be called on the party and the compartment made ready for sleeping. At this point it was discovered that despite our friends' purchase of a bottle Festas' generously stocked wine cellar of six bottles had been depleted!

The train affords the passenger the luxury of effortlessly travelling hundreds of miles whilst he slumbers, but luxurious it aint. On one side of the compartment three bunks can be made stacked one on top of the other while the other side contains a further two beds. Dominic and Emanuella volunteer to take the long climb to the top while we try to make the best of the rest. It's not until you try to fit on something that was a seat moments previously that you realise how little room there is. Then you get to wondering how many fat arses have spent their time farting through the upholstery upon which you are now resting and realise why the wily Germans are on the top bunks.

Saturday - Alessandria - Monaco – Auron (220miles 4hrs 45mins).

I didn't sleep well, if at all, I couldn't get comfortable on a surface that wouldn't stay still. It's not something you really notice while sitting on a train but the cornering forces when lying down can feel quite strange. Outside the day was well underway and the thin curtains, that barely covered the window, struggled to keep out the sunlight. From above various feet and legs began to descend to the tiny compartment with accompanying groans. It wasn't easy finding and then pulling on garments discarded late last night as floor space was at a premium. There was confusion to as to whether breakfast, such as it is, would be served but something did eventually arrive wrapped in plastic but its identity remains a mystery. Still, what we needed most was something to drink and tea and coffee were gratefully consumed.

Ablutions under these circumstances require careful balance and often a strong stomach as lots of people wish to perform the tasks at a similar time. There is, of course, the usual horror of the toilet room but along the corridor we also have the addition of a small room containing a sink and mirror. Once inside the cleaning of teeth and washing could be attempted up to a point. That point being where one bends towards the sink. This is when one discovers the limitations of the room as ones bum contacts the door or wall and ones' head contacts the mirror, it's really quite small in there.

As the train pulls into the station we stand in the corridor and allow Dominic and Emanuella space and time to change into their bike gear and assemble stuff ready for departure. Unfortunately this heroic gesture leaves us with very little time to do the same ourselves as we are urged to vacate the train as quickly as possible. Our solution was to pull down the compartment window and pass our gear out and onto the platform. This worked well and we then proceeded to get changed into our biking attire on the platform...just as a loaded passenger train pulled up on the adjoining platform, probably not the best sight to begin their day with.

Changed and repacked we then plodded our long hot way to the end of the platform to await the arrival of the vehicle carriages. It seemed to take ages before the train eased up to the offloading ramp and then even longer before the man in the florescent jacket gave the signal to collect our bikes. In the car park, as we loaded our bikes, Dominic and Emanuella stopped to say farewell. They rode a beautiful black

1200cc Ducati Multistrada which seemed very lightly loaded for the two of them but, as they explained, they were heading for the beach and didn't need much. With handshakes, very British,, a hug and a kiss, very continental, over they remounted and disappeared into the morning traffic heading for the coast.

So where are we now? Maybe I should explain that the overnight train has brought us around 600 miles from Dusseldorf in Germany to Alessandria in Piedmont Italy, some 55miles south east of Turin, rich in artistic heritage, including a famous Cittadella, vast squares and eighteenth century palaces, apparently (though none of this is evident at the scruffy railway station). This town is rather handy as it allows us access to both the Mediterranean coast and the French Alps.

We head off into the heat and traffic and I am amazed to find that I have remembered much of the escape route out of town and am able to lead us straight to a garage for petrol. Now we can really get started as we join the A26 toll road south before turning right onto the A10 / E74 to run alongside the Mediterranean coast line. The motorway crosses many bridges and cuts through a surprising amount of tunnels as we journey westwards. It is very busy and congested in places and we need to make full use of our bikes filtering abilities to maintain good progress until we need to stop again for fuel close to the French border. This is a good time for an ice-cream, a bottle of water and the remnants of Kryten and Festas copious packing up.

Back on the motorway again and we part with the best part of €20 at the toll booth before entering France and later taking exit 58-Roquebrune-Cap Martin. This leads us to a small lay-by where we park up and walk across the road to an area with stunning views of the deep blue of the Mediterranean and the Principality of Monaco and Monte-Carlo. For me it feels that this years' trip is now about to begin, like stepping off the aeroplane at your holiday destination with the anticipation of all that lays ahead. We extract cameras from tank bags and photograph each other and the view with perfect timing as we are soon joined by a coach full of people about to do exactly the same as us.

The road down to the centre of Monaco twists and turns repeatedly and is busy without being congested. At times the streets seem very narrow and I am not confident I have chosen the right route. After a right turn into very narrow busy street we emerge onto a roundabout that is the Virage du Portier and the entrance to the tunnel under the Fairmont Hotel on the Grand Prix circuit. As we enter the darkened tunnel I can almost hear the sound of F1 racing cars echoing off the walls and Murray Walkers excited commentary as Damon Hill raced to his 1996 world championship.

I really wanted to drop down a couple of cogs to give the Leo Vince exhaust chance to announce our presence but I also wanted to take in the moment and fully appreciate where we were. This is the fastest part of the GP circuit and F1 cars reach speeds of around 170mph through here. I managed a very sedate and legal 30mph taking in the views through the concrete supports to the sea on the other side, the concierge service at the Fairmont's' car park entrance and the steady curve of the bumpy road before the blinding sunlight of the exit. Now we are in the harbour area, through the chicane we go then on alongside the posh boats to Tabac corner where we peel off into a car park and come to rest.

Man it's hot here, surrounded by cars and high walls we soon head for the small amount of shade offered by the doorways of some dilapidated old garage lock-ups that are built into the walls below some cafes that peer over from above us. It's here we dump as much of our riding gear as possible before we head back across the road to stand on the harbour wall and admire the myriad fancy boats. Leaving Festa and I to keep an eye on the bikes Kryten takes off with his camera to capture some images returning briefly before heading off in the opposite direction to where the bigger boats are moored up. An open topped Rolls Royce glides past behind us before coming to rest a little further along at a place I wouldn't dare park my Mondeo. An immaculately dressed gent steps out and proceeds to make a telephone call as if waiting for his valet to appear with his boat.

Kryten returns and it's my turn to take a look at the posh boats and motors just along the quayside. First I pass a small jetty where it appears riff-raff can sit and dangle their feet in the clear water maybe partaking in one of those trendy fish pedicures at the same time. Then the really posh stuff starts, beginning with a black Bentley Continental GT and the odd Porsche in the car park and ending with some outrageously expensive looking boats (should we call them yachts?) attended by neatly presented crew and menacing looking dudes in dark shades and black suits.

Back at the bikes I re-join a hot looking Festa and Kryten (oh dear that sounds very wrong, I feel I must stress they are hot because of the heat and not, err, well, moving swiftly on...). I take a deep breath and we move back onto the F1 circuit passing La Piscine, rounding La Rascasse and heading off into the traffic to make the steady climb up to the Casino. Unfortunately we can't enter Casino Square as we are waved on by Monsieur Le Plod and have to take a slight detour before finding our way back to the corner at Mirabeau and the famous tight hairpin on the decent outside the Grand Hotel. Lined up here are loads of scooters and bikes with their owners watching the traffic negotiating the unexpectedly tight bend. From here we pass under the hotel and arrive back at the Virage du Portier roundabout and the end of our lap of the circuit. We turn left this time and head along the Avenue Princess Grace which takes us close to the beach and some undoubtedly expensive hotels before we climb back up the maze of narrow streets to re-join the A8 motorway heading briefly back east.

Soon off the motorway we now head north to the village of Sospel where I take a wrong turn and we have to stop alongside the river Bevera and consult the instructions and a map. As Kryten has produced the magic mobile phone I decide that I ought to have a glance at mine to check the unlikely possibility that someone may have contacted me. A most fortuitous decision as it turns out. My wife had received an email back home saying that the hotel we had booked for tonight was full but she had booked us into an alternative, The Igloo (should we expect a warm welcome?).

Out of Sospel we spy the sign that confirms we are on the right road once again, D2566, 'Moulinet and Col de Turini'. This road is a regular stage fixture of the Monte Carlo round of the World Rally Championship and has been used by such driving notables as the Top Gear team in search of the best driving road, the Fifth Gear team to test the Audi RS3 and none less that James Bond (Pierce Brosnan) in an Aston Martin DB5 for a scene in 'GoldenEye'. Research also reveals there are 34 tight hair pins (lacets) on the way to the 1607m high summit. All jolly exciting and as we begin to climb we soon encounter the slightly intimidating grey walls that support the road at its steepest points and feature in many of the images of the famous Col. I say we, but by the time I reach this point I can only just about catch sight of Festa and Kryten somewhere above me seemingly less intimidated than I. It's a lot cooler here, away from the heat and traffic of Monaco, with trees providing a shaded canopy at times and the day rapidly turning into late afternoon.

Eventually I pass the little brown sign announcing 'Col de Turini – Alt. 1607m' and turn to join my companions in the rather uninspiring car park. After such a climb the high point is, well, a bit of a low point, an anti-climax to be honest. The immediate area is surrounded by trees so there isn't a great view to behold; there are a couple of German bikers but no Subaru Imprezas, Mitsubishi Evos, Mini Coopers or Paddy Hopkirk, no Top Gear presenters with exotic motorcars and certainly no James Bond.

Ok, after the delights of Monaco this area may have lacked a little something so we head off downwards threading our way around a varied selection of bends to join the more purposeful D2565 road. We stay with this road for a while until we need to join the D2205 at an amazingly tight junction we arrive at after a steep descent. From here we enter the rather pleasant Gorges de Valabre with the road mimicking the meanders of the river it accompanies and begin to look for petrol for the smaller fuel tanks of the GSR and the Triumph. Kryten is in front when we spy a potential petroleum retailer and he doesn't see us turn in to the empty forecourt. Rather than try to chase after him Festa and I decide to try to fill up using our credit cards. To our slight surprise and relief this works and we quickly return to the road to attempt to re-join Kryten.

It's not long before we reach the roundabout that will lead us to our overnight stay in the village of Auron but Kryten is no-where to be seen. There's nothing for it but to press on (much like the chaps from Top Gear on one of their challenges) and hope that his navigational skills have lead him along this very path. When we enter the village we do indeed find him parked up and enquiring where we had been. Kryten reported that he had located our original hotel and had been told that our new hotel was somewhere to the rear. With the centre of the village chained off we had a slight detour round via a slightly unusual route to get to another street where we thought the hotel should be. The Igloo was no-where to be seen but after some head scratching and a little luck we stumbled upon the sign for Hotel L' Oustalet with a somewhat smaller sign above its door saying 'The Igloo'.

We have the luxury of two fairly basic rooms and while Kryten and I fanny about Festa is soon showered, changed and out on the town in search of a beer, nothing new there then. I like to take stock of things and enjoy a leisurely shower before being ready to face the world again. I suspect Kryten, who has a room to himself, is doing something similar as well as catching up with those all-important text, Twatter and Basefuck messages. Indeed when Festa returns we venture into the world of Kryten to discover, not too unexpectedly, that he appears to have emptied the entire contents of his top box and arranged them randomly around the room.

Most importantly though Mr. Kryten has excelled himself this year with the introduction of two new pieces of essential touring gear in the form of a kettle and a flask. Yes dear reader I kid you not, along with tea bags and milk! Now on the face of it one may question the inclusion of such items but when you consider the general contents of a hotel room in foreign parts it is a genius move (although, as we discovered, the kettle will not work on the train). So here in the Alps we drank tea, ate biscuits and listened as Festa reported the price he had just paid for a pint of beer, that'll be €8 merci monsieur.

Time to find somewhere to eat and after a brief meander around the small village square we decided to go for what has become standard tour fayre, beer and PIZZA! Here a small amount of French lingo was all it took to order what turned out to be one of the biggest one person pizzas I have ever seen (other than on Man v Food). Maybe my French isn't as good as I think it is but I don't believe I ordered family sized. After dining we moved across to the hotel we should have been staying at which was very busy or should I say lively? Here Kryten introduced me to Hogarden Wheat Beer which immediately went onto the list of my favourite tipples.....at the bottom.

Sunday - Auron to Les Salles sur Verdon (160miles 5hrs 45mins).

Awoke after a most agreeable nights' sleep, it being our first night in a bed that wasn't moving. It wasn't long before we were packed and ready to move on as we had decided that breakfast in the hotel would be an over-priced bread and jam affair and anyway Kryten had prepared a nice big flask of tea. So with the bill sorted and the top boxes clipped into place we headed back out of the village the way we had entered returning to the D2205. After a short ride we enter Saint-Étienne-de-Tinée and briefly accompany the Tinée River along a valley floor before joining the D64 where the road begins its climb to our first destination, the Col d la Bonnette. The road is fairly typical of Alpine passes being quite narrow with unforgiving rock one side and even less forgiving plummets to the other. The views become increasingly spectacular as we climb leaving the trees below us to join the multitude of mountain peaks that rise up all around us. Close to the top we pass a couple of grim looking grey machine gun posts, remnants of WW2 and part of an extensive network of tunnels and fortifications that formed the Maginot Line (we are close to the Italian boarder here).

This is one of the highest paved roads in the Alps (arguably the highest for those to whom these things are important) at 2715m (8907ft) but includes a road that loops around to the Cime d la Bonnette giving a final height of 2802m (9193ft). It's here we pull up alongside a large black stone with a plaque and the many other people that seem to be up here on this bright and sunny morning. There are exhausted cyclists, families, couples and our fellow motorcyclists taking it in turns to have their picture taken in front of the black stone as we are joined by a large 30 to 40 strong motorcycle club.

It's a great atmosphere but Festa and Kryten are keen to climb to the very top along the winding rocky path that leads upwards from the car park. I volunteer to watch over the bikes and they are soon racing to the top. On their return I decide that since I have come all this way I too should make the final pilgrimage to the very top. It's not far but it is slippery with loose rocks and stones making my ungamely progress dressed in leathers and Alpine Stars boots more tricky. At the top there is a Table d' Orientation on a raised mound and a 360° view of mountains as far as the eye can see. As I make my way back down I can make out Festa and Kryten and the many bikes that line the road but then have to perform a double take as I think I see someone cycling up towards me! On second viewing my eyes did not deceive me as there really is a Lycra clad individual pedalling his skinny tyred racing bike up the path to meet me. I step to one side and a guy, not in the first flushes of youth, passes me and makes it all the way to the top. On his return his friends are congratulating Mario for having completed this challenge without putting a foot down, Mario? Super Mario surely?

The plan was to stop for tea somewhere here but it felt a little too exposed so we elected to move on and find somewhere more secluded. Back on the bikes again we rode downwards for ages on a road that starts off as the D64 passing the abandoned French military Camp Des Fourches and revels in the name Le Pis just after another abandoned military base at Caserne de Restefond. Lower down we ride the busy road to the town of Barcelonnette before turning off onto a minor road, signed D902, and begin to enter the Gorges du Bachelard heading towards the Col d la Cayolle.

The small road grows increasingly narrow as it ducks and dives along the tranquil gorge shadowing a swiftly flowing river but we meet very few others along the way so progress is steady and relaxed. I am still looking for somewhere to stop for a tea break but each possible location I spy has a reason not to stop and I am left with the feeling that if we stop here there will be something better just around the corner. Shortly after the tiny hamlet of Saint Laurent I finally pull over to a gravelled area with a view back down the valley, this'll have to do. We are well ready for a break by now and Krytens' genius flask of tea makes its first outdoors appearance. It's a very warm day and it's nice to stop and enjoy the surroundings, the view of the tiny church, the steep sloping sides of the gorge and the river below barely audible alongside the gentle ticking of cooling motorcycle engines.

After what are politely termed 'comfort breaks' we continue our journey along the gorge crossing over the river on a narrow bridge and following the road into pleasantly cool woodlands. We hadn't been riding long when, wouldn't you know it and almost as predicted, we enter a delightful valley and cross over a bridge that reveals a waterfall that cascades out of the trees, tea break anyone? Beyond here the road continues to climb until we reach the barren 2326m summit of the Col d la Cayolle and a stone marking the border between the French departments of Alps-Maritimes and Alps-Haute-Provence. Over the Col we pass through an Alpine village with a more practical than picturesque persona before passing through several tunnels and entering the village of Guillaumes.

Not long after the D2202 leads us into cool woodland before presenting us with a change of colour in our scenery. A short tunnel is carved out of red rock and leads into the Darius Gorge where the road splits into two as our side goes through another tunnel in the rock and the other side of the road goes around the rock. Everything here is red and we stop to have a more detailed look around. The Pont de la Mariee is a pedestrian bridge that crosses the gorge high above the river and lurking in the middle is a white van and a young chap selling bungee jumps for €30. Sod that, would you buy a bungee jump from white van man?

The bridge does, however, afford a decent view along the gorge and we pose for more photographs with this unusual backdrop before riding through the gorge a couple of times to make sure we hadn't missed anything. At the southern end we exit and turn left towards the town of Entrevaux. The road is wider and quicker and is joined by a railway line as the two follow a widening river along the open valley floor.

Entrevaux surprises me as it seems to appear unannounced after a tight bend in the road, its fortified buildings perched on rocks above the river. Then there's the little bridge that leads into that part of town and almost distracts me from the turn I need to take into the market square. It's a curious route at this point as we seem to be heading into a car park but the road cuts through this, runs by shops and turns to cross a narrow bridge heading towards the Col du Buis, which today is Ouvert. At this point the road is exceptionally narrow and it feels like we are riding up someone's' driveway until we break free from the town and head into the hills. The road continues narrow and the surface had often fallen away making progress cautious but steady as we gained height once more. With the height came the views across the landscape towards the mountains. Further on the roads became wider with much improved surfaces and we were able to crack open the throttle with much more enthusiasm as we raced towards our next point of interest, the Gorges Du Verdon, known as Frances' Grand Canyon (probably only in tourist brochures though).

The D71 approach road to this natural wonder gives no hint of what to expect as it is surrounded by scrub land with occasional decent views but appears fairly uninspiring after our day thus far. The road surface is good and as time is marching on we take the opportunity to quickly get some miles behind us while thoughts of locating fuel are also beginning to creep in to Festa and my concentration. Then just around another rocky corner the drama of the gorge begins to be revealed as a metal Armco barrier is all that protects us from a huge drop. I want to look over to my right but know that I must find somewhere safe to park up first. We leave our bikes in a cafe car park and walk across the road to peer over the tiny retaining wall. Wow! The drop off the other side is sheer and the view is astonishing, it's huge. I admit to being a little sceptical when I initially read 'Frances' Grand Canyon' but this truly is Grand.

A little further along we find a gap in the wall that leads to a viewing platform via some steep concrete steps. I can't imagine who would build such a thing but we venture down and stand scanning the vista before us, it's like sitting in an eagles nest. For me this is quite enough but for Kryten and Festa standing on the wall that protects us from entering the next life with a splat is the only way to be photographed at such a place, I can hardly bare to watch, but decide to film the stunt just in case I can capture some footage for You've Been Framed'.

Alas I don't get to claim my £250 and we return to the bikes all in one piece. I watch as a large motor home passes by its driver craning to see into the gorge and I want to shout 'Just watch the road' as he seems blissfully unaware of the precipitous drop a meter or so behind the low wall. As we make our way further along the road the gorge is once again hidden from view, but I know it's there and ride even more cautiously than normal. It's not long before another corner unveils the impressive arch of the Pont de l'Artuby which spans the gorge 182m above its base. We crossed this bridge when we came to it (ha ha) and parked up alongside the many cars that were already here. The attraction? Another bungee jump from what was claimed to be Europe's' highest bungee jumping bridge. This one was different though as when I enquired about the possibility of jumping off I was told I had to produce a doctors' note certifying I was completely insane and had nothing left to live for. We watched a couple of lunatics perform their leap of faith before returning to the bikes for the last part of the journey.

It took longer than I expected to complete todays 160 miles but we eventually arrived at our hotel for the evening in the village of Les Salles sur Verdon. It's still pleasantly warm and we are keen to get showered and changed and are looking forward to a well-earned beer. Inside my French seems to be holding up and we are directed to our room on the first floor (premier étage). It's just the ticket, large and airy but with one major plus, the view from the balcony over the vivid blue water of Lac Sainte-Croix, bonus! This lake is really a reservoir completed in 1974 and used to provide hydroelectricity, the original village is now completely submerged.

Anyway, Festa and Kryten get showered and changed and then head into the village while I faff about and eventually achieve cleanliness. They return with wine which we drink while admiring the view before heading back out to locate nourishment. The village has a small, neatly block paved square with one or two likely restaurants and we enjoy food that isn't pizza for a change. It's a short walk back to the hotel and we walk down to the lakeside to see people swimming before returning for a chill out beer on the hotels patio, all jolly civilized.

Monday - Les Salles-sur-Verdon to Le Monêtier-les-Bains (180miles 6 hrs).

Wake up after a sound nights' sleep and stand on the balcony admiring the privileged view we have across the lake and surrounding hillsides. While the UK endures another miserable summer we anticipate fun in the southern French sun while sipping Krytens morning tea, another day avoiding overpriced coffee and croissants! That said I would like to have had the time to sit on the patio with breakfast contemplating a day exploring the surroundings here, but we must keep moving.

I start by taking a deep breath and mentally practicing my language skills ready to enquire the whereabouts of local petrol. I rehearse my speech but also try to imagine what may come as a reply. Amazingly I manage to make myself understood without resorting to hand flapping or the traditional British method of indignant shouting. The reply was, I assumed, a detailed account of the location of the garage from which I managed to deduce was on the edge of the village back the way we came in. The bikes showed signs of the distances we had travelled thus far and still had the remains of early morning dew attracting airborne dust as we reattached our luggage and made ourselves ready for the day,

With full tanks we follow the D957 out of town as it falls gradually to meet the shore of the lake offering tantalising glimpses of an unreal turquoise blue through the scrublands along the way. It's not long before we stumble across the Pont de Galetas and stop to wonder at the sight that greets us. The bridge isn't particularly high but it crosses the river Verdon squeezed between the steep rock faces that hold it in place. There are brightly coloured canoes and pedeloes beneath us making their relaxed way further into the gorge and I think we all felt we would like to have joined them on this warm and sunny day.

We push on for another mile or so before turning onto the D952 at the sign that says 'Gorges du Verdon' and once again the road width diminishes and starts gain altitude through a series of bends shrouded in trees. To our right there is a strong sense that we are climbing along the gorge we saw from the bridge and occasionally there is a framed view back to the lake. It's a good feeling winding open the throttle out of the tight turns and feeling the bike surge forwards with the trees rushing by outside my visor. With little traffic to encounter the surges gather pace as confidence increases until we break out of the trees and slow to observe the ever changing scenery. The road is now clinging to the sides of the gorge and it is clear that its' route has been carved out of the rock face. Below us we can see the blue water of the river, but it is a long way below us and the tiny stone wall that lines the road in places seems barely adequate. We pull up in what may be a passing place and leave the bikes to walk back a few meters and have a look over the edge of the small wall. It's a sight that has me taking a step backwards before returning better prepared for the vision that lurks beyond, that is one heck of a drop, and I've just ridden past it!

If the precipitous drop wasn't enough for one day the sight that greeted us just after we set off was something else. As we rounded another curve on our mountain road I had to double take the vision of a senior citizen striding out purposefully towards me dressed only in a pair of red Speedo swimming trunks, nothing else, no shoes or hat even, just red Speedos! Maybe I was suffering altitude sickness?

Progressing further we thread our way through the narrow streets of a tiny hamlet before stopping in the car park of a recommended view point called 'Point Sublime'. It's very hot now and we debate whether or not to leave clothing with the bikes before heading off to find the view. It's a tricky route we tread over shiny smooth rock in our biking boots to access the viewpoint which is set on a prominent rock surrounded by rusting protective fencing about 400meters from the car park. An excellent view for sure, but 'sublime?' We have already seen better today from our bikes. Oddly, when we return to our bikes, the promising looking stalls that border the car park can only sell us honey or tat but not the ice cool drinks we would have gladly purchased

Back on the bikes again we follow the road as it forces its way between rocks and hard places sometimes round tight and sinuous bends and sometimes as it breaks into a gallop with the occasional straight bit. We are heading downwards and eventually join a fast flowing river where the road accompanies it at times under overhanging cliffs. The valley is less steep sided and as it levels out and widens we start to pass large holiday caravan sites and more houses. Eventually we turn away from the river and the road becomes wider allowing us to crack on at a more lively pace. It's not long though before we encounter water once again this time in the form of the Lac de Castillon whose shoreline we follow closely. The

Lac is another manmade affair, beneath which lies another sacrificed village, and after a bend in the road we find ourselves crossing the huge arc shaped dam that EDF use to produce hydroelectricity.

After leaving the lac behind us we turn onto the D955 through some anonymous countryside that would be great anywhere else but in such Alpine company pales to insignificance. Still the pace is good and the road surfaces allow us to make swift progress towards the town of Colmars where we are greeted by the sight of a Savoy fort (built in 1693) perched on a hill above the road. On the other side of town the D908 leads us away from the tree lined streets of Colmars through the village of Allos and on to the ghostly ski town of La Foux D'Allos situated seemingly at the dead end of an ever steepening and encroaching valley. We ride through the tall mostly wooden ski chalets that line the road until it appears we will be riding along public footpaths in order to continue our journey. At the last moment a sign announcing 'Col d'Allos – Ouvert' is spied and the road diverts sharply right following rocks that line the sides.

Now the road is an unfeasibly narrow strip of tarmac not much wider than a family saloon car and it's climbing, snaking its way to join the path of a redundant ski lift. This is less daunting on the bikes due to our narrowness and luckily we only need to negotiate a couple of cars coming the other way as we gain height leaving the trees below us to eventually pull into a car park where the road crests the hill.

It's a quiet and peaceful place once our engine noise drifts away on the slight breeze but the views are not so spectacular as we are surrounded by more hills. It seems like a good place to stop though and crack open the flask for a brew and a bite to eat. Festa feels the urge to do the Kate Bush thing and goes 'Running up that hill' in order to see if the anticipated view can be had higher up. He returns to report it is no better and we sit on the hill in the mid-day sunshine above the car park admiring what is, after all, a splendid vista of Alpine peaks, it's a bit reminiscent of a scene from 'Last of the Summer Wine' although this is clearly not Holmfirth..

On the bikes and over the top we pass the 'Refuge du Col d'Allos' with an inscription that reads A.T. 2250m and it sure feels like we're up that high with the surrounding peaks slightly below us. The road is a little wider and doesn't feel too threatening so we feel we can relax a slightly and enjoy the twisty descent into the valley. Well maybe I relaxed a little too much or maybe it was the tea but I very soon needed a 'comfort break' and stopped in woodland near a small hut where it soon became apparent many such 'comfort stops' had occurred. Locating a reasonable place to, err, get comfortable I looked out and realised just how far up we were and how far down we still needed to go and, I could see the road we would be taking. The road looped back on its self, holding on to the sides of a valley but with very little to stop one leaving it suddenly and irreversibly, eek!

With the narrow twisties behind us and back down to a more reasonable level we joined the D900 then D954. These were in contrast to the mountain roads, faster A roads allowing us to open the throttle a tad more enthusiastically. Soon after joining the D954 there were brief views of water through the trees and then, after a bend, the rich blue waters stretched out before us. This was the 'Lac de Serre-Ponçon' one of Western Europe's' largest artificial lakes and another to have required the evacuation and flooding of a village. On an island stands the little Chapelle Saint-Michel that once stood on the top of a hill above the village.

We shadow the lake shore for a while and then turn away following the road gradually uphill with some very nice sweeping bends and a smooth surface that inspired confidence. Like commentators curse on any sporting event just as we were getting into a groove following Krytens inspiring lead we so nearly come a cropper. With far more speed than skill coming the other way is a clown on a red Ducati Hypermotard. He was hanging off the thing that far that although the bike may have been on his side of the road (there were no white lines) he most certainly was not. How Kryten managed to avoid the idiot heaven only knows but a well-timed reaction swerve saved the day and we pulled up to the side of the road to catch our breath.

Further along, as Festa this time pushes on in front, there is an excellent photo opportunity in the form of a tiny church perched on the hillside overlooking the lake, its exposed bell tower revealing two bells framed in arched stonework. Kryten and I can't resist then, with images captured, we race to re-join Festa waiting further down the road. After some tricky navigation we join the busy N94 passing Embrun before returning to the more pleasant D902 that traces the Guil River for some of our journey and forms part of the Route des Grandes Alps.

The Route des Grandes Alpes (Great Alpine Road) is a 425 mile long route through the French Alps. It extends from Menton (next to Monaco) to Thonon les Bains near Lake Geneva and includes some of the highest and most beautiful mountain passes in Europe. The construction of the route started in 1909 when the Alps were still a fairly isolated region of France. Construction was completed in 1937 with the opening of the Col de l'Iseran but variations were made in 1995 to include the Col de la Colombière and the Col de Aravis.

We are now in the steep sided Guil Gorge where the road is once again narrow and meandering but are brought to a halt by roadwork traffic control lights on the approach to a narrow bridge. Here we sit patiently waiting while being joined by a couple of cars. As the lights flick to amber the headlights of two motorcycles appear in my mirrors as they filter past the couple of queuing cars. Kryten, who was in front, moves off as the road in front was clear but the two BMW GS bikes hurtle past causing us all to swerve and brake violently as they bully their way onto the bridge and speed into the distance (what a pair of chimps). Kryten is on a roll, his second near miss of the day, could he make the hat trick before our destination?

Onwards through the village of Arieux before turning left and working our way to the 2361m summit of the Col d'Isoard. A quick dip into Wikipedia reveals that this Col is a frequent challenge for the competitors in the Tour de France. If you are interested in such things it is particularly memorable for the exploits of Fausto Coppi, Bernard Thevenet and Louison Bobet but I couldn't be bothered to find out why. Anyway, there is a small cycling museum here along with an obelisk type memorial to Coppi and Bobet. More fascinating to me was the guy putting his bike back onto the roof of his car. Why? Because the bike only had one pedal as its owner only had one leg! 2361m on one leg, that guy deserves his own obelisk!

After the essential photographs are captured in front of the summits plaque we squeeze back into helmets and gloves before remounting to begin our descent to the town of Briançon. Kryten and Festa manage a far quicker pace than I dare of course and Krytens overtaking prowess means that I am soon left dawdling along behind several cars. Not that I mind, I believe that it is very important that in any group riding all participants should ride at a pace they feel comfortable with and not be drawn into trying to keep pace with faster, more skilful riders.

I catch up with the duo as they wait for me near a petrol garage since we need to replenish our dwindling fuel supplies. The town is busy as it is around going home time and this is a much larger place than we have encountered over the last couple of days. I have been here before though with my family so I soon work our way out of the melee and on to the D1091 heading for our evening halt at Les Monetier les Bains. Having passed through several small villages that line the base of this valley we arrive in our destination and are obliged to follow a horse and cart containing a very jolly family whose kids delighted in waving at us.

With only a slight navigational error we park up outside the tall chalet styled hotel and climb the stairs to the reception. It has an out of season feel, we are shown a nice secure garage for our bikes and our room is basic but pleasant enough. Kryten points out that it is his turn to choose where he is to sleep and a discussion ensues which culminates in him sleeping on the bottom bunk in his own part of the room. That resolved and washing and changing completed we head out into the town and locate the Sherper Supermarket to purchase a few luxuries (ok beer mainly). The town continues its' out of season feel when we search for somewhere to eat and find, after a couple of laps, most places are 'Fermé'. Fortunately we stumble upon an "Open all Hours" style shop that seems to employ various family members in the rear cooking pizza (our traditional diet). Whilst we await the pizza we are distracted by the shops' many other temptations and eventually leave with an arm full of stuff, Arkwright would have been r, r, rubbing his hands together!

Tuesday - Monetier les Bains to Annecy (160miles 5hrs 15mins).

I slept well following the beer and pizza extravaganza and am keen to get started on todays' adventure. Once again we decide against overpriced petit déjeuner and enjoy the delights of Krytens travel kettle tea making facilities. In the garage we are reunited with our bikes, still huddled together in one corner and are soon loaded up and ready for the off.

Out of Les Monetier les Bains we continue along the D1091 valley road for a mile or two until the Col du Laurtaret where we turn onto the D902. This road is narrow and starts a steady climb clinging onto the side of what at first seems to be a gently sloping hill. I wave Kryten and Festa past me and assume my now customary position at the rear with a good view of their lines. The gentle bit soon gives way to some attention grabbing steep rocky hills and we are on the outside of the road.

There is no attempt to engineer any form of protective barrier between us and a very rapid decent to the valley below, just a thin grass and stone verge. I struggle to keep up with Festa and Kryten but maintain a view as they overtake the various shaped motor-homes wheezing up the hill in front of us. There are cyclists to on this popular Tour d'France climb along with cars and fellow motorcyclists.

As we labour relentlessly upwards Krytens' normally excellent judgement is briefly over-ridden by a desire to get past yet another ponderous camper. We are approaching a tight right hander with a small stone bridge supporting the road and a stream cascading to our right and beneath the bridge. Krytens' view seems clear past the camper but as he begins his overtake rapidly descending cyclists fly over the bridge and into his intended path. There is no room on this narrow road for the camper, cyclists and Kryten but miraculously everyone emerges unscathed, except for a few choice hand gestures and unrepeatable French words!

The higher we go the scarier the road gets with doubtless magnificent views all around us. But I'm not looking, I daren't look, I have to keep focused on the road, one tiny mistake and, "They think it's all over...it is now". I do manage to look up occasionally, more in desperation of end to this "fun", and spot a building which I hope signals the summit. It kind of does and we pass a roadside monument to Henri Desgrange, (instigator and first director of the

Tour d' France. Apparently whenever the tour crosses the Col a wreath is laid here in his memory. The "Souvenir Henri Desgrange" is awarded to the first rider across the summit of the highest mountain in each year's tour). This is not the summit however, it is close to a tunnel which is a single lane through the mountain and controlled by traffic lights (one of the highest such installations in Europe, 2556 m for those anorak wearers amongst you.

We pass the tunnel and continue our climb but the road surface here has changed to a rich dark black smooth tarmac and I begin to feel like I may live to see the summit after all. A few tight corners later we arrive at a car park, 2645m up on top of the Col d Galibier.

Now get ready to don those anoraks once more as we learn more about this famous Col. It was first used on The Tour in 1911 and the first guy over the top was Emile Georget who, along with Gustave Garrigou and Paul Duboc, were the only riders not to walk up! In 2011 the tour climbed up twice to commemorate 100 years since its first inclusion and Andy Schleck won the first ever summit finish here which was also the highest ever stage finish of the race.

Anyway, we take a little time to find some fairly flat ground that we feel will ensure our bikes are still upright when we return to them in this bumpy loose gravel car park. As usual with such a place there are vehicles from varied European countries and even a 1050 Triumph Tiger from the UK. Finally convinced our bikes would be safe we head up a gravel track that leads to a vantage point from which we can clearly see the sinuous road that led us here. We are surrounded by Alps to all sides. Below us the lower slopes are a patchwork of green that looks as if it has been worn through in places where the grey rock protrudes. To the sides and in the distance the high peaks remain covered in ice and snow, there are no trees here, we are too high up. It's an excellent place to strike a pose and photograph each other standing tall against such a rugged backdrop taking time to absorb the scenery that surrounds us.

Back down in the car park we meet the owner of the Triumph who hails from Scarborough telling us he is here on his own and sounds like a well-travelled chap. We watch him go, listening to the sound of the triple motor reverberating off the surroundings then soon after begin our own descent. The road surface demands our attention as there is a scattering of gravel in awkward places but at least we don't feel quite so intimidated by the steepness of the sides. So, while concentrating on several things, I am a little surprised when we turn into a corner and find a bloke with a camera in the road taking our pictures (later, at home, I remember the name he had on the side of his van and find three pictures of each of us. It transpires that vain motorcyclists and cyclists can purchase their photos as a memento, so that's what I did. 12 Euros plus 4.5 Euros postage may sound expensive but that's a lot cheaper than the photo the police took of me a few years ago!).

We pass through the village of Valloire and soon begin to climb once again. This time the climb is easier as the road is comparatively straight, has a small protective wall against the side and is amongst the trees. The views are no less spectacular though as we are climbing the Col Du Telegraphe. We pass some odd sights on the way as well, there's a bloke on a silly looking low rider bike and a chap Nordic Skiing up. We ride over the 1566m summit without stopping and continue down to the bottom of the valley where the road meets L'Arc River which we follow to the bigger town of Modane. It's cool in the mountains but much warmer and has a far more industrial feeling down in the town.

Quickly out of town we begin to climb once more passing through small villages and out of season ski resorts to join the D902 road that takes us up our third big Col of the day the Col de l'Iseran. Once more we leave the trees behind but this time we enjoy a far more relaxed journey as the road advances through a high valley tracing a fresh Alpine stream and in places crossing it using rustic looking stone bridges. Outside of the village of Bonneval-sur-Arc the road becomes noticeably steeper as it gains the final 950m in height to reach the summit. There are a few mighty unprotected drops on the way until we come to rest in the large car park to have a wander around.

There is a sign here that informs us we are on the D902 and that the Col de l'Iseran is at an altitude of 2770m (9088 feet), it's a splendid place for another photo session. This Col also lays claim, along with several others, to being the highest paved road in Europe which may account for the number of YouTube videos available and the unusually large car park we are standing in. Unfortunately, being the highest is about all this place has to offer as it is not the most attractive and oddly doesn't provide us with the best views either.

Back on the bikes we pass the uninviting looking grey stone cafe to begin our descent and it soon becomes clear that this will require full concentration. The views in front are spectacular but this is because the side of the road falls away sharply with little to stop an ill-judged turn turning into disaster. I am acutely aware of this but can't help but keep glancing at the view which nearly results in me running into the deep ditch on the "safe" side of the road. Eventually the view gets too tempting and we pull over to sit, admire and photograph it, our front wheels pointing towards the ski town of Val-d'Isere way below us.

For me Val-d'Isere evokes fond memories of watching Ski-Sunday on BBC 2, David Vine sporting his woolly hat in an exotic location far removed from where I lived. Now I am here the town seems like many others and I have no real desire to hang about preferring instead to see all I need to from the seat of my bike as we pass through. The road out of town seems hemmed in by the imposing rocks that rise above it until we reach the Tunnel de la Daille with its five Olympic rings hinting of the towns' past winter sporting importance. This tunnel, and the several that follow, introduce us to the bright blue waters of the Lac du Chevril briefly before plunging us back into darkness once more. It's a fine place to practice the juvenile pleasure of dropping down a cog or two and blasting out the glorious tones of a 750cc Suzuki engine through a Leo Vince can against the bare stone walls of the tunnel that surrounds us.

Later we are still on the D902 but here it isn't such a pleasure to ride as there are many more vehicles and the road is much busier all the way to Bourg-Saint- Maurice, another large and missable town. After the town the D902 takes on a completely different character as it narrows considerably to climb through some densely wooded areas with some very tight bends leading me to wonder if we are even on the right road. Eventually we leave the woods and are unexpectedly gifted a wide open and flowing road that almost wafts us through a delightful valley floor. At the end of the valley as the road begins to climb once more there is an opportunity to look back at a most excellent section of tranquil road. At what must be the summit the sign reads Cormete Roselend and informs us we are 1968m up. There's a small car park containing a couple of stalls selling stuff we didn't fancy much and then a vehicle rolls up loaded with cyclists. These guys set themselves up to freewheel down the way we are heading so we remount and begin another rapid descent.

This time the road begins gently sloping and it feels a bit like the start of a rollercoaster ride as it picks up momentum gradually. We can see the road with its many twists and turns below us and there are very few other users about to spoil the run. Lower down we ride alongside the Lac de Roselend briefly before rushing into the small town of Beaufort in search of petrol. Fortunately we locate it the form of a small Elan pavement style garage with a single pump. On the way down Kryten had spotted Festas' bespoke top-box holder had come loose and things had got a little sideways. What was required was a small nut and bolt and this, being a garage, was the perfect place to source one, if only we knew the French for nut and bolt. After a little deliberation Festa decided to check his extensive (not) range of spares located under his seat. As luck would have it he had miraculously packed the exact part and we were soon back on the road again.

Time was getting on a bit by now and the roads were nice, we are in the Alps after all, but more purposeful and busier with lorries and coaches, the sort of traffic one rarely finds on high Alpine passes. As we draw closer to our destination I spy an oasis that we had been looking for some time, a fruit seller. It's a welcome break from the road and from the biscuits and nuts that normally form a large part of our travelling diet. The stall has all manner of tempting juicy offerings and I come away with a small bag full. Sitting in the warm afternoon sun slurping up the juice that ran down my chin felt very refreshing and set me up for the final push into town.

Not long after we turn off the main road onto the D909A which leads us to the very edge of the beautiful Lac d'Annecy. The road literally runs right along the east shore separated from the beach only by a log style low fence. There are many people enjoying a whole range of water sports and I would love to have been able to stop and jump in as the water looked clear and inviting. That said, I feel I would have picked a more conducive place to lob my beach towel than 2m from the road edge as some had chosen to do.

As we made our way along the shore the road seemed to narrow further and get busier while we caught up with more ponderous motor-homes and slow moving lorries. At times the beauty of the view was in stark contrast to the diesel filled atmosphere we were riding through in this stop start congestion. As we entered the town of Annecy the traffic frequently ground to a complete halt and it was so tightly packed that filtering was impossible, still that meant I had more time to navigate.

After a long crawl through the heat and a tight confusing bend I realised that we needed to turn off next to the Hotel Splendid and follow the signs to "Police Municipal". Now the route got interesting, we had to push through tiny streets alive with pedestrians and at one point go through a tunnel between shops, it felt like being in a scene from the Italian Job (the original one not the crappy remake).

We popped out of this labyrinth onto an extraordinarily busy junction where I had to pull over and think of the right way to go next. I chose correctly leading us through numerous contortions until I recognised the road upon which I remembered our hotel was located. This was great but someone had decided to dig it up and there was much confusion. Another roadside head scratching session ensued before we finally arrived outside the front doors of the hotel, an advantage of the motorcycle being where one can park in such circumstances. Inside the glossy facade of the Best Western was not matched in our pokey room with its view of the road-works below.

With three adults and three lots of bike paraphernalia space was tight but we each managed to claim a small piece of floor as our own and were soon showered, changed and out in search of Annecy's' medieval town centre. After a couple of adjustments we found ourselves amongst the canals that help earn this place the tourist nickname of the Venice of Savoie (probably only by tourist brochures again). We photograph each other on a bridge in front of the "Palais de l'Isle" (the old prison) which is a symbol of the town and one of the most photographed monuments in all of France (it's nice to be original). The area is thronged with the people of many nations but we finally manage to sit in a canal-side restaurant as the sun begins to depart and the area is lit by many coloured lights that adorn the charming town and reflect back from the waters of the canals.

Wednesday – Annecy to Culoz (35miles 1 hour).

After a miserable excuse for an "American style breakfast" we are soon out of the 'Not at its Best Western' hotel heading towards Culoz, a small town in the Ain Department of the Rhône-Alps region. It's a pleasant enough route over a modest hillside and through some wooded sections but the tight narrow roads make for slow progress on a day when time could be against us. What's the hurry? Well today is when the path of our Alpine tour crosses that of the 99th. running of The Tour d'France cycle race, made more exciting as Britain's' very own legend Bradley Wiggins is leading the race and is expected to do well at the end.

There are times though when I doubt my carefully planned route will ever lead us to Culoz as the roads get smaller and seem to drift away from where I feel we should be heading. There are some very tight turns and at one point we circumnavigate three sides of a small roadside cottage. Once over the crest of a hill there are tantalising glimpses of the River Rhône and Lac du Bourget but they still seem to be a long way off.

Eventually our perseverance pays off and we cross the Rhône on the Pont de la Loi joining the many vehicles that all have a similar aim to ourselves, that of parking up in the town and gaining a vantage point from which to watch the race pass by. Our bikes give us a huge advantage in the congested and chaotic town as we are able to ride into an already full car park outside Le Poste and squeeze neatly into a space. Once parked we then use an advantage afforded us by the excellent top-boxes we now all sport. Riding gear goes into the box and walking gear comes out giving us the freedom of not having to worry too much about lugging bike gear around with us, oh yeh 'Joie de vivre' brothers. The sun is out, the sky is a clear blue and after applying copious amounts of sun cream we set out to find the start of the climb.

Today is stage 10 on the tour and the riders will be travelling 194.5km (about 120miles) from Macon to Bellegarde-sur-Valserine. Bradley Wiggins has the leaders' yellow jersey but will not be the first rider we see today as others are more capable mountain climbers. We are going to be on the 1501m Col du Grand Colombier, the second of todays' big climbs. This is a 'hors catégorie' climb which is a French term favoured by Le Tour and used to designate a climb that is 'beyond categorization', ie Well Hard! When you learn that the length of the climb is 18.3km over which distance the riders climb 1255 meters with an average percentage gradient of 6.9% you can start to appreciate just how difficult a route this is and how fit the riders must be.

I freely admit that I'm not fit, well at least not as fit as my fellow bikers so I am relieved at the relatively easy start to our climb. It is through a very average looking street of houses and as we start we stray into the clutches of the Tat peddlers and end up purchasing overpriced nonsense as mementoes of the day (one of mine being a €20 baseball cap for my son which on return to the UK he never wore preferring his £3 chav-hat bought from Sports Direct, but I digress). Clear of the tat the crowds that line the streets lower down begin to thin out as the road becomes increasingly steeper and the sun ever warmer. I am struck now by the amount of people that have chosen to cycle up here, not just the macho lycra-clads but the many shapes, sizes and ages. For some reason I hadn't expected anyone to be allowed on the road during the day until after the race had passed by. I suppose it would be something to be able to say one had ridden the route on the very same day as the Tour.

After leaving the houses and tat behind and walking through some small vineyards we decide to leave the road and turn onto a rough track that seems to head upwards promising to cut out some of the bends while also providing shade under some trees. One or two others share this view it seems as we make our way along soon leaving everyone else behind. At a clearing we have a commanding view back over the town, the plain and the River Rhône so stop to catch our breath and admire the panorama laid out before us. In the town the crowd was continuing to grow in anticipation of the spectacle soon to pass through. Onwards then and relentlessly upwards we trek with me slowly loosing contact with Kryten and Festa and the jolly banter we shared at the start slowly dissipating into puffing and blowing. This made for a very peaceful walk that after some time became a little too peaceful. Gone were the people, there was just the three of us spread out along the rocky track lost amongst the trees. Where was the road that we had left behind such a long time ago and would we even see Le Tour at all? It wasn't looking good and time was ticking by.

Just as all hope began to fade we stumbled out of the woods and onto a tarmaced road, there were parked cars and people and they all seemed to be heading in one direction...yes! The road was in sight and we emerged 5km from the summit, right next to the sign that announced this as it happened. There was no appetite for continuing to the top so we worked our way back downhill for a few hundred yards to pick a spot on the roadside to plonk down, drink Krytens tea and wait. It was quite a party atmosphere with the folk of several nations (notably Australia and Norway) engaging in good humoured banta. At one point a struggling lady cyclist passed through being pushed up by her partner and an Australian shouted "You're doin' a great job of pullin' that guy up Sheila, keep goin'" There was much laughter followed by a huge amount of encouragement from the crowd with the 'Hup, Hup, Hup' cries accompanying the applause, banging together of tubes and the clanking of cow bells, brilliant! There were many 'amateur' lycra clad enthusiasts that passed us this day but the one that struck us most was the young (14 yrs ish) lad who arrived on his bike alone and settled in to watch his heroes having ridden 13kms up a very challenging road, good effort fella.

It was a long hot wait with texts being fired in from our UK cycle nut who updated us with progress from in front of his Eurosport TV. Eventually helicopters could be heard above us as the tour began to grind its way up towards us. This was preceded by police motorcycle outriders, numerous brightly decorated sponsor vehicles hurling freebies, read Tat, at the most enthusiastic spectators, that'll be Kryten then, media motorcycles and an occasional late cyclist, namely an Italian who seemed to want to be in all our photographs!

It was a riot of colour and noise, vehicle horns blasting out in competition with the music from the advertisers' vehicles and the engines of the circling media helicopters. Then suddenly the first racers came into view. I've no idea who they all were but take your pick from such names as Team Sky's Boasson, Hagen, Porte, Rogers and Froome, then Voeckler, Van den Broeck, Scarponi, Sanchez, Devenyns, Voigt, Casar, Fovonoy or Evans. I did manage to spot the group containing the yellow jersey of the since knighted Sir Bradley Wiggins, (Go Wiggo! I believe is the customary popular parlance) he swished past to eventually finish in 13th. place on the day and to overall tour victory and Olympic glory later. The first over the top today was Thomas Voeckler who went on to win the stage and the 'most aggressive rider' of the stage.

And that was it, the last clang of a cowbell rang out and the sound of the helicopters drifted into the distance leaving us to pack up and head back down. It was at this point that we realised that if we were at the 5km from the top marker of an 18km road then we now had a 13km walk back to the bikes, still, it was all downhill, how hard could it be? As we headed down it soon became clear just how hard this could be. Thing is, Newton's elementary Law states that what goes up must come down and this was precisely what began to happen. All of the Lycra Loonies that had pedalled up now began their descent and there were a lot of them, most of whom seemed to be in a very great hurry. Now you might think that isn't so bad but then we also must negotiate the various motor-homes that are turning in the road along with the cars. Put this lot together, random manoeuvring vehicles and suicidal cyclists all on a narrow piece of mountainous French B road with us pedestrians, our backs to the approaching mayhem, and it makes for a very nervous retreat.

After an hour or so of total chaos the traffic began to thin out and we were pretty much the only ones left on the litter strewn road. It became a relentless, unforgiving march with occasional views to lift our flagging spirits but never, not once, a nice level bit. In places the road was incredibly steep, especially on a couple of tight bends, making one wonder just what kind of fitness is required to cycle up such a challenge. As we at last approached the town we were greeted by a drunken Norwegian, dressed in his national flag, staggering about in the vineyard short cut we had chosen, but I had no time for his singing or his enquiries about the Queen, my feet hurt, I was knackered, hot, thirsty and just wanted to be back on level ground again.

The first glimpse of La Poste and the bikes came as a great relief. God knows how long it had taken us to get back but the sight of those three bikes standing alone in the car park was like the end of double maths lesson on a sunny afternoon. It wasn't long before we were letting the bikes do all the work as we headed back to Annecy almost retracing our route (I got a bit lost in places) which seemed far longer on the return trip. Back at the hotel after an inspection of the complaining feet and a quick change we head back into the photogenic part of town. Weary and hungry we retraced yesterdays' steps.

Thursday – Annecy to Epernay (330miles 6 hours).

Slept like a log after yesterdays' walking and awoke with my legs letting me know how they felt about it. I wasn't looking forward to this day as it would be one primarily designed to move us around 330miles north requiring around six to seven hours of riding. We were also in no mood to speculate a further twelve Euros each on a crap breakfast and would be relying on the magic of Krytens' tea flask once again for sustenance on the journey.

We joined the busy morning traffic heading out of Annecy and were soon on a motorway leaving the town behind before turning onto the smaller roads. Although we needed to cover a fair distance I planned for us to at least start the day with a little countryside riding (The alternative would have been to try to ride the motorways around Geneva and I couldn't imagine that being a barrel of laughs). It was pleasant enough passing through the villages in this flat plain landscape although navigation on such back roads is always slightly more demanding. We crossed over the busy A40 motorway and made our way around the French / Swiss border to the much larger but uninspiring town of Gex. From here the D1005 would lead us to what I had planned as the last treat of the day, climbing the 1323m of the Col de la Faucille,

One of the best known climbs in the Jura Mountains for cyclists the Col has appeared on several occasions in the Tour de France since

1951. In 2004 Lance Armstrong, despite already clinching the Tour, chased down an escape as it contained Filippo Simeoni. Simeoni had testified in a doping probe and tried to implicate Armstrong. Armstrong had called him a compulsive liar, which given events in 2012 was a tad un-sportsman like as it turned out.

Anyway, cycling politics aside, the Col de la Faucille proved to be a disappointing ride due to it being quite a busy road and it having no real character to its curves. Towards the top it began to get cold and grey so by the summit there was nothing that made any of us want to stick around. The descent was most notable for the length of time it took us. We seemed to be riding downhill for absolutely ages and it felt as if we were coming out of an Alpine festival weekend back down to a school on Monday reality.

When we arrived back in the real world we very soon found the links to the motorway we needed all contained yellow signage with the legend "Route Barrée". Oh dear! We carried on regardless half expecting to find we could squeeze the bikes through whatever was Barrée - ing? the road but eventually ground to a halt where the road surface had been removed. Turning back was never really considered as an option as that would be admitting defeat. Then, like a shining beacon in the dead of night, Kryten produced his dormant sat-nav. and a route to circumnavigate the obstruction was duly plotted. It proved to be quite a pleasant alternative along some unusual roads that passed by a deep looking gorge at one point before the welcome signs for the N5 motorway began to populate the roadside. It was a jolly good time to stop and enjoy a celebratory cup of tea.

From here we had a long dull two hundred mile dash up the French motorway system. There was nothing else for it but to get our heads down and blast away the miles as quickly and safely as possible. As the time dragged by anonymous French landscape changed to different anonymous French landscape and gradually I noticed the speed creep up until I felt comfortable with 90+mph showing on the speedo. There was little to do but keep a wary eye out for wayward French drivers and inch my arse around my sparsely padded seat in search of a position that allowed blood flow to continue. My shoulders and neck took a bit of a pounding as the tiny nose fairing could only offer limited protection to my large frame. I did experiment by pressing my head into the tank bag from time to time but this looked and felt so ridiculous that I soon gave up. In my mirrors both Festa and Kryten too could be seen performing similar "adjustments" with Krytens' arm waving techniques being the most visual and no doubt confusing for surrounding motorists.

The further north we ventured the greyer, colder and wetter the weather became making it even more difficult to summon up enthusiasm to remount the bike following a petrol and pee stop at a service station before the last 'big push'. Eventually signs we were getting there began to become more frequent until we left the motorway to join the A road to our destination, but not before coughing up around €20 for the use of the road (maybe it's time to start charging Johnny Foreigner for using our roads?).

By the time we arrived at our hotel it was cold, dark and raining and the entrance wasn't exactly easy to find. The Hotel web-site boasts "Our luxurious hotel suites are housed in a renovated former military building which provides views across vineyards, and offer everything you need for a comfortable stay. Each suite is equipped with a kitchenette, a fridge and a microwave, and other amenities such as free Wi-Fi and cable / satellite television" which all sounds tickerty-boo. There were the usual language issues as the guy that could speak English was tied up and I tried my best to understand the unusual directions to our room. Back outside in the rain, then to the third building along, up some stairs to the premier étage (first floor as you learnt earlier), along the corridor to our room, the number of which was higher than I could count in French, my head nearly exploded!

The room was ok, basic and bear it contained a small kitchen / dining area, a bedroom, bathroom and living area. After the usual bed allocation debate we were able to cast off our sodden ridding gear. I was fortunate to have the grown-ups room to myself and set to dangling my riding gear over any available hanger. Festa had dragged out a low put-you-up style thing and had performed his usual lightening transformation into civilian attire while Kryten searched for extra bedding. "If I can't have an extra blanket I'll freeze to death" he complained. We returned through the rain to reception to try to explain this to the non-English speaking receptionist. Eventually our request was successfully translated and we were lead back around the many rooms at a brisk pace by a very, let's say 'happy' fella in search of Krytens auxiliary insulation.

With Krytens' insulation issues resolved and a glass or two of Festas' red wine consumed the pressing issue now was the location of an evening meal. The hotel didn't seem to be an option so we headed back out in the rain for the twenty minute walk into town. Few places look great in the rain and Epernay is no exception, its' grey streets and rundown buildings did little to lift the spirits. The lights that signalled the centre were a welcome sight and we took very little time in deciding on a busy pizza restaurants' inviting glow (who'd have thought we'd end up in a pizza place?).

Inside the atmosphere was pleasant and many local folk seemed to frequent the place. Beer, pizza and more beer made it a difficult place to leave for the return hike, in the still pouring rain, uphill to our hotel. That evening I was very pleased to receive a text telling me my son had done exceptionally well in his SATs tests and would be in the top set at his new school. I slept, surrounded by drying apparel, hopping for at least a little sunshine for what I had planned for the following day.

Friday - Walking tour of Épernay attractions.

Oh dear, it's Friday 13th. And so much for thoughts of a rain free day! Out of my window there were indeed vineyards on the surrounding green hills but these were shrouded in mist and rolling rain clouds. There was no hurry to eat breakfast once we had trudged across the soaking car park to the main part of the hotel to find it. Later during a break in the rain we made our way back into town. Épernay is home to many of the world's most famous champagne houses and beneath its streets in some 100km of subterranean cellars / caves an estimated 200 million bottles of champagne are being aged. These caves are vast vaults cut into the chalk rock on which the town is built. Companies such as Moët et Chandon (the largest), Pol Roger, Mercier, and de Castellane are here amid the neoclassical villas and Victorian town houses on Avenue de Champagne. In 1950 Mercier hosted a car rally through the caves without the loss of a single bottle! A couple of years previously my family and I were fortunate enough to stay in Mr. Merciers house, which is now a hotel, a jolly grand place indeed (and it was defiantly sunny then!).

Anyway, I led us into the Avenue de Champagne and, after posing in front of a statue of Benedictine monk Dom Pérignon (it was he who perfected double-fermentation for creating champagne apparently) we enter the hallowed portals of Moët & Chandon, partly for a look round and partly to get out of the rain. There's not a lot to see, a small art gallery and the usual over priced merchandise, unless you take the 16.50€/tour.

The most recommended cave tour is with the lesser known brand of Castellane which is at the opposite end of the Ave de Champagne and round the corner a bit. Castellane is housed in an imposing building listed as a historical monument with a prominent 66 meter high tower announcing its presence. Inside we book the reasonable 10€/tour and have time to wander around the large museum and climb the 237 steps of the tower to enjoy the views of Epernay and the vineyards of the Marne valley. The tour, in English, involves us walking around some of the 9 Km of caves learning about the Champagne making processes (of interest mostly to home brew king Festa) and ends with a dégustation (that's a wine tasting don't you know) and jolly nice it is to. Back at the entrance is an "opportunity" to purchase a selection of the produce which we are all tempted into.

Outside the light rain that had plagued us today had turned to heavy rain to torment us. Festa and Kryten opted to spend the afternoon in a town centre bar while I trudged a very wet and disgruntled path back to the hotel with our purchases. Disgruntled not with my companions but because today was Defil Mania day, a huge gathering of mainly French motorcyclists which I had planned for us to join (translates roughly as Mad Parade). On my way back to the bar I called in at the gathering site and stood with the dozen or so stalwarts in the rain to watch a stunt motorbike show, shame the weather was so bad.

Back at the bar Festa and Kryten were in good spirits and told of a conversation with a couple from Leeds who had also seen the Tour d' France and made the long journey north into the rain. By now though it was about time to look for somewhere to eat again and we began the search close to the bar. There was little choice it seemed but after a few false starts we climbed the steps of a Chinese restaurant to find we were its first customers of the evening.

The bread and beers arrived but it wasn't obvious just what was on offer from the menu which had an 'assiette de charcuterie' translated as 'delicatessen with fireworks'. Eventually we deduced that it was a French version of an all you can eat buffet and went up to select our dishes. It looked most unappetising and we were about to run away when they turned up and started filling all of the empty containers with a variety of food. Veggie Kryten then decided to try his hand at a little French directing "Non Carne" at a puzzled waiter. Non Carne, Kryten assures us, is Italian for "No Meat" but probably translates into a French Chinese waiters ears as "No book of tickets".

On the way back to the hotel we call back into the Defil Mania show and look around the gathering of assorted bikes before sheltering from the rain under some trade stands. We watched as the bikes then began to leave on their parade lap around the town, something I would have loved to join having seen it in the sunshine on a previous visit but not after a day in the rain. Close to the entrance of the hotel we arrived just in time to witness the parade pass by in all its glorious noise to a background of fireworks being chucked willy-nilly, tomorrow was the 14th July and Bastile Day.

Saturday - Épernay to Bruges (190miles 4hours 30mins).

Well what a surprise, rain! It turns out this is northern Europe's' wettest year for some time, thank goodness we went south to start with. We made our way to the breakfast room but soon spun round and gave up as the place was stuffed full of a coach load of German tourists and there was no room at the inn.

Todays' journey of around 190 miles could be taken at a leisurely four and a half hours through the forests of the Ardennes or a dull three and a half on the motorway. It's grey, wet, cold and miserable not the kind of day to navigate around intricate European roads and villages, so motorway it is then! (Whoop-de-do). Fully wet suited and booted I eased myself onto the bike with all the dexterity of a medieval jousting Teletubby and we set off.

I may have mentioned I am no fan of motorways and todays' journey on the A26/E17 Peage only serves to cement that feeling. Through the limited view I have from the shattered rain drops that cover my visor I find myself peering into passing car windows for once envying the occupants sitting warm and dry maybe listening to music as the miles drag by. Brief rest bite comes at the ubiquitous petrol station stop where the rain is beginning to ease off and tea is taken courtesy of Krytens' flask. Once again though, we must remount for that 'final push' to tonight's' stopover in the Belgium town of Bruges.

Three hours seemed like an eternity today but we eventually arrive on the outskirts of town only to get caught up in the aftermath of an overturned car on the motorway with the emergency services still in attendance, a sobering scene. A little further up the road and the on board internal navigation system crashes (probably due to rain and boredom) meaning that I lead us right past Bruges and begin heading towards Zeebugger! My excuse being complicated and extensive road works but it's not a disaster and we are soon back within striking distance of the medieval town. Once travelling along the narrow cobbled streets Krytens' arse adjusting dance on his self-proclaimed 'best bike in the world' is played out in my mirrors while my carefully written instructions go to work to guide us to the hotel. The last line I wrote was "Turn left at The Chocolate Corner into Wijngaardstraat to find the Hotel". Now you may have your own interpretation of 'Chocolate Corner' but let me assure you, dear reader, that Bruges is famous for its' fine coco based confectionary products and this is the name above the premises of a purveyor of such consumables, just in case you were wondering! Our bikes are stowed in the tight car park beneath the hotel and we are pleasantly surprised by the standard and size of our room, three good sized single beds, result!

So what do we know about Bruges? The Lonely Planet tells us "Suspended in time centuries ago, Bruges is now one of Western Europe's' most-visited medieval cities. Picturesque market squares, dreamy canals and old whitewashed alms-houses all evoke a world long since gone. Stay overnight or late on a midsummer evening, when the carillon chimes seep through the cobbled streets, and local boys cast fishing rods into willow-lined canals.

Visit in spring when daffodils carpet the tranquil Begijnhof (a walled community once housing a Catholic order of women)" etc, etc, who writes this flowery nonsense? Anyway, they go on to say "Bruges has been renovated time and again to retain its medieval appearance. Whereas what you see reflects that of centuries ago, much of the architecture dates only from the 19th and 20th centuries".

So there you have it, in a nutshell Bruges is a nice place. Festa had been keen to come here since seeing the 2008 film In Bruges but now it's time to evoke 'Beer o'clock' and there can be few places better to continue this fine tradition than here in Bruges. A beer ticking friend of ours alerted us to two particularly "authentic" venues; De-Garre Staminee (down a small alley) and T-Brugs-Beetje. Unfortunately the former was heaving full but we found a table in T-Brugs-Beetje and got bedded in. What a contrast to the corporate cloned theme pub bollocks of the UK, a real feeling that the place had existed in pretty much the same form since man first mashed, boiled and fermented Barley, water, hops and yeast before slurring "I love you" to everyone on his way home. There was a ludicrously large beer menu on the table and when the waitress came over (oh yes they come to you here unlike standing at an English bar with a limp tenner being ignored) she pointed out a "specials" board which narrowed the choice down to half a dozen all quoted with a brief description and their alcohol content. Each arrived in its own unique glass and our beer mat was marked accordingly, you take the mat to the bar and pay as you leave, now that's how it's done.

If the place had a decent food menu we would probably still be in there, but after working our collective way through the specials board we felt the urge for another British beer fuelled tradition, a curry. The only place we found wanted to charge 20 Euros for that pleasure so we soon side lined the idea and settled for the welcoming white linen table cloths of a posh restaurant rejoicing in the name Gruuthuse Hof. Our two rather camp hosts were immaculately turned out in proper black and white waiter gear and the three course meal we enjoyed came to 16 Euros each, which was all rather splendid!

On the way back to the hotel we couldn't find a supermarket but passed a small shop where we purchased a bottle or two to accompany the compulsory playing of Krytens chosen tour hymn, Iron Maidens Fear of the Dark, an understated little ballad with soothing overtones that complement the contemplation of a fine dining experience at the end of mixed day. Whilst I was busy contemplating the day and Festa was occupied contemplating another beer, Kryten was contemplating his own Fear of the Dark ..."I'm going to be cold, anyone seen a spare blanket?"

Sunday - Bruges to Europort (100miles 2 hrs).

Had a great nights' sleep but woke up to the sound of more rain peppering the window. This time we timed our run to the four star Hotel breakfast room just right and were able to feast at will before the rest of the blurry eyed guests descended upon us. Looking around and listening to the chatter there seemed to be a real mix of cultures and nationalities in the room and it always fascinates me to see what other people consider to be breakfast food.

Unlike many of our adventures Bruges is a mere 100 miles from our ferry in Rotterdam and we can afford the luxury of extra time to wander around the town before setting off. We check out of our room and pay up but leave our gear stored in a large cupboard opposite the reception desk. If he is to be believed the guy behind the desk will be flying to London soon to be Madonna's DJ at a function, but no he couldn't get us a pass. Outside the rain has cleared and the sun is chasing away the last of the clouds. We are heading for the large bell tower in the market square from which a man jumps and then splats on the cobbles below before delivering a short speech to his mate before finally croaking in Festas In Bruges film (I must get round to watching it someday). On the way we come across a light aircraft that has apparently crashed outside another church tower but this seems to be a quirky art installation or something.

The bell tower, known in Flemish as Halle en Belfort, is about 83 meters tall and leans to the left by 1.19 meters. There is a steadily moving queue when we arrive but very soon we are climbing the 366 steps up to the excellent view of the market square, the town and surrounding countryside. Here we see the 47 bells of a carillon, no I didn't know what one of them was either so allow me to illuminate –

'A set of chromatically tuned stationary bells, usually hung in a tower and played from a keyboard' so now you know and you can impress at the next pub quiz. Back down and below the bells there is indeed a man playing the keyboard that dings the bells and plays a variety of melodies although Krytens' request for 'Fear of the Dark' fell upon deaf ears.

Back on terra-firma our meanderings take us to the unrealistically entitled 'Lake of Love', a smart modern fountain and over several canal bridges that explain why some tourist guff compares Bruges to Venice. The obvious differences being that Venice has no cars and you are unlikely to be squished by a quartet of Chinese tourists in a horse drawn carriage. At some point our thoughts turn to home and we hurriedly seek out a vendor of chocolate before returning to the hotel discovering a large supermarket round the corner in the process.

Back in the bowels of the hotel we cast off the flimsy, carefree clothing of the casual tourist and slip into something less comfortable. The skies have cleared and the afternoon temperatures have crept up making our exit from the hotel underworld back into daylight startling. The narrow streets are packed as we pick our way carefully through to cross a canal guarded by a keep that signals we are leaving the town behind us. We join a busy dual carriageway that follows the canal before turning away by a well-kept traditional looking windmill heading towards the Belgium and Dutch border.

At the border we use our bikes filtering potential to slip past a traffic jam with no obvious cause and continue on into Holland. Here we are in flat open countryside, no surprise there, and progress is easy, enjoyable and relaxing with only minor navigational points. On the N62 the road dips into a tunnel beneath a river and I take full advantage to give my ears one last taste of 750ccs of exhaust gas passing through a Leo Vince can as I drop down a cog or two and push the rev counter needle a little further round the dial. It's a stupid childish act and maybe not a wise one given that Festa and I are running a little low on fuel, but it makes me smile.

After searching for some time and noticing Dutch fuel prices are quite steep it seems odd to finally draw up to a tiny two pump, unmanned self service station and find two things, one that the price is 1.70 Euros (not bad for here) and two, our credit cards work! From here our route takes us along the sandy coastline and, being a Sunday, there are many folk out enjoying the sunshine. We pass sand dunes, open water, yachts, sail boards and kites and, being Holland, we traverse bridges over wide rivers were turbines are driven by the ebb and flow of the tides, it's a brilliant way to get to the ferry. It's also a bit of a surprise just how soon we arrive at the ferry terminal as one minute we are on holiday by the sea and next we are joining the queue to board the ferry, most agreeable.

Inside the ship we lash our bikes down and engage in conversation with some Welsh scooter riders who are returning from a rally in Germany. It seems they were there for over a week and it rained every day, always a great shame I feel. Still below decks entertainment is provided by a guy with a racing car mounted on a trailer towed by his Range Rover. Unfortunately he and it have become stuck in the doorway of the car deck as he is unwilling to park his precious vehicles with the freight lorries on top, can't say I blame him.

As Kryten and I continue our usual faffing about Festa disappears off to the bar. Inside the cabin multilingual 'Safety Notices' and 'Sales Pitches' begin to assault our ears but one in particular makes me smile. Clearly the person on the microphone was new to the role and was reading from a script but at some point lost the plot, "...or why not take advantage of our special offer tonight and get two for the price of fifteen" she chirped.

As the ship spliced its main-brace or whatever and left the port Festa and Kryten settled into their seats in the sundeck lounge and began to consume another bottle of red wine. I met up with them soon afterwards, they had been requested to leave as it seems one is not permitted to consume ones' own alcohol in public places on board. I had chosen to feast in the luxurious surroundings of the Costa Coffee bar and having partaken of a sandwich and said coffee I then wandered to the rear of the ship joining many others watching Holland slip away from the rather breezy deck. We complete our evening in the cabin quaffing red wine from the plastic cups found in the bathroom accompanied by a final fanfare of Fear of the Dark.

Monday – Hull to Home (40miles 1 hour).

Bing bong, blah-de-blah-de-blah we are sailing up the Humber after a tranquil crossing but the Tannoy announcements fail to rouse us. Being seasoned travellers we are now well aware that we still have an hour or so before even Kryten and I need to start moving. Once the call is made we join the crush to the car deck and arrive in time to hear the extraction fans strike up heralding the start of the evacuation into the grim Hull dawn. Outside the usual queue at passport control snakes around the florescent jacketed officials until we are finally released into England's' green and pleasant bits. It's Monday morning and the army of continental travellers collide with the great and the good of Hull heading to work. It's time to filter once more and led by Kryten and Festa I am followed by a German couple on a BMW GS as we wriggle our way through the resentful commuters (you can tell you're back in England when cars see you in their mirrors and close the gap rather than let you through). We cross the toll free for bikes Humber Bridge and with barely a nod Kryten and Festa power off into the distance like a couple of school kids released from parental control leaving me, the old man I've become, to watch them go.

Back home I arrive in time to receive a lovely greeting from my young son and hand over the merchandise I have acquired from foreign parts just before he heads off to school. It's back to the reality of garden maintenance and stinky washing. How is it unpacking and returning things to their allotted place seems to take forever? Another adventure is over but it's been a good one.

Chapter 9.

Croatia & Slovenia. (11 days).

The planning and booking work is a distant memory as I begin to pack for this years' foray to visit our European neighbours. I have to admit that things hadn't gone entirely to plan as I had got certain dates mixed up resulting in some frantic re-arranging with booking companies, fortunately without any cancelation fees!

So what's my ride this time? Well I used "man maths" (a method by which any purchase of goods or services can be justified as having an overall financial benefit. Indeed numerous such calculations have revealed what is commonly known as a "Bargain" over the preceding years) to convince myself I 'needed' a change of machine. Thus, following current trends and the devotion of Kryten to his VStrom, I decided to invest in a Triumph Tiger 800XC "Adventure" bike in gleaming white. Well I say white but, apart from the tank and a front mudguard, it mainly consists of black scaffolding to which I added a rack for my top box, a tank mounting ring for the tank bag and some engine bars for no real purpose (isn't man maths great?).

As I prepare for the trip I perform all of the usual checks and decide that the coolant level could be increased as we are probably going to encounter some heat as we head south. I read the manual and find triumph recommend a very specific coolant so head to my local bike shop who have never heard of it. Why would an "Adventure" bike require a specialist coolant? What if my adventure takes me away from the nearest Triumph dealer? I go with just a quick distilled water top up.

Anyway, that's all behind me as I complete my OCD packing the day before we are due to leave, passport, driving licence, log book, tickets, Euros, HRK (Croatian Kuna) maps all present so I can sit back feeling rather smug, oh, wait a minute, did I pack my . . ? Better just check.

Saturday – Home to Hull (40miles 1 hour).

Departure day being a Saturday means my fellow OCD sufferer Kryten has the entire day to lay out all of his belongings before flapping them three times and folding them neatly into his top box. I begin to receive text messages . . . "Four hours to go!!" . . . "Two more hours!" Kryten is excited though I suspect our imminent departure has barely registered with Festa, other than a check on his red wine stock naturally.

I arrive first at our meeting point and await the distant sounds of approaching motorcycles. I am always slightly apprehensive having planned the adventure but the sight of my companions inevitably promotes a smile. Krytens' excited arrival is announced by a loud "Yeeehaa!" from within his Arai and I know we are embarking on another great trip.

On reflexion I think we are quite a well matched group. Krytens' infectious, almost overwhelming enthusiasm, Festas cool unruffled demeanour and my contribution as planner and chief worrier combine well. My companions now refer to me as "Dad" by the way and it's a title I recognise as quite appropriate.

On board the Pride of Hull the familiar ritual of securing the bikes is soon over and my minimal overnight luggage is swiftly transported to our cabin. Not as swiftly as Festa though as he is just heading for the bar as Kryten and I enter the room. After our traditional faffing around we join Festa who has a ring side seat in front of the big screen. Its world cup football night and England are playing Italy. I have a choice, I am not a big football fan but then again the entertainment offered by the P&O Players is, well, an acquired taste? England 1 Italy 2 P&O Players 0. Time for bed.

Sunday - Europort Rotterdam – Dusseldorf (170 miles 3 hrs).

Off the ferry and straight onto the now familiar A15 Dutch motorway that leads us away from the busy city of Rotterdam carving its way eastwards through the low laying countryside. For the first time in years of travelling this route I manage to lead us onto the N323 then N322 that take us south to roads crossing the border into Germany without a detour.

Even entering the daunting city of Dusseldorf goes remarkably smoothly but alas this run of navigational excellence can't continue. Sure enough as I glance in my mirrors I notice Krytens' Suzuki headlight is a good distance behind me but he usually catches back up. This time however I pass through an amber traffic light and while concentrating on directions don't notice Kryten and the following Festa have stopped. I am excited because I realise I am on the right road and near to our destination. I realise I am alone as I prepare to turn into the street where a Lidl supermarket is located and decide to wait on the corner. I know Festa has the route on his tank bag and feel sure he will be able to reunite us.

It's a long wait so the mobile phone calls begin. Turns out they have successfully negotiated their way to the station about a mile away but will return to meet me at the shop. What I hadn't accounted for was that this was a Sunday and, unlike the UK, the residents of Germany can somehow survive a whole day without the opening of a giant supermarket. After a brief hunt around nearby streets for supplies we return to the station empty handed.

Queues were forming but no-one was going anywhere. We had a long and hot wait during which time we observed a bizarre old BMW sidecar outfit and spoke to a Dutch guy who was heading to Albania. Eventually we shuffled past the check in hut, "Englisch sprechen bitte? Nein", queued a while longer then braved the un-nerving ride through the low undulating decks of the railway carriages to park up. Remember to take your key; remember to take your key! I forgot to take my key and had to return to my bike which was by now firmly wedged into its travelling position.

We got changed out of our riding gear on the platform, not the most endearing vision I realise, and then Festa and I go in search of provisions for the journey ahead. We found a bustling underground shopping area sprawling beneath the platforms and returned with a multitude of unhealthy food stuffs. There's nothing to do now but wait. Mobile phones are in evidence and I receive a welcome Father's Day message from my son.

As usual it's a confusing wait. Garbled messages in German do little to aide the situation as a train pulls onto the platform. People surge towards the carriages but word gets round that this is not our train. After more waiting our coaches are shunted onto the platform and after more confusion we eventually find our cabin. This time we have upgraded to a three berth with a sink in order to avoid having to share with person or persons unknown. Unfortunately it turns out my wardrobe at home is bigger than this tiny space and we struggle to squeeze ourselves, riding gear and helmets in. Every available inch has someone's gear and we sit so close together it feels like we will have to breathe in unison.

Once the train edges out of the station and into the German countryside we begin to consume our rations while being treated to spectacular views of the River Rhine and some of its' many castles from our narrow carriage window. When darkness descends there is little left to do but get ready for bed. It's a bit like playing that old childhood game of twister as we convert the seating into a stack of beds.

Monday -Villach (Austria) – Kirk Island (Croatia) (185miles 5 hrs).

It hasn't been a particularly comfortable nights' rest, the train stopped somewhere and was shunted around a bit just as I was nodding off. Still, using the train has saved us riding the 900mile 14hour route from Europort to our destination in Croatia. Unfortunately we have missed breakfast somehow and must now alight pronto or risk being whisked off to destinations unknown.

We hurriedly dress then jettison our belongings onto the sunny platform. Looking around it would seem everyone else had been up and about for hours as they calmly enjoyed watching our antics. (A bit like most of my camping experiences were everyone is up at the sparrows' fart cooking bacon, walking to the shower block with a towel round their neck and whistling loudly). Even so, there seemed little hurrying the arrival of our bikes so we were able to regroup and get changed on the platform (seems to be a bit of a habit this).

After the arrival of the bikes and the frantic unloading we were riding out of the station and away, only to turn around two hundred yards down the road as I had turned right instead of left. That's when we spied a Spar supermarket and decided to postpone our start in favour of breakfast. This also meant our return trip could be a far more nourishing affair.

By now it will come as no surprise to learn that soon after our re-start I led us wrong again, but we were fortunately halted at a road works were I realised my mistake. On the right road we avoid impatient drivers on mobile phones and smirk like school kids at local signage like "Wank Hof". We have a brief foray into Italy where we buy a Vignette (like the old road tax sticker) before entering Slovenia via a sleepy customs check point. Instantly we are presented with the mountains of the Triglavski Narodni Park and a cartoon of a motorcyclist falling off. Route 203 twists its way along this sinuous mountain pass offering glimpses of the Trdnjava Kluze fortress, streams and life beyond the trees that shield them from the road.

As we drop out of the mountains we ride across a large open space and in the village of Bovec stop at a café for refreshments. It's around one o'clock and the sun is high above us in a cloudless sky as we sit in the shade looking out across the fields to the mountains that surround us, not a bad start then. Onwards again we enter Nova Gorica where we avoid the motorway south in favour of the R204 which leads us through rural villages and beautiful open countryside to Kozina.

Here we must make use of the speed of the motorway as time is beginning to press on and we soon encounter the police checking vehicles for their Vignettes. We plunge into the city of Koper and are confronted by a huge section of road works and the opportunity of getting lost again, which of course I grasp and lead us to a dusty coastal car park. Festa and I consult the map while Kryten finds a suitable area to catch some rays as it is baking hot.

After some frustrating false dawns I do manage to lead us to the border with Croatia. You can tell you are close as any number of shacks spring up at the side of the road offering to exchange Euros for the Croatian Kuna "Best Rates Guaranteed". Here we are surprised to find a long tailback of people queuing for passport control. It was a helmet off full on check, which we were not expecting given we are all now "European".

Free at last we follow the motorway signs for Rijeka knowing that our destination is not far beyond this goal. After slightly longer than expected we pass Rijeka and turn off the motorway towards signs for Otok Krk and stop to pay the 18kn / £2ish toll that allows us to cross the long bridge onto the island of Kirk / Krk. The weather has changed considerably from that in Koper and the bridge is windy with a hint of rain in the air. The main road on Kirk, D102, is well surfaced and fast (very fast if you are local!) and after passing the airport we drop down into the village of Malinska and to our hotel.

It is set on a hill and does not appear to be particularly inviting having that 'out of season' feel as we look for somewhere even and flat to park our bikes. Kryten assumes his usual bike guardian role as Festa and I seek out the not terribly obvious reception. We check in and wander off in search of our room. The approach is non-too inviting either but the room is pleasant enough with a view across the pool and restaurant to the sea below. There is a twin bedded room and a room with a double. As I am now known as Dad I am allowed the double while the children fight over beds in the twin room. Krytens' "YeeHaa!" call echoing around the tiled floors and bare walls indicates he is happy and soon the IPod is set to work with the delicate melodies of the Foo Fighters accompanying the football on the telly. Hardly Dads' ideal way of settling into a room after a long day on the bikes, so I elected to go for a shower.

Once we are all showered and changed we head down to the hotel restaurant where we are shown to a table by very pleasant staff and it feels far more welcoming. It is a buffet style affair that Festa and I approach with relish. Krytens' no compromise vegetarian commitment means he must find a waiter to explain the mysteries of the myriad dishes.

Unfortunately, none of the available staff spoke enough English to understand the concept of vegetarianism and a panicked Kryten was forced to try his luck in Italian. Hopelessly waving his hands he repeated the phrase "Non-carnet". This, he believes is Italian for No meat. Quite why a Croatian would understand Italian any more than

English is any ones guess but these were desperate times. Still, even if Italian was understood niente carne (Italian for no meat) should not be confused with Non carne (Italian for no dog!). Once resigned to a cheese salad Kryten joins us again only to complain that our chosen table is in a draught and he his cold (it's a lovely warm evening). One can understand the puzzled looks but find that where ever we are in the world a smile is universal, as is the word Beer accompanied by the requisite number of fingers.

Tuesday - Tour of Kirk Island (Croatia) (60miles 2 hours).

It's a beautiful sunny morning that greets our blurry eyed view of the blue Adriatic just visible beyond the confines of the hotel. I feel the warmth of the early sunshine as we make our way past the pool and down to the delightful breakfast buffet. The glass doors are opened to allow a gentle breeze to carry the tempting aroma of fresh bread towards us.

After a leisurely feast we are soon on the bikes and heading out to explore the island. I appreciate it isn't the safest form of rider apparel but it is so warm that we have all chosen to wear jeans today and it feels very liberating. The bikes have been unburdened from the weight of luggage and feel eager to be on the roads. It's a steady climb out of town and up to the main D102 road that traverses the island and we join it heading for our first stop in the town of Krk. The road is well surfaced and lined on both sides with tall dense reed like grass as it undulates towards our first stop.

Once off the D102 we head downhill passing white painted houses with red tiled roofs and after a roundabout we find ourselves riding alongside the harbour in busy traffic. This is where it is advantageous to be riding a bike as parking seems at a premium but we soon find a very convenient place close to the promenade. Helmets and jackets are secured into empty top boxes and we are free to wander.

It's a busy but friendly atmosphere and we determine to walk round the wide paved promenade to the small light house that sits on the end of the man-made wall that protects the harbour. The water is fairly deep but crystal clear as first we pass the pleasure craft bumping together on their moorings. At the far end are a couple of slightly larger commercial fishing vessels and here we lose most of the people as we turn towards the lighthouse.

Looking back across to the town from the lighthouse, the bell tower of the small cathedral protrudes above the roof tops and stands close to the Frankopan Castle. A tourist boat begins its journey out into the bay and it would be an idyllic spot to while away the morning but we had more riding to enjoy.

Leaving the by now bustling town uphill through its' narrow streets we soon turn right onto the D102 again. For a short while to our right are the shimmering blue waters of Punat bay but then we begin to climb, almost surprisingly, upwards. The road here has an excellent surface and begins to snake its' way through the stubby trees and scrub land. A multi-lingual "Welcome to Baška" sign appears and then the road throws up a few tricky bends as we crest the Treskavac pass and briefly glance at a view across the wide open valley before rapidly descending into it.

The ride through the valley is a delight, the traffic is sparse and the smooth even road visits a couple of sleepy towns cradled by fairly gentle hills. Eventually the road runs into the popular southern resort town of Baška with its old stone houses and narrow streets. We opt to drop down, almost literally as the road is so steep here, to the harbour area and again use the bikes size to find suitable and convenient parking.

It's warm and breezy as Kryten announces it's time for tea-up while producing the faithful flask and ingredients from the confines of his top-box. Tea in hand we wander up onto the sea wall and watch a decent swell crash against it throwing up the occasional spray in our direction. Looking back towards town there is the 800-meter-long Vela plaža (Great Beach) and tucked away the other side is Bunculuka beach a smaller, "clothing optional," pebble beach, to which our eyes are drawn as elbows nudge other elbows. Normally such places are populated by some fairly hideous sights, but not so this one today! (We later discover this end of town houses the large Bunculuka naturist camping site).

Remounted we head back the way we came along the valley and climb out into the mountains (Obzova, at around 570 m, is the highest point here if that is considered a mountain otherwise we are in the hills). On the descent we turn right to a far smaller road and I have to pause for a natural break. With the bikes turned off the only sounds are of the Crickets chirping away and the staccato plinking of the cooling engines.

Not much further on we arrive at the tiny harbour in Vrbnik with the town perched above on a limestone outcrop. It's very peaceful and quiet and we have the small car park come harbour area to ourselves. This presents an ideal opportunity for arranging the bikes in various positions so many posed photographs can be captured with such an enchanting background. Images captured we leave the bikes and make our way the short distance to the protective sea wall. Here we find a small tunnel in the cliff that leads to a tiny hidden beach with white topped breakers disturbing the serenity of the blue water of this hidden cove.

So, with Vrbnik ticked off the list we are off again along narrow coast roads towards a village called Čižići. Just before the village we ride alongside Meline beach in the Bay of Soline and stop to take in the views. In the distance the mountains of the mainland rise up from the shimmering blue water with villages dotted around the foot hills. The foreground however, reveals more unexpected views. Maybe the word beach is a misnomer when applied here as the area seems little more than marsh land. On closer inspection there are families set for a day out, deckchairs and kids playing in the mud. Investigation uncovers the reason to be that the mud supposedly has healing properties and health benefits which possibly also accounts for the small grass covered structure with the words "Massage Shack" hand painted on the driftwood sign (we didn't investigate further).

More tiny roads follow until we stop in Njivice the final town of the days' brief island tour. Njivice is the newest-built town on the island and it looks it to. Still human in size but clearly constructed with tourism in mind making the most of the long and narrow sandy beach backed by trees, a neat harbour with small pleasure craft and a swimming pool built into the sea. It was mid-afternoon, the sun was very warm and I think we all wished we had our swimming shorts with such an inviting sight. We had a quick shuffle round a gift shop, probably because it was the only one we saw, where I bought a Croatian Pirates T shirt for my son (worn once just to appease me I think), before we hightailed it back to our hotel.

It's a bit early for "Beer o'clock" so we opt to earn a drink by walking from our hotel to see what is around the other side of the bay. There is a path that hugs the shoreline and it's a delightful amble in the warm sunshine but we soon become pre-occupied by our quest for refreshment. A sign for a bar at the end of a jetty catches our eyes but when we get there it's disappointingly shut. Shame as it overlooked the sea to one side and a protected area filled with kids' waterborne inflatables the other.

After a further promenade we plonk ourselves down under the shade of a beach side umbrella attached to a bar and are rewarded with three large glasses of cool beer, the condensation rolling down the outsides. After the hour or so walk to get here it's a refreshing pause but not one that is refreshing enough for Kryten. After mumbling away about being hot and attempting to entice Festa and me to join him Kryten plunges into the nearby sea and bobs back and forth while shouting to Festa and me how great it is. We observe our friend with amusement from the comfort of our seats shaded by the umbrella but amusement turns to alcohol fuelled laughter when he decides to re-join us. The return route is a stony one and the sight of Kryten flailing about on all fours like some kind of Darwinesque re-enactment of the accent of mankind from the primeval swamp has Festa and me in hysterics.

The walk back to the hotel seemed much longer than the walk out and the three pints I had consumed made it feel even longer so it was a great relief, in more ways than one, when we finally arrived back. We didn't linger though as it had been decided we should all go for a swim out to a row of floats that surrounded our hotel beach. One does tend to do daft things once alcohol has taken effect, a point I began to appreciate as the water got deeper and cooler about two thirds of the way to the line of floats. The beach looked much further away when I turned to take a breather and having made it to the floats I was glad to make it back and feel the sand between my toes again.

In the evening we discovered that the 'Free Buffet' of yesterday, err, wasn't so free, it was just that our brilliant friendly waiters had omitted to check our room number against their list. Still, it was a lovely meal again, dog or non-carne! After dinner I left Festa & Kryten watching football and returned to sit on the beach watching the sun go down, The twinkly lights from homes across the bay, the waves gently lapping the sand and distant football related shouting and bloody awful singing!

Wednesday - Kirk to Numag (140miles 4hrs 45mins).

Woke up early and opened the curtains to a glorious sunny day with the pool in the foreground and shimmering sea beyond filling the horizon. We are moving again today and after a peaceful breakfast soon have the bikes loaded up. A final essential pee and we set off for the short ride to the ferry dock in Valbiska. On the dock we join many German and Austrian bikers and cyclists waiting for the Jadrolinija Ferry to transport us the short 30 minute £3:50 hop from Krk Island to Merag on Cres Island.

Once released onto Cres Island we follow the eager stream of vehicles up the steep gradient that leads to the main road junction. Curiously everyone but us seemed to be turning left and it wasn't long before we discovered why. The nice smooth and warm tarmac of the D101 turned abruptly into the gravel and dust of ongoing resurfacing works. Cautious adventure biking ensued as we encountered numerous changes of surface, a narrowing track and increasingly long drops as we climbed over the central high ground, great views though!

After what seemed like an age I began to question my limited navigational skills as the route should have been a brief 20 miles to the next port but we ploughed onwards. Suddenly, after not seeing a soul, vehicles began charging towards us kicking up clouds of dust and stones making picking a safe route slightly trickier. As we progressed we realised that these must be vehicles from a recently arrived ferry and began to quicken our pace.

Eventually the gravel abated and we rolled down decent tarmac into the village of Porozina to be greeted by a man franticly waving his arms and pointing to the ferry. It became clear that the ferry was about to leave but we had no tickets and so missed boarding by minutes. There was nothing left to do but buy tickets for the next one and dig out the flask for tea up.

We had one and a half hours to kill before the next ferry and by now the sun was beating down onto the surrounding concrete of the quayside. The water was crystal clear and very deep with the occasional shoal of fish glinting into view before darting to safer water below. I tried to hide in what little shade was available while Festa and Kryten stripped off their outer garments to wander around in dubious shorts. Eventually the ferry returned and after disgorging its passengers we were soon on board for the 20 minute £3:50 crossing to Brestova back on the mainland.

Time was moving on so a planned visit to a Roman amphitheatre in Pula had to be scrapped for a re-planed onward journey using a very basic Google map I had printed off as a guide. The road out of the port was again a steep one and navigation towards Pazin was tricky on the undulating roads, not helped by the limited amount of road signs. We got very lost trying to find a village called Baderna but did see an impressive castle somewhere along the way, no idea where though. After a frustrating couple of hours in the mid-afternoon sun we stopped on the edge of a village at a bench and table with a stunning view. Tea and biscuits were taken in the traditional English way but we were in competition with some exceptionally large ants in the process.

Once we were ready to continue we felt the need to thoroughly inspect our helmets and gloves for unwanted passengers before squeezing our hot and sticky selves back into them. It was a further hour or two before we came down from the hills following a long straight dry road into the much larger town of Ulmag. My instructions read 'Turn left at the concrete tennis balls on the roundabout' and it was with a certain amount of relief that they came into view and soon after the welcome sight of our hotel.

It wasn't a great hotel just an adequate one that I couldn't imagine staying in for more than a night or two. It did have air conditioning though which we made full use of while peeling off our biker gear and scrambling into more suitable attire for beer o'clock at a small bar close by. Energised by the refreshing qualities of Croatian beer Kryten and Festa decide to throw them-selves into the nearby sea. I couldn't be arsed, the frustrations of the day left me just tired and hungry so I watch the two bald heads bobbing up and down amongst the waves their laughter bouncing off the walls of the slipway I am sitting on.

Emerging from the sea there is a renewed urgency to order food as kick-off time is rapidly approaching. Tonight our hosts Croatia will play Cameroon and an excited crowd is gathering around the big screen in the hotel foyer. I leave the boys to enjoy the game and head out to explore the fairly deserted marina area. There are some spectacular craft moored here on the bright clear water and the area seems clean and well maintained in contrast to the jaded appearance of the area surrounding our hotel. I return to the hotel in time to catch the final minutes of the match. Croatia won 4-0 and there is much joy and happiness.

Thursday - Ulmag Hotel (Croatia) to Škocjan Caves (Slovenia) (50miles 60mins).

There had been some debate about today. I had planned for us to visit the Škocjan Caves across the border into Slovenia but Kryten was keen to soak up some sunshine by lying on the beach all day. We all went down to breakfast to discover queues at the bun fight but when we eventually managed to sit down Kryten decided he would join Festa and I heading for the caves.

There was no way any of us were going to visit caves wearing full motorcycle gear in the heat we were experiencing. We emptied the top boxes to allow for storage of our gear and rode out wearing jeans and trainers and boy oh boy did that feel good, so wrong but so good!

Off we rode with my carefully planned route tucked into the window of my tank bag. All did not go well once again as I struggled to even find the way out of town. We passed through some very pleasant countryside but there seemed to be an un-nerving amount of speeding white van men hurtling towards us on bends. My thoughts when route planning have always been to steer clear of motorways and fast A type roads to enjoy the more tranquil side of a country. As the day progressed I got the feeling I had over-thought this idea as I lead us deeper into the countryside. I stopped on a hill with a fantastic view to re-orientate myself on this confusing route before we dropped down into a nice village, but this was wrong also. There was a public map of the area displayed at a cross roads which led to more confusion. Were these actual place names or the names of people who lived there? The revised route took us uphill again using a very tiny road back into a small village where the smell of Wisteria was amazing. We passed a tramp walking in the middle of nowhere before finally locating the planned road to the Croatia / Slovenia border crossing.

The road gently meandered uphill through dense woodland with no other person around until we found the border. It was a rather comical vision with a red and white pole blocking our way and two sleepy guards seated in a small hut. One weary guard rose from his chair and approached us as we fumbled for our passports. He spoke very little English but we became aware that this was a border for local people only and not for tourists. We could see a village beyond and thought this was probably Royston Vassey (from the BBC series League of Gentlemen). As we stood rather bemused more motorcyclists arrived from the Royston Vassey side. It looked like they were German and they were also turned back. I guess we are all getting so used to a borderless Europe.

We had no choice but to return to the "Official" border crossing on the D21 motorway about fifteen miles away. I was hot and frustrated and this lead to some unusually 'spirited' riding of the Tiger as we retraced our route. When reason caught up with me I stopped and swapped bikes with Kryten riding his softer sprung VStrom until we stopped in a restaurant car park for tea and directions.

Onto the motorway we soon found our progress grinding to a halt as we approached the border. A single line of cars edged painfully slowly forward down a hill with a number of bends. We tried to ride past as many as we could using our bikes width advantage but we were constantly met by two lines of fast moving cars hurtling towards us and had to seek refuge in between vehicles that had little intension of letting us in (like being in the UK).

Eventually we put all of the border worries behind us and arrive in the car park of the Škocjan Caves, entered on UNESCO's list of natural and cultural world heritage sites in 1986. It's now time to dump the motorcycle gear into the empty top boxes and don our far more suitable cave exploration attire, in Festas' case that equates to shorts, T shirt and flip-flops. We locate the ticket office and pay the €16 fee for a guided tour in English and German and find we have just enough time for another tour favourite, the Magnum moment.

We are led to a locked steel door which forms the entrance to the cave system and follow our excellent guide along the pathways that take us deeper underground. Here I have lifted some of the text from the guide to explain more about the caves:

"This system of limestone caves comprises collapsed dolines, some 6 km of underground passages with a total depth of more than 200 m, many waterfalls and one of the largest known underground chambers. Škocjan Caves Regional Park is situated in the Kras Plateau of South-West Slovenia. The protected area of 413 ha conserves an exceptional limestone cave system which comprises one of the world's largest known underground river canyons, that was cut into the limestone bedrock by the Reka River. Along its course, the river suddenly disappears into the karst underground, before passing through a vast and picturesque channel of up to 150 meters in height and more than 120 meters in width, often in the form of dramatically roaring rapids and waterfalls. The canyon's most spectacular physical expression is the enormous Martel Chamber, which exceeds two million cubic meters in volume. Like the canyon, the vast underground halls and chambers of the cave system expose stunning variations of limestone bedrock and secondary cave formations"

So there you have it. I would strongly encourage anyone who is anywhere near these caves to pay them a visit. The Martel Chamber mentioned with its narrow walkways and bridges suspended above the rushing waters is incredible and could be included in scenes from any Lord of the Rings or Indiana Jones movies and there are some wonderful pictures to be seen on Google Images.

When we return to the bikes there is a suspicion that someone has been rifling through our tank bags. Not that we left anything worth nicking but still annoying and a reminder not to take chances in the future. Back into the bike gear we return to our hotel and make remarkably swift and easy progress along the motorway and through the customs check-point for an early start at Beer o'clock.

There was time for another walk around the harbour but the sea proved to be too rough for a swim, probably just as well. After a pleasant dinner taken with red wine Festa and Kryten settled down to watch England v Uruguay while I went for a swim in the hotels' salt water pool (note to self – take goggles next time!). Later, as the football lingered on and the darkness began to draw in I went for a walk along the sea front. Initially I had the sounds of waves lapping on the beach to one side and Crickets chirping on the other. Later I was assaulted by a mixture of an Elvis tribute group, the sounds of Boney M (Rivers of Babylon) and German Ompha music. No twinkly lights out to sea just impenetrable darkness, bit like England following their 2-1 defeat after a brace of goals from Luis Suarez I am informed on my return.

Friday - Ulmag (Croatia) to Ribcev Laz (Slovenia) (140miles 4hrs 30mins).

Awake to another warm and sunny morning following a sound nights' sleep. After the breakfast bun fight we gathered together in the room to collect all our available Croatian Kuna. After loading up the bikes we were joined at reception by a tall Australian lady, owner of a CB600f, who was touring alone. We paid for our stay from the cash we had pooled but still seemed to have plenty of Kuna.

Back at the bikes I squeeze earplugs in then push my head inside my Arai helmet, tighten the strap then throw my right leg towards the tall seat of the Triumph Tiger catching my foot with my right hand to help my leg to clear the seat. The day was already warming up as I poked my sunglasses into place over my ears then wriggled my hands into my Alpine Stars gloves before pulling in the clutch and pushing the starter. While the engine ticked over and we waited for Kryten to adjust himself I sat and stared at the detailed instructions I had prepared and placed in the window of my tank bag. For me there's always a sense of nervous anticipation at the start of a day. We have never really used GPS so navigation can be tricky at times and although it doesn't really matter that we lose our way I hate the waste of time. Finding fuel at the right time occasionally jangles the nerves to but these negatives are soon flushed from my mind as we set off.

Unfortunately, and despite my prior careful study of instructions, I lead us the wrong way at the motorway and end up having to pay two Kuna each on the toll road to turn round and go back. Great start! What follows is much more of the hot and scary filtering down to the border crossing. We pass the Australian lady patiently queuing on her CB600 in the heat and manage to clear customs but things don't get any easier. As we approach Koper we encounter more nightmare filtering through the cauldron of un-surfaced road works that seem to encircle the city. It's hot, dusty and dangerous as cars jostle for that extra meter that gets them in front of the next car. It's a chaotic start to the day and I'm not enjoying the experience one bit.

The motorway does at last start to turn away from the city and regain a decent surface with defined lanes and a bit more order. As the traffic thins out our speed can increase and then air can pass over us supplying a welcome cooling breeze. Then, just as we thought it was over, we notice cops checking for Vignettes using binoculars. Fortunately we have the required stickers prominently displayed in our screens so pass by untroubled.

After a fifty to sixty mile dash along the motorway we can finally turn off onto the 409 which I had hoped would keep us away from the manic traffic and immerse us in rural Slovenia. Unfortunately this wasn't to be entirely the case. The road surfaces became unpredictable and the journey a little tedious, I picked a quiet spot for a break soon after only to be followed in by a lorry then lots of cars driving past. The unsatisfactory break was followed by the equally unsatisfactory realization that another navigational error had occurred requiring a map to attempt to discover our location.

Turns out we weren't too far off and after a brief diversion we made steady progress until another tea break was called for. We stopped on a small road junction near a café under trees and were soon approached by some locals. I think they had noticed the GB plates on the bikes and had come over to say hello, I love this about travelling on a bike. They confirmed we were on the right road and one told us he used to drive a truck in the UK. We were invited to join them in the café but as time was limited we had to decline.

As we prepared to set off again a huge truck thundered down the hill past us then struggled to turn at the junction. I could only take this as a warning of what might be around the next bend as we continued our journey onwards. Uphill, downhill through forests and open meadows but more often than not stuck behind a car, van or lorry on the twisty roads, at one point we were passed by a determined local who used the gravel on the inside of us to complete his manoeuvre. We were also passed by a guy on a Ducati sports bike who clearly could see round corners and through rock.

Within the last few miles of the ride the rain that had stalked us finally caught up but only managed a short sharp shower despite the leaden skies. Our hotel was located next to a small wooden cycle hire shed on the approach road to the small village and was easy to find. When the sound of the engines dissipated it was replaced by the kind of silence found only well away from urbanization. While removing helmets and earplugs and gathering our thoughts we were joined by a very pleasant lady who mercifully spoke excellent English. She took us into the hotel and explained that as she wasn't busy we could have a choice of rooms. We chose one to the rear of the building which meant we could park our bikes right outside it and pass the gear over the veranda straight inside.

Soon it was beer o'clock and we sat with views over to the mountains watching a gathering storm. Once the storm had fully gathered it unleashed a fairly spectacular display of light and sound which echoed around the valley. We watched one unfortunate cyclist take shelter under the canopy of the cycle hire shed before the mobile phone summoned his wife to rescue him. As there was still time before dinner, Festas' head in a book and Kryten enthralled in the 'Joy of Text' I returned to the room to attempt a bit of washing. Temperatures in Croatia had been above 30°c and, well not to put too fine a point on it, I stunk! Well at least my trusty under leathers clothing did so it was sleeves rolled up and out with the travel wash.

By the time we were ready to eat the storm had passed and sunshine returned to cast shadows across the valley floor. Much to my fellow travellers amusement I found the waitress oddly attractive as she patiently answered questions about the menu. She too had a firm grasp of English and a very appealing accent but that didn't prevent Kryten agonising over his choice. Vegetarianism hasn't really caught on with many of our European neighbours and even Krytens' fluent "Non-Carney" met with a blank expression. Eventually Kryten tried "Do you have any fish?" "Oh yes" came the reply "We have Trout . . . it's over there in the tank. Which one would you like?" Kryten looked across in horror at the fish swimming around in the tank. Today he would choose salad and chips.

After dinner we took a walk a short distance to the lake. The air was still, the lake surface reflecting the calm after the storm and the atmosphere blissfully tranquil as we joined others who were enjoying the evening. We stood on a bridge that transverses the lake outlet and looked out to the snow-capped Julian Alps beyond. Mist clung to the tops of trees and below us brown trout darted, which one would you like Kryten?

The silence was broken by the local church bells informing us of the hour. It's a 15th century church dedicated to John the Baptist and built in Gothic style if you're interested in such things. Oh yes and the lake is called Lake Bohinj in the north western Upper Carniola region, part of the Triglav National Park and is the largest natural lake in Slovenia covering 318 hectares, 790 acres. It's a glacial lake and apparently much more water leaves Lake Bohinj than enters it, which is explained by subterranean sources of water. So there you go, a bit of history and a bit of geography to, class dismissed.

Saturday – Day off the bikes.

Apparently I was snoring last night and resisted all attempts to stop me. I think I was a bit knackered after the heat of Croatia and the navigational inaccuracies of previous days. I can report a great nights' sleep though and today we had planned to leave the bikes huddled together behind the hotel and go off exploring on foot. After a continental breakfast, (cereals, bread and jam) flasks were made, bags packed and we were soon off down to Lake Bohinj to check out the sign saying 'Canoe Kayak Hire'

It would be hard to conceive of a more perfect start to a day. Last nights' rain had gone, the sun had got its' hat on (hip-hip-hip hooray), there was hardly a breath of wind and a pervading air of serenity filled the valley. The very friendly man at 'Canoe Kayak Hire' spoke a little English but managed to convey we could take whichever vessel we wanted and he would take payment from us when we returned. Festa and Kryten both chose the small sit on things, sports GTi models, were as I, being the Dad, chose the larger safer sit in version, Volvo estate! This meant I could carry flasks, food, cameras etc. with less of a chance of flipping over. My canoe rumbled over the gravel at the waters' edge then all was quiet again as I began to glide over the surface of the lake.

It's interesting just what I am prepared to do or can do on a trip such as this. I mean this as no detriment to my family but travelling with friends just is different to travelling with family. I once heard a man say that a good test of a marriage is if you can canoe together and wallpaper a room together. It was this thought that brought a smile to my face on Lake Bohinj and I am happy to report my wife and I have survived both ordeals with only minor emotional scars.

After the initial uncoordinated flapping and paddle slapping we eventually began to make progress across the lake with a delusion of competence stopping briefly to photograph each other in this idyllic location. Soon though the challenge of paddling the 2.7 miles to the other end of the lake took a hold of Festa and he drew further and further away (I'm not convinced he knew it was 2.7 miles when he set off though). Kryten and I continued at a more leisurely pace admiring the scenery and pausing now and then to glide silently along.

A while later and about two thirds of the way along the lake Festa came back into view and we decided to beach the boats for a brew stop. It was another 'scorchio' day with the sun reflecting back off the water. The brewing of tea would have to wait though as we plunged into the crystal clear water to cool off. Cooling off, I have to report, was fairly rapid as the lake is fed from the melting snow of the Julian Alps and was, not to put too fine a point on it, f**king freezing. It took a while to acclimatise to the temperature of the water but it was such a pleasure to swim and dive under that we stayed in trying not to be the first one to crack. Kryten was last to emerge though and once again demonstrated all the poise, balance and dextrous coordination of a child's first steps.

Surrounded by pine trees with the backdrop of mountains we sat in this peaceful location drinking tea and eating biscuits with our clothes drying in the warm sunshine. As if this wasn't enough the inhabitants of the lake, Brown Trout, Chubb and Perch seemed to get braver and braver when we jettisoned fallen biscuit crumbs into the water.

Back in the boats we took the return journey at a more leisurely pace hugging the shoreline for a good deal of the time marvelling at the clarity of the waters and the views beneath its' surface. With a final flurry of speed the boats ground up the pebble beach and we paid the man thanking him for a very pleasant morning. Back in the village we found a small supermarket and were able to replace supplies by buying more biscuits, English breakfast tea and Slovenian sweets which we took back to our hotel for another brew stop.

We were only half way through the day so over tea we made the decision to circumnavigate the lake, about 7 miles, for the afternoon and set off suitably equipped for the trek (flask of hot water, tea bags and biscuits). We chose to walk anticlockwise and so crossed the little stone bridge before turning left onto a tarmac track just before the church. We were rewarded with more beautiful views with paragliders landing in the meadow to one side and families bathing in the lake on the other before the tarmac gave way to a narrow stony and undulating path that led us through the wooded banks of the lake. It was nice to be out of the direct sunlight shaded by a lush green canopy.

At the end of the lake the path opened out into what appeared to be wooden holiday style lodges before climbing upwards. We were following signs for the Savica Waterfall and our efforts were rewarded with the discovery of a small café. This café offered cold beer which was most welcome and Slovenian Mushroom Soup, Gobova Juha, which didn't look too appealing but tasted fantastic.

From this area it is possible to take a trip in a cable car 569m up to the Vogel ski centre but unfortunately time was slightly against us so we elected to try the waterfalls instead. On arrival though we found a pay booth charging a €2:50 entry fee to see them but uninspiring photos meant we turned away. Heading back we went slightly off-piste trying to find a short cut away from the road. Soon we felt completely lost in dense woodland and started worrying we might hear the sound of banjos. Being blokes there was no way we were going to admit defeat and turn back so we stumbled on until eventually, and with some relief, reconnected with the small road that shepherded us back to the village and our hotel.

It had been a brilliant day and to celebrate I drank a pint of water to rehydrate followed by a refreshing shower while Kryten and Festa went off for beer and football. I returned to the TV room to watch the final few minutes of a game before we went for dinner. After this another match had started and more beer was required but I chose to return to the room where I fell asleep to the sounds of crickets in the night air, like in the movies.

Sunday – Into Austria trip (130miles 4hours 30mins).

Another bright and sunny morning was unveiled when the curtains were pulled aside by a blurry eyed Kryten. The bikes just beyond the window glistened with the early morning dew that signalled the day was rapidly warming up. Breakfast in the bright and airy room was a busy affair as every guest seemed to have responded to the weather and was keen to get out and enjoy it.

What follows is an example of how our European adventures have developed over the years. For our first trips we all stuck together and everything we did was about riding the bikes. As we progressed year by year we grew in confidence, went further afield and began to include activities unrelated to motorcycling. Last night Festa decided he would like to hire a mountain bike for the day to explore some of the trails that led out of the village. I had planned a days' riding into Austria and Kryten was torn between both ideas before electing for Austria. I found this a very positive milestone in the relationship we share. I would have happily ridden to Austria on my own and Festa was happy to take himself off.

As Kryten and I loaded our bikes we noticed that there were a lot of bees around. About 25 meters away in the trees the hotel owners had numerous hives and it seemed the bees were preparing their own adventure. The owners were alerted by our murmurings and came out looking very concerned. Masses of bees now circled the hives and I understand this is a sign that they will swarm and fly off to find a new hive, best get underway quickly then!

We head off back down the winding road that leads us along the valley floor following the course of the Sava Bohinjka as it flows out from Lake Bohinj. Soon we are heading through the far busier tourist town of Bled next to the lake of the same name before heading east. I had a couple of navigational errors before heading across a wide open plain towards the border with Austria. As we approached, the tree covered hills that were in the distance loomed larger and having passed a small white washed church in Zgornje Jezersko village the 210 road began its' sinuous journey upwards to the Seeberg Saddle at an elevation of 1,218 m (3,996 ft.) and the Austrian border.

There were the usual customs buildings, welcome signs and warning signs but no guards or passport checks. There were, however, an abundance of cyclists who, as you may imagine, are quite slow on the way up demanding extreme vigilance on the blind bends. Slow they may be going up but descending they were verging on suicidal given their clothing, use of all of the road and the varying quality of the surface.

In Austria the 210 road became the 82 but continued to wriggle downwards passing through Bad Vellach before it levelled out. We stopped for a quick look at the map just outside the spa town of Eisenkappel-Vellach and I realised we had just passed our turn off. Still, this seemed like a good place to stop for tea and biscuits. Sometimes it's difficult to choose a good place to stop as one always thinks there may be a better place just around the next corner. This turned out to be just such an occasion. As we sat drinking tea and munching biscuits it became apparent we were stopped on a fairly popular cycle path.

Not long after and having located the correct L131 road we stopped at a view point overlooking the green valley with very little traffic to disturb us, a far more contusive spot for a brew. Having said that, we were briefly joined by two German BMW GS riders who stayed for a moment before speeding off noisily into the distance. The sign read 'welcome' in four languages beneath Gemeinde / Obcina. Zell Sele. It was a great place and a fitting start to the delightful 45miles we rode along the valley towards the town of Ferlach. Unfortunately this is where the delight ended and the disappointment began.

Ferlach came as a bit of a shock after such a pleasant ride to get there. It appeared more urban but it led to what I had hoped would be another scenic pass. The Lobi pass took us back into Slovenia and was disappointingly busy and unattractive seemingly a more major route for lorries and people in a general 'me first' hurry. I soon gave up on my carefully written directions deciding to wing it back on the motorway to Lake Bled as soon as possible.

On arrival Lake Bled was every bit the popular tourist destination it is renowned to be. We rode around the narrow lane that encircles the lake but, even with motorcycles, couldn't find a spare piece of even ground to park up and explore (that we wouldn't have to pay for). We had to leave the bikes at the side of the busy road where we found a clearing to hastily snap a few pictures. Disregarding the traffic noise it was an idyllic scene, tourist information time: The Lake has the only island in Slovenia upon which stands the Assumption of Mary Church which can be visited by traditional wooden boats called Pletnas. The best views of the island are from the 12th century Bled castle which has stuff going on most of the year. Anyway, we didn't do any of that but I have to say the brief glimpse of the island set in the blue waters with people swimming, paddle-boarding and rowing looked very inviting especially since the temperature was now 32°c.

Back at the hotel there was no-one at reception but our arrival had alerted a lady who came hurrying with our room key. Having peeled off the riding gear in the cool of the room and 'slipped into something more comfortable' another cup of tea seemed in order. It wasn't long before a hot and red Festa re-appeared. It seemed his route had been a slightly over ambitious one having ridden an estimated 60miles up hill and down dale in the full heat of the day.

We were all hot and sticky and there seemed only one thing we could do. We all got suitably attired and proceeded to throw ourselves in the lake. It didn't take too long for the waters to reduce our body temperatures and it certainly felt good. Gosh is that the time? Its beer o'clock so we had a shower and sat on the hotel balcony sipping traditional Slovenian beer until it was time to eat. Tonight it would be the by now traditional tour favourite of pizza which, according to the menu, had been cooked in a stone oven.

We sat and watched the world go by with another beer or two while Kryten buried his head in the joy of text. I noted that the Adventure bike craze had not found its way to Slovenia yet judging by the amount of sports bikes that entered the town and then high-tailed it out again their exhaust sound resonating around the valley. But all good things etc. and so it was time to pack up ready to move on.

Having spread out the contents of his top box over his bed Kryten was able to demonstrate his three flap method of preparing clothes. Basically hold the garment in both hands and flap vigorously in a downwards direction three times. The garment may then be folded, or rolled, safe in the knowledge that it contains not one crease. Festa questioned this method as he witnessed the ritual imparting the phase "don't sweat the small stuff" before taking all of two minutes to pack and return to his wine and book.

Monday - Ribcev Laz (Slovenia) to Villach (Austria) (60miles 2hrs 15mins).

It's the usual elbows out bun fight at the bread and jam breakfast buffet but I have thoroughly enjoyed our brief stay here. The people have been very welcoming, the weather near perfect and the quiet location with the lake and surrounding mountains made the whole experience a very pleasant one.

After chucking the gear back over the balustrade and onto the bikes we had the final sweep of the room before locating the owner to pay our bill. Cash was requested here and we each delved into our pockets to produce the requisite amount. Reminding me of days long since past when I would empty my pockets in the sweet shop trying to find enough pocket money for some tooth rotting confectionary.

Onto the bike and into the routine, helmet on, suit zipped up, gloves on and a final glance at the route before, oh bugger, forgot the ear plugs! Gloves off, helmet off, plugs located and inserted, helmet back on, gloves back on, deep breath, glance over the shoulder for the ok and we're off.

The route begins over the little stone bridge and past the church affording us one last glance at the glassy lake before turning right along a narrow tree lined road. Soon the 633 road leads us steadily upwards through tiny hamlets that feel as though we are heading back in time. As we climb through the forests I flip open my visor and breathe deeply to take in the wonderful smell of pine. At many places along the road there are piles of sawn logs surrounded by the shavings that suggest fresh activity.

Over the crest of a hill we enter a large clearing of open meadows and witness 'traditional' style harvesting of the hay by hand. There are quite a few people engaged in the activity which seems to culminate in the hay being draped over racks to dry in the increasingly warm sunshine.

This was the kind of riding I love, no great need for speed, no real time constraints just an emersion in the surrounding landscape that the cosseted confines of an air conditioned car fail to deliver. In fact I was so wrapped up in fluffy thoughts that a slight navigational inexactitude occurred and I led us into a farmyard.

Extracted from the farmyard and with concentration fully restored we begin our unexpectedly rapid descent from the mountain. The road wriggled through the surrounding woodland and Festas report of his previous days' mountain biking experience came to mind. He had encountered something similar and had ended up overtaking more cautious four wheeled road users. I have watched riders in events like the Tour d' France and winced at those unfortunate enough to take a tumble wearing nothing but lycra. Having led us into a farmyard not too long ago I was one of those more cautious folk on this descent.

The time travel rural idle soon dissipated when we left behind the last of the trees and approached the busy town of Jesenice in our search for petrol. A motorway ran alongside our road and we were back into the world of the ubiquitous corporate signage festooned filling station. A little further on and out of town we pull into an elevated lay-by for tea and biscuits. There are views back across the river to the mountains we have just vacated but the motorway has had the good grace to disappear into a tunnel somewhere heading into Austria.

Back on the road we turn onto 201/109 Wurzenpass Straße which takes us out of the valley onwards and upwards toward the Slovenia / Austria border. Close to the top there's the unexpected sight of a Russian T34 tank left over from WW2 its barrel still aimed at Austria. It provides a photo opportunity before we cross the unmanned border into Austria and begin our final descent into Villach.

We locate the small Spar supermarket opposite the railway station which presents the opportunity to stock up on reasonably priced provisions for the overnight journey. I volunteer to remain with the bikes and offer up my financial contribution to Festa and Kryten with the request that at least some portion of it be used to purchase non-alcohol based solid food items. As I wait it is clear that we are not the only hunter-gatherer train travellers as numerous people emerge with various packages and head straight to the station.

In the holding area for the train Festa and Kryten display what appears to be a veritable feast but are concerned that maybe we are under stocked in the beer department. This proves to be fortunate as at this point Festa realises he has left his wallet in the shop. Festa swiftly returns to successfully retrieve the wallet and has equal success with the acquisition of a satisfactory amount of beer.

With all things sorted there's nothing to do but wait. It's very hot and there's an unpleasant smell of cigarettes, but it's a good opportunity to indulge in a spot of people watching. There's the usual assortment, mums and dads trying to entertain kids, the bossy wife of a retired couple, the young couple with rucksacks and the loud jolly German bikers with their BMWs and Harleys. We got talking to a husband and wife from Goxhill, just down the road from where we live, who, it turned out, shared a mutual friend with

Kryten, small world at times. They had suffered heavy rain and hail on the way and were busy drying out some of their gear.

There was much excitement when people in orange Hi-Viz started unlocking things and generally fussing about. It makes me smile to watch the reactions as word spreads that the train is on its' way and people get ready to be first on board. We all have tickets and we have all been allocated a space on the train, be cool people.

When it was the turn of the motorcycles to be loaded there was much revving of engines before each in turn took the cue from Hi-Viz man and began the perilous journey along the undulating bed of the carriage. Best to keep your helmet on, keep your head low and keep moving, which is easier on a sports bike than the tall upright adventure type machines.

Having struggled in the past this time we had unloaded all our gear and left it on the platform before riding onto the train. Now there was just the performance of actually finding our compartment and wedging ourselves and our gear into it. We were ushered onto the train by an over made up blond lady and, as always, our compartment was at the opposite end of the busy corridor. Once inside the humorous removal of bike gear and transformation into 'evening wear' occupied us for some time before we could finally settle back and reward ourselves with that 'click and fizz' sound that accompanies the opening of the first can.

When the train pulled out of the station we were well into the fine dining experience that Spar had provided and could watch the drama of another scenery change as the daylight began to fade. When it had faded completely there was little else to do but get some sleep and this should have been a simple enough task. Our compartment was, as you may have gathered, a little compact but we managed to convert it into three tiered bunk beds. Kryten on top, Festa in the middle and me on the bottom only something wasn't quite right. When Festa tried to crawl into his bunk he found it so close to the bunk above that he looked like the filling oozing out of a sandwich toaster. We tried in vain to correct the situation but with poor light and the rocking motion of the carriage we failed. Festa decided that he would just have to go with it and we gave up.

Sometime in the night the train stopped at a station for a while and I noticed a guard standing on the platform. I made myself decent and went to seek his assistance with the Festa sandwich situation. When he saw Festas' predicament he burst out laughing and once he finished asked Festa to step away from the bed. Within a couple of seconds the bed was deftly positioned in its' correct location and the guard went away chuckling to himself. Three stupid English with varying degrees of engineering skill couldn't put a bed up properly. Festa was greatly relieved, unfortunately it was the kind of relief that Kryten was the first to encounter and it required the opening of the window to its' widest point!

Tuesday - Dusseldorf to Amsterdam (150miles 3 hrs).

Another day dawned, but it hadn't dawned on us that we were approaching the station in Dusseldorf as we sat tucking into our sparse AutoZug breakfast. We had acquired extra tea from the helpful cabin steward and sat blissfully sipping it as the train ground to a halt on platform 2.

To say that we were unprepared for the arrival of the 7:15 from Villach would be to put it mildly. The compartment contained the discarded remnants of last nights' consumables mixed with our possessions and riding gear. All of this was hastily bundled out onto the platform were we finally stood blinking in the warming rays of the morning sunshine looking like we had been evicted for non-payment of rent. There was little else for it but to change into our riding gear there on the platform, no doubt putting many commuters off their early morning croissants and coffee.

Once we had reunited ourselves with the bikes and regained a small amount of composure we headed out into the Dusseldorf traffic. I was feeling good and congratulating myself that I had managed to lead us flawlessly through the city and onto the autobahn like a local. There is, however, a saying in the UK that mentions 'Pride' and its' appearance before a fall. It thus came to pass that while confidently overtaking many vehicles a slow realisation crept up on me that the road signs were no longer suggesting this was the correct course. Still, what's a mere thirty miles between friends? Oh, better make that sixty as it was thirty miles back again!

We approached Amsterdam with a degree of trepidation and stopped for a final pee on the outskirts to gather our thoughts. I had previously Googled the route into the city and read my description a number of times before positioning it in the window of the tank bag. The route took us alongside canals and over bridges all the while desperately looking out for the magic sign that said 'CENTRUM'. Aside from the cars there were trams, pedestrians and mopeds coming at us from all directions but worst of all were the cyclists. It should come as no surprise that cycles are popular in Amsterdam, but there are thousands of the buggers all hurtling around like worker bees that have just smelt smoke. Plus, and this maybe just me, the Dutch are all tall and ride bikes from the 1950s like Marry Poppins.

As I sensed we were nearing our hotel I was once again allowing a certain amount of self-congratulation to enter my being as I was sure the next turn into a narrow street would reveal journeys end. I was right, it did! Unfortunately our route was somewhat impeded as someone had parked a large cherry picker across our path. To go back would mean we would have to navigate around the one-way system that surrounds the central Dam Square and I didn't fancy that one bit. Kryten was the first to attempt the squeeze between the offending vehicle and the brick wall. Once through Festa and I followed and to my relief the hotel was straight in front of us.

I had picked this hotel as it ticked so many useful traveller boxes. It was reasonably priced, fairly central and had that most rare city facility, the underground secure garage parking. Inside the surprisingly spacious lobby the friendly multi-lingual receptionist gave us the keys to our room which was on the top floor. Mercifully there was a lift and three single beds!

Once encamped in the room we discovered it was exactly 'Beer O'clock' so we headed out across Dam Square looking for a couple of places recommended by our trusted beer ticker work colleague who knows about these things. (In truth I think Festa is more than capable of locating purveyors of fine ales anywhere in the world without help!). The first place was packed to the rafters so we moved further on to find 'de Wildman' situated in Kolksteeg 3 and a former Amsterdam distillery.

This turned out to be an excellent choice with a selection of 18 beers on draft, 250 different types of beers on bottle and an expanding range of ciders. The selection of beers focuses mainly on Dutch and Belgian varieties, such as beers from the Trappist breweries but includes German and some English to. All music to Festa and Krytens' ears with the only agony being which to choose. The barman was very helpful seeing our indecisive state and we were soon sat taking in the atmosphere with a couple of excellent choices. Our host was also key to the location of a restaurant which he recommended and was located close by. It was a small and not overly endearing café but it did provide examples of the tour staple pizza and chips with an accompanying beer.

Sufficiently replete with both pizza and beer we set out to discover what else there might be to entertain three gentlemen of an evening in Amsterdam. Oh yes, I remember now, we took a tour of the red-light district. Although the city is well known for this area for me, as a first time visitor, it came as quite a shock / eye opener. Not only were there windows full of gyrating ladies beckoning anyone who made eye contact but there were 'funny smells' and very scary looking 'toy shops' with all manner of unusual objects for sale. The gyrating ladies in the windows reminded me of the tank full of trout back in Slovenia and my reaction was similar to that of Kryten when asked to pick one. I didn't like this seedy part of the city, it felt unclean and a rather sad place.

It wasn't long before we returned to de Wildman for more beer and then Kryten and Festa were keen to move on to find a bar that contained a screen for football viewing. I wandered off back to the hotel for a shower and a bit of OCD packing ready for the next day.

Wednesday - Hotel to Europoort (60miles 2 hrs).

The day began with a pleasant breakfast taken in a modern setting, like an Ikea inspirational kitchen-diner. The outer wall was floor to ceiling glass and offered a view of Dam Square, if you craned your neck and pressed your nose against the glass. Breakfast over we packed our stuff onto the bikes, placed our riding gear in the hotels store room and were out on the streets by 10:00.

Having negotiated the traffic in Dam Square we made our way to Anne Franks' house, the place where she went into hiding and wrote her famous diary. It didn't seem like much of a hiding place as everybody seemed to know where it was judging by the enormous queue of people stretching back around the block. We had a little time to kill but not enough to join this. Much aimless wandering followed but the city seemed to ingratiate its' self the further away from the 'centrum' we travelled. We shopped for cheese and chocolate gifts to take home until we came across a 1hr canal cruise for €9 to pass some time.

On board we joined the newly-wed and nearly dead listening to the English commentary illuminating us about the passing surrounds. As we glided by the Waldorf Hotel we were told that in the sixteenth century servants used to cut off the heads of those who would attempt to rob the clientele. We passed through locks into a dock basin where a sailing ship built by the unemployed was moored next to a building reminiscent to that of The Deep in Hull. There was a brief stop to photograph the canal with seven arches before we were told that on average one car per week falls into a canal.

Back on land after our nautical adventure we could not resist one final naughty adventure (see what I did there?) back through the red light district, only in the daylight. Yikes! If it looked sleazy at night it looked desperate in the daylight. "Services" were still being offered even at mid-day but the choice was much more limited now. Our choice was to head back to the hotel to pick up our things. We got changed into riding gear in the garage, did a couple of schoolboy engine revs inside, cos it sounded great, then exited into the mid-day Amsterdam traffic mayhem with more trams, mopeds, cycles and pedestrians to dodge around. Perhaps unsurprisingly by now I got us lost again but this turned out to be a simpler route than the one I had planned and after a brief head scratching stop we were soon onto the A4 motorway.

It wasn't too long before we were able to leave the motorway at Afrit 13 to join the delightful N223/N468 which ran alongside canals with ducks and swans, passing windmills and secluded houses with unbroken views over open fields embracing the rural aromas. A much slower pace now than the frenetic urban motorway system and such a contrast to the sleazy centre of Amsterdam.

We arrived in plenty of time on the dockside of the small Maassluis to Rozenburg car ferry which gave us enough time to read the sign on the ticket machine. Enough time because it was in Dutch, so we tried just sticking a credit card in it to see what happened, result, nothing. When the ferry arrived we watched others board and noticed the attendant taking cash so joined the queue. It was a short trip across Het Scheur and meant we were only a couple of miles from the Europort with time to spare.

A couple of minutes ride took us to EIC Mainport Rotterdam (Education and Information Centre Mainport Rotterdam) a visitor centre in grounds which seemed mainly deserted. We parked up next to a tall tower atop which was a viewing platform. With this part of the world being so flat the short climb up was rewarded with extensive views back towards the ferry and onwards overlooking the docks and an oil rig in for refurbishment. Directly below were the ubiquitous Dutch cycle tracks leading off in several directions. All in all a great place for the final tea stop of this varied trip.

It was a simple ride to meet the Pride of Rotterdam and in such contrast to the lane changing merging nightmares of earlier returns to the port. Tickets and passports checked and cabin allocated we rode straight onto the ship securing the bikes and heading upstairs with little fuss. The only inconvenience was when the shower head fell off and had to be fixed by an engineer.

Festa and Kryten were keen for beer o'clock and more football so I was last into the shower and took my time to enjoy the freedom of an empty cabin. Dressed in my by now crumpled but least stinking clothes I skipped the beer and football and headed out to watch the loading process. There were all shapes and sizes of containers along with tankers which made me wonder what else is travelling with us. I stood there on deck marvelling at the engineering and organisation that makes such a large port operate so efficiently. A few more people joined me as the last of the containers was loaded and secured and the ship slid away from its moorings heading out past the multitude of storage tanks and wind turbines that line the banks.

Back below I return to find Festa and Kryten front and centre of a large screen TV showing another match. Festa has his head in an eBook while Kryten worships at the altar of the IPhone. I decide to venture off to the bar for a Guinness then to watch the entertainment provided by the P&O Players. I am joined at my table by two older Dutch ladies who seem to gain more enjoyment from the stage than I do.

An hour, that seemed like two or three, past by before I gave up and returned to the football room. Kryten and Festa were now watching another game and had been joined by a fellow who had promptly fallen asleep. There was little else to do but return to the cabin for an early night and to reflect on the end of another splendid adventure.

The End

.

Final Thoughts.

So we've made it to the end of the book together and I sincerely hope you've enjoyed the ride. I suppose you could be wondering which was my favourite trip? To that I would have to reply Norway, with the Pyrenees a close second. We were very fortunate to be able to travel there with comparative ease at the time and we did pretty well for weather to. It might be the contrast to my home county of Lincolnshire or the experiences we shared but the sheer natural beauty of the place blew me away. I realise that strictly speaking Norway is Scandinavia and not Europe, as the book title may suggest, but hopefully you can forgive that geographical error.

You may have gathered I have used several varied machines for the trips so the answer to the next question is the CB1300 was my favourite bike. It's not perfect but it suited me and any riding style I may have. I am 6'2" tall with an expanding middle and that bike felt so comfortable and so easy to ride. It was also the machine I used in both Norway and the Pyrenees and the only bike I regret selling.

If you have never ridden your bike abroad I would like to think I have convinced you to at least consider it and maybe one day to give it a go? One of the most helpful web-sites I can recommend is **https://www.seat61.com/**. It always seems to be kept up to date and I have used it a lot. If you have ridden abroad, where-ever your journey has taken you, I hope reading this book has jogged a few pleasant memories.

All that remains now is for me to thank all of the guys I have ridden with and who have made these trips and the memories so enjoyable. The remaining three of us, Kryten, Festa and I, still venture to foreign parts when we can so if you see us please come over and say hello. If you skipped the introduction bit you may have missed the opportunity to enjoy the multi-media experience that is "Motorcycle Tales from Europe - The Picture Show". It's the film of the book and can be found by simply typing "**Motorcycle Tales from Europe**" into the search box on **YouTube**. It's twelve minutes of your life you won't get back but hopefully it will put some faces and places to the text. If you wish to email me (heaven knows why you would) then you can try **jim.rendall185@gmail.com**.

Acknowledgements.

I would like to thank my incredible wife Jayne for putting up with me and my daft ideas over our many years together. I started these trips into Europe when our son wasn't very old and she waved me off and wished me well each time I left her holding the baby. Her quiet, selfless and caring nature makes her one of humanities great ambassadors, a truly amazing lady.

To my son Adam I would just like to apologize for all of the disappointingly naff presents I have returned home with each year. Unfortunately that's what happens when your mum isn't there to make the right choices. Thank you for appearing to like them and for the welcome I received on my return home.

Of course I must acknowledge those who have made my trips so enjoyable, so special and who I am proud to call my friends; to Wayne, Nigel, Martin, Ian and Kevin a huge big thank you for having me tag along. There is absolutely no way I could have done any of this without you guys.

I must not forget all of the people we met along the way, we may not talk the same languages but in many ways we do and every encounter adds something extra to every trip. A special mention here must go to Simon, who we met in Germany. Simon, your food was crap, your beer was better but our ride-outs with you were just unbelievable, cheers mate.

Also I must thank my friend Steve Blythin for allowing me to use his music to accompany the pictures of the trips on my YouTube channel. The opening track makes me smile each time I listen.

Finally I would like to dedicate this book to our friend Ian (Dizzy) who we lost to illness far too early.

Thanks for reading and remember;

"Never ride faster than you Angel can fly".

Printed in Great Britain
by Amazon

33673631R00141